THE SYLVAC STORY

The History and Products of

SHAW & COPESTAKE LTD.
SYLVAN WORKS,
LONGTON,
STOKE-on-TRENT

AND

THOMAS LAWRENCE (LONGTON) LTD.
FALCON WORKS,
LONGTON,
STOKE-on-TRENT

1894–1982

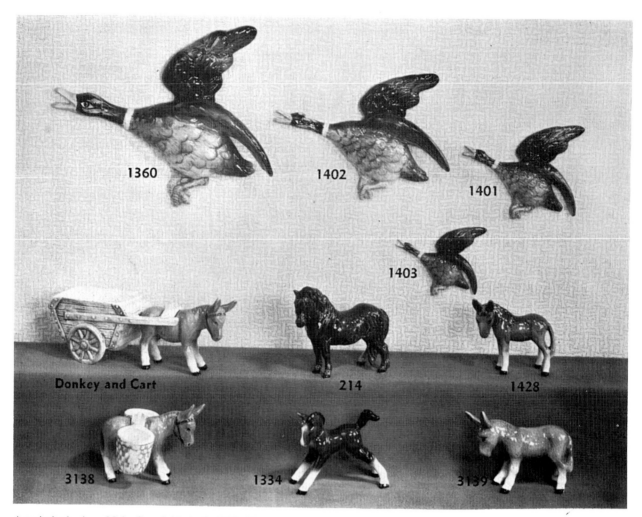

A typical selection of SylvaC available in the 1960s. Here you see the four flying ducks, the smallest of which, Number 1403, was a much later addition. They were sold in two sets. Large size set consisted of 1360, 1402, and 1401. Small size set contained 1402, 1401, and 1403.

CONTENTS

ACKNOWLEDGEMENTS

In compiling this information I have received considerable help from many people. I would like to thank Mrs. G. Thompson, whose late husband Mr. R. Thompson gave me so much information, and Mr. Thompsons daughter Mrs Jeanette Holdcroft, for their kindness and patience during our visits. Mr. Malcolm Chapman, who has contributed greatly to this information. Mrs. Kath Day, who gave us our first leads in our research and her many friends. Mr. George Matthews, Mr. E.J. Dennis, Mrs. E. Hull, Mr. G.G. Barlow, Mr E. Roy Taylor and Mr. W.D. Holt for additional information. Miss Angela Lee, Curator of The Gladstone Pottery Museum for access to their records. Miss Valerie Baynton, Curator of the Sir Henry Doulton Gallery. The Staff of the City Museum & Library, Hanley, Stoke-on-Trent. The fact that this book was written at all is due to Olive and George Caple who first suggested I should publish the information I had gathered. They have encouraged me throughout and George Caple has made a wonderful job of taking the majority of photographs in this book.

Thank you Jayne L'Epine-Smith, David Richards and Olive Caple for lending items from your SylvaC Collections.

Above all I am indebted to my husband Peter for all his support and encouragement during the last two years. He has accompanied me around Stoke-on-Trent, and all the Antique Fairs, searched through volumes of books and taken video films and photographs. He has been largely responsible for the publication of this book.

Photographs by Mr. Peter Lepino, Mr. Harold K. Bowen – who kindly went to the Gladstone Pottery Museum to take photos from the Pottery Gazettes.
Majority of Photographs taken by Mr. George Caple.
Special thanks to the Gladstone Pottery Museum, and Tableware International, for allowing photographs to be taken from the Pottery Gazette.

Published by Pottery Publications, 7 Merton Park Parade, Kingston Road, London SW19 3NT.

Printed by The Oxford University Press Printing House, Walton Street, Oxford.

1st January 1989.   ISBN 0 9514889 0 2

A display of SylvaC in the old Shaw & Copestake showrooms about 1940.

▲   Miss Dorothy Ridgeway, Company Secretary Shaw & Copestake Ltd., in the company showrooms c1950.

▼   Mrs. May Alcock, Company Secretary Thomas Lawrence (Longton) Ltd., in the company showrooms c1950.

FOREWORD

Most of the world's greatest artists only achieved fame after their death. In a manner of speaking, the same situation applies to Shaw & Copestake Ltd. When in 1982, at the instigation of professional advisers, it was recommended that the company cease manufacturing and go into voluntary liquidation, none of the directors or the employees realised that the firms products would become collectors' items.

During the life-time of the company and its associate company Thomas Lawrence (Longton) Ltd, an immense number of ceramic products were developed and produced. The variety of these creations was fantastic. In many cases unique market leaders in their own field. From the very ornate highly decorated Victorian styles of vases and bowls of the early days, to ingenious table accessory items, to natural animal studies, to coloured glaze cachepots and floral containers, and of course the matt finish rabbits, dogs and other caricature animals which are so much sought after to-day, to name but a few of the vast SylvaC range.

As each new shape was modelled, it was given a shape number and in some cases a name. Unfortunately from the collector's point of view, these shape numbers did not follow in strict numerical or chronological order. This, to a large extent was due to the combination of the product numbers from two different factories. At this point I must mention the tremendous work undertaken by the author in compiling some sort of order out of the chaos of these numbers – a task made all the more difficult by the disappearance of the limited documentary evidence in existence at the time of the closure of the company.

Many of the company's products were the inspiration of the late Richard Hull Junior, who although no artist himself, had the unique talents of knowing what the market required and of being able to guide both artists and technicians into the production of the items which he had in mind. In its way this book may be regarded as a tribute to the man whose inspiration was responsible for the creation of so many of the pieces which collectors seek to-day. I am sure that he would have appreciated this narrative which records so much of the work to which he devoted his life.

I knew Richard Hull for most of my life, until his death in 1977. For nearly thirty years I was employed as accountant, company secretary and subsequently director of the company, which he did so much to build. It was very much a 'family' business in which the employees felt so much a part of the family. Richard Hull always endeavoured to foster that atmosphere to the extent that he earned the factory nick-name of 'father'. Throughout my time it was always a happy company. When in the recession of the early 1980's I had the unpalatable job of announcing the closure of the company, there was none of the bitterness amongst the employees at the prospect of redundancy usually associated with such events – just a deep sense of sadness at the end of an era of which they had all been a part. It is nice to know that Shaw & Copestake Ltd, will 'live on' through this book.

Finally may I congratulate Susan Verbeek, who together with her husband Peter, has undertaken months, even years, of research work in compiling the material necessary for this book. I am sure it will be of a particular help to collectors and to all who are interested in SylvaC Ware.

MALCOLM D. CHAPMAN
Ex Director of Shaw & Copestake Ltd.

INTRODUCTION

I started to collect SylvaC in 1986. Up till then I had never heard of SylvaC, and knew nothing about it. My first SylvaC piece was a green matt dachsund (Number 1332). I soon became very interested and now have over 700 pieces in my collection. I tried to find out if there were any catalogues or brochures, all the information I could find was that it was made by Shaw & Copestake Ltd, Stoke-on-Trent, and had been taken over by Crown Winsor.

1986, was the year of the Garden Festival in Stoke-on-Trent. We had planned to go, and were studying the brochures sent. Idly glancing through the factory visits I noticed the name Crown Winsor (Formerly Shaw & Copestake). We arranged a visit and met Mr. W.D. Holt, general manager, who gave me my first treasured catalogue and brochure, and showed us round the show rooms. Unfortunately, no early records of Shaw & Copestake Ltd., had been retained. A visit to the factory shop was our first meeting with Mrs. Kath Day, manageress, who has since been so helpful, and is always pleased to see SylvaC collectors. Kath told us where to find Mr. Malcolm Chapman, former director, and we called on him that very day. We made quite a bit of progress on that first visit.

Our second trip to Stoke-on-Trent was very exciting. Having followed up various leads, we met Mr. Reginald Thompson, who had been with Thomas Lawrence and Shaw & Copestake for over 60 years, he sadly passed away in April 1988. By this time we had our video camera, and everyone was subjected to an interview. Mr. Thompson gave me several more catalogues and brochures, and I was well on the way to learning the SylvaC story.

We returned to Stoke-on-Trent five times, gathering more information and researching in the Museums and Libraries. Information has been obtained from the Pottery Gazette Diaries, the Pottery Gazette, the Pottery and Glass Record, and Pottery & Glass. In between we visited the British Museum Newspaper Library in Colindale, and searched the Antique Fairs for pre-war items. I also made contact with many collectors of SylvaC.

I was gradually gathering together a considerable amount of literature and a Register of Numbers, but there were quite a few gaps in the Register. One of the most exciting finds, by Mr. Malcolm Chapman, were the mould makers registers, which certainly filled in most of the gaps. I have been in constant touch with Mr. Malcolm Chapman, who has a wonderful knowledge of the history of the company, and its employees. Much of the information in this book can be attributed to Mr. Chapman.

I wrote to the printers of catalogues, every agent still traceable, for catalogues or photo negatives, contacted the Tableware International, formerly The Pottery Gazette, and the local Staffordshire newspapers without success. Not surprisingly printers do not keep examples of all their work, and no-one could have forseen such interest in Shaw & Copestake. Photographers do not seem to keep negatives for any length of time either, so many of our photos have been reproduced from catalogues or the Pottery Gazette, which may reduce the quality of the print slightly.

However, I have managed to collect a large number of catalogues, dating from 1940, which I hope to reproduce at a later date, also brochures, leaflets, and the SylvaC & Falcon Bulletin, which was issued spasmodically throughout the life of the companies. Thanks are due to the former directors and staff who have dilligently searched out this treasure trove of information for me.

There are still many avenues to explore, and much more to learn, and although it is possible to keep on researching and finding new leads, other collectors and antique dealers are eagerly waiting for this information, so the time has come to share my extensive researches with you. It has been a very interesting project, and my husband Peter and I have met many friendly and helpful people during our two years of research. We have looked forward to our visits to Stoke-on-Trent, and hope to continue finding more interesting information. I hope you find this book interesting and helpful in your quest for SylvaC.

PART ONE

CHAPTERS 1–9

CHAPTER 1

COLLECTING SYLVAC

Collecting SylvaC can become compulsive. It creeps up on you gradually. It may have started quite innocently with a green bunny or flying duck, but the consequences can be total absorption in a fascinating hobby. There are many different types of SylvaC collectors. The matt green only brigade, fawn matt (green being considered unnatural) lobby, jam & honey pot specialists, wall vase enthusiasts, cat collectors and another only vases, but the majority once having started, collect any Shaw & Copestake item. It has to be admitted some SylvaC is really awful, and is wrapped up out of sight. The floral lines, with handpainted flowers usually have pride of place, and no one can be called a true SylvaC collector unless they have a good sprinkling of rabbits.

The quality of SylvaC varies enormously, some items are very poorly finished, but the flying ducks, character jugs, prestige pieces and the hand painting on some of the vases fill one with admiration. The pixies and gnomes must also be part of a good collection, and the large novelty jugs and vases are undoubtedly a very good investment. Any large animal is also bound to increase in value, and is becoming quite a rarity. There are so many vases to collect, that one wonders if it is worthwhile, but surely now is the time to add to your collection while prices are still reasonable. I always buy anything which is reasonably priced, provided it is perfect. It also pays to inspect dealers displays carefully as the most unlikely items very often turn out to be SylvaC, and one can be quite pleasantly surprised.

A surprising find was a maroon highly glazed clog, with a Dutch embossed scene 4½″ long Number 2863, very clearly marked SylvaC. But my pride and joy has to be the Shaw & Copestake clock set, very ornate, with the early daisy mark in gold. Having sought one for a long time it was a real triumph to find it. There is so much to look for, and this is why you will find the Number Register so useful. Not all ware is SylvaC marked, their system was very haphazard, and it will be useful to look the number up to see if it relates to what you have. The most important attribute a SylvaC collector needs is a sense of humour, if only to cope with the squirrels and fawns nestling in woodland, and the crying onion!

The ash-trays are also an interesting part of SylvaC, although the bases may be the same, there are many different adornments, mostly unrecorded.

Fortunately is it not an expensive hobby with reasonably priced items still available. It is still possible to buy small posy bars and vases for just a few pounds. The price of SylvaC varies such a lot, according to condition and size. Obviously the larger items cost more, and the bunnies are now much scarcer. I have to admit to seeing very highly priced SylvaC Ware, and it obviously depends how much you desire the item in question. It is not really possible to give you a price guide, I can only advise you to compare the prices the dealers are asking.

Should you collect the Falcon Ware? In my opinion it is equally as interesting, and as much of Falcon Ware is also SylvaC it must be the same value. Equally Falcon Ware stands on its own merits, and the quality of original Falcon Ware is excellent. They brought out some very original ideas, but it is not quite so easy to find as SylvaC, or so well marked. Other potteries also used the Falcon Ware mark, so be sure it is from the Thomas Lawrence Potteries in Longton.

I have to admit I have slipped up on a number of occasions, and bought ware I thought was SylvaC, which has turned out to be, in most cases, by Price Bros. (Burslem) Ltd, Top Bridge Pottery, Burslem. They produced a very similar range to SylvaC, but it is very easy to make a mistake. Other potteries such as Devonmoor Art Pottery, and Crown Devon, also made similar wares.

RARE ITEMS

Obviously the items not yet recorded must be rare. But apart from those there are quite a few different wares to search for. The Mr. SylvaC ashtray, Number 3542, of which there were only 600 made for the dealers, is not going to be easy to find. Likewise the Leyland lorry ashtray, made for British Leyland offices, 1000 produced, Number 5404, is unlikely to find its way to the ordinary collector.

Very rare are the horse and rider and pony and rider, Number 4707 previously Number 21, and 4708. These were originally Falcon Ware made. The ski-ing bunnies Numbers 25–29, are unlikely to have the numbers on the base as they as so small, as are the three figures Pam, Paul and Peter, Numbers 3111/2/3.

Number 920, The dancing lady, is a questionable Shaw & Copestake model. The numbers are very similar in style, the date of the number fits in with the 1930s style of the model, and the colour matches. No other pottery has been seen to make this model, so I think we can safely assume it to be Shaw & Copestake. It has also been seen in blue matt. There are other figures to be seen on posies, Number 1336, shows a lady possibly bathing, Number 1326 also has a lady on the front of the posy. Number 1327, has a lady this time reclining on the side of a curved posy. Number 1337, has a flower seller behind a posy. This does prove Shaw & Copestake were capable of making figures.

The Falcon Ware designed by Mr. Thompson, Jeanette with the flowers, the girl on a swing, girl sitting and the Bretton girl, are all very desirable models.

The matt coloured flying ducks are very rarely seen, and the wall plaque seagulls, and swallows are difficult to find, especially complete sets. The seal posy which was replaced by the smallest duck wall plaque, Number 1403, would be a real find, and I have yet to see the large leopard, Number 1458.

Other rare items are the garden ornaments, the gnomes. How I would love to have one of these. We have to assume that as they were cellulose finished, and outdoor items, it is unlikely they would have survived the years, although they were still making them until the 1950s.

The SylvaC birds are not seen very often, Numbers 1328,30,31,49,50,51,57,75 & 76. Although I do have 1357 on a ashtray.

The early SylvaC commemorative ware is relatively rare, as is any of the advertising ware. A Harrods doorman character jug was made especially for Harrods in 1981, Number 4497, and this must be quite rare.

▲ A selection of SylvaC and Falcon Ware catalogues collected during research, dating from 1940. Centre front are the mould makers registers.

◄ The author, left, with Mrs. Kath Day, manageress of the factory shop, at the start of researching "The SylvaC Story", in 1986.

PRICE'S
MATT FIGURES

Elephant · Cat · Puppy Dog · Donkey · Pig
Squirrel · Seal · Duck · Roger Dog · Nigger Dog
Kangaroo · Running Rabbit · Penguin · Sitting Rabbit · Tim Dog

The above range for Export are offered in four colours: Matt Green, Blue, Fawn and Oatmeal, fifteen different figures, all at the same selling price.

PRICE BROS. (BURSLEM) LTD.
TOP BRIDGE POTTERY
BURSLEM

An example of some Price Bros. animals, showing similarity to SylvaC ware. From the Pottery Gazette c1950s.

3339

5211

3459

5209

▲ The Prestige Range.

◀ The Budgerigar range. Jug 544, Basket 545.

Pages reproduced from the 1940 catalogue.

Pages reproduced from the 1940 catalogue.

1334	1119	1433	1426	1372	1399	1425	1182	1424
Approx. height 4″	4″	3½″	3¼″	2¾″	2½″	2¾″	2½″	2¼″
Price per doz. 13/3	7/-	7/-	7/-	7/6	5/-	7/-	4/-	7/-

1340	1394	1393	1413	1403	1457	1455/1400	1454/1450	1454/1432	1420	1421
12½″	8½″	5″	Posy	Posy	Posy	Ash Tray	Ash Tray	Ash Tray		Pixies
42/-	21/-	13/-	21/-	8/3	15/-	10/6	10/6	10/6		6/6
(SHIP, made in 3 Sizes)										

1270	1366/1357	1366/1182	1311	1181/1270	1181/1265	1064
Match Holder	Ash Trays		Book Ends	Ash Trays		Match Holder
Price doz. 6/-	13/3		36/-	11/9		6/6

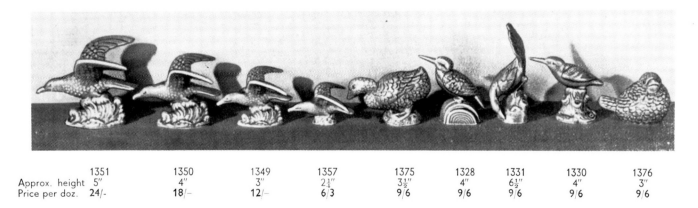

1351	1350	1349	1357	1375	1328	1331	1330	1376
Approx. height 5″	4″	3″	2¼″	3½″	4″	6½″	4″	3″
Price per doz. 24/-	18/-	12/-	6/3	9/6	9/6	9/6	9/6	9/6

Pages from the 1940 Catalogue. Note number 1403 second row, the number which was re-used later for the smallest flying duck.

"SYLVAC" NOVELTIES—MATT GLAZE

SEAGULL WALL PLACQUES—1543   1544   1545

| 1506 | 1500 | 1426 | 1521 | 1522 | 1520 | **LAMBS**—1505 (6 in a Box) |

| 1547 | 1485 | 1494 | 1573 | 1519 | 1561 | 1590 | 1504 | 1531 |

| 1528 | 1508 | 1518 | 1548 | 1512 | 1497 | 1534 | 1527 |

"SYLVAC" NOVELTIES—CELLULOSE FINISH

| 788 | 769 | 1022 | 1086 | 992 | 1132 | 1320 | 1140 | 961 | 1211 |

Pages from the 1940 catalogue.

18

CHAPTER 2

HISTORY OF SHAW AND COPESTAKE

It is generally accepted that Shaw & Copestake was established in 1894. I have been unable to confirm the exact date of the founding of the Shaw & Copestake factory. Shaw & Copestake produced a 'History in Brief' for their customers, in which they gave the date as 1894, also adding that Mr. Richard Hull Senior joined the company in the same year. The obituary of Mr. Richard Hull Senior, in 1935, published in the Pottery Gazette, states he became a partner in the firm in 1900. Whereas the obituary of Mr. William Shaw, the founder of Shaw & Copestake, also to be found in the Pottery Gazette in 1951, gives the date of the partnership with Mr. Hull as 1898. Having studied all the relevant documents from the year 1894, the first mention of Shaw & Copestake is found in 1902. The address given is Drury Works, Normacot Road, but by 1904 the address has already changed to Sylvan Works, Normacot Road, as can be seen in the first advert. It has not been possible to establish if the name Drury Works was changed to Sylvan Works, or if it was a different location. From 1902 there are frequent mentions of Shaw & Copestake, in the Pottery Manufacturers Directories. So there are four different dates recorded, 1894, 1898, 1900 & 1902. Presumably the 1894 date, was recorded by the original directors of the company, in company records now no longer available, and we have to assume it to be correct.

The old works was situated opposite the site of the existing Sylvan Works in Normacot Road, Longton, Stoke-on-Trent, but has now been demolished. The site is used as a car park, only a short piece of wall remaining.

Mr. William Shaw and Mr. Copestake founded the business. Whether Mr. Copestake was connected with the well known Dewes & Copestake Pottery of Viaduct Works, Caroline St. Longton is not known. Mr. Copestake did not stay in the business long, only about six months. There are also other Shaws in the directories at around that time one being James Shaw, Albion Street, Longton. One can only speculate as to whether they were related. As William Shaw was very young when he founded the business, probably in his early 20s, one can reasonably assume he was financed by a relative, perhaps already in the business. He would also have had to be familiar with the business, and it seems more than likely his family were already associated with the Potteries.

Mr. Richard Hull senior bought Mr. Copestakes interest and became Mr. Shaws partner. This partnership continued until Mr. Hulls death in September 1935, when his son Mr. Richard Hull junior became Mr. Shaws partner.

In 1936, the business became a Limited Company. Mr. William Shaw continued to be a director until his retirement in May 1942, he died at the age of 76 on 31st December 1950. After Mr. Shaws retirement in 1942 Mr. E.J. Dennis became a director.

In 1938, Mr. Richard Hull and Mr. E.J. Dennis acquired Thomas Lawrence (Longton) Ltd, Falcon Pottery, Waterloo Street, Longton, Stoke-on-Trent. The Falcon Pottery was built in 1898 especially for Thomas Lawrence, and is still in existence. It is now used by the John Beswick Company, (part of the Royal Doulton Group). When Beswick took over the Thomas Lawrence Factory they found a room full of the Falcon backstamp, the room is still known as the Falcon Casting Room. The name Falcon appears quite frequently in the Beswick shape book, and it is more than probable these were pieces made in the Falcon Casting Shop. The name of the road was changed in the early 1950's to Barford Street.

Falcon Pottery was owned by Mr. Thomas Lawrence who founded it in 1888. In the 1920s or maybe shortly before, the business was taken over by his nephew Mr. John Grundy, whose daughter Miss Eileen Grundy married Mr. Richard Hull junior, thus amalgamating the two factories.

During the war years, the Shaw & Copestake Factory was requisitioned by the Government and used for storage. only the office and packing departments were available for use. Part of the Falcon Pottery was made available to Shaw & Copestake, and limited production continued under their own name. Shaw and Copestake were able to re-open their own factory in 1945.

A landmark in the history of the two firms was the opening of their own London Showrooms in 1953, at 30 Brooke Street, Holborn. Mr. H.W. Town was in charge of the Showrooms, he had previously been the Representative for London and the South East. Before they had their own premises they used London Agents, Mr. J.E. Holt, 60, Shoe Lane, Holborn, London for many years, and then Mr. J. Artis, Morley House, 26 Holborn Viaduct, London. The Scottish Agents were Mr. J. Crowe, 30, Gordon Street, Glasgow, and Messrs. Doleman &

The new combined offices and showrooms. The factory is at the rear. Photo taken about 1962 before the existing factory shop was opened.

▲ The very first Shaw & Copestake advertisement appeared in the Pottery Gazette on June 1st 1904.

◄ An article and photograph appeared in the Pottery Gazette on 1st April 1904. The following is an extract: "The group shown comprises the set of four pieces, consisting of centrepiece and stand, 21"h, with two side ewer-vases, 16"h. These have dark green ground with rich gold decoration. The same set is supplied in many decorative schemes; one with bronze green ground, richly gilt birds, foliage and handles, makes a handsome set well suited for a present. The vases are all artistic in outline and in ornamentation. The firm are very successful in their colour combination. Pale green and salmon ground, with hand painted flowers and gilt handles, celeste and gold ground, ivory and salmon ground, with colour and gilt foliage, make rich decorations."

Steward Ltd, 172, Buchanan Street, Glasgow. The Northern Ireland Agent was Mrs. H. Dean, 41, Donegall Place, Belfast, and the Eire Agents were Messrs T.G. Jones & Co., Ltd 1 Aston Place, Dublin.

Mr. Hull and Mr. Dennis's ambition for many years had been to build a new factory to combine the Shaw & Copestake and Thomas Lawrence Works, and this ambition started to be fulfilled in 1955. The new premises were positioned opposite the old bottle kilns in Normacot Road. In fact they had acquired some land on this site and offices and warehouses were already situated there. When more land became available, it seemed the ideal opportunity to build the finest and most modern factory in the Potteries. On January 22nd 1957 the first piece was made in the new building. The office block, showroom and warehousing units were completed in 1962. At this time they were employing 140 people. In 1962 Thomas Lawrence (Longton) Ltd, ceased trading under its own name and became fully merged with Shaw & Copestake Ltd by 1964. No more items with the Falcon Ware mark were produced after this date.

The post-war years saw not only a vast change in production techniques, but also changes in the marketing of the products. The export market continued to flourish and Shaw & Copestakes products were sent world-wide, about 30% of production being sent abroad.

Mr. E.J. Radford joined the Board in 1947, Mr. M.D. Chapman in 1962, and Mr. E.R. Taylor in 1974. Mr. Radford passed away in 1974, and Mr. Richard Hull in 1977. Mrs.

Richard Hull continued to be connected with the business until 1982.

During the late 1970s there was a steady decline in output due to the recession and Far Eastern competition, and 5 years later in May 1982 Shaw & Copestake went into voluntary liquidation. All production by the company ceased in that month. The land, buildings, plant and equipment were purchased by the North Midlands Co-Operative Society now known as the United Co-Operative Society, and leased to a workers Co-Operative known as Longton Ceramics. All the moulds, remaining stock and the name SylvaC were taken over by Longton Ceramics. This concern only lasted for 18 months, when the United Co-Operative Society took over the business, which is now run in the name of Crown Winsor. Crown Winsor are still producing some of the original SylvaC and Falcon Ware designs.

Mrs. Kath Day, former secretary at the Shaw & Copestake Works, and now manageress of the Crown Winsor factory shop, has organised several Shaw & Copestake reunions at her home, and I have been able to meet many of the former workers, and what wonderful characters they all are, with a fund of amusing and interesting tales to tell about working at the pottery. (Which is all on video tape). There is no doubt there was something special about working at Shaw & Copestake. Conditions in the new factory far surpassed most of the old potteries, and the management went out of their way to make sure everyone was happy. It was a very sad day for all when the firm went into liquidation.

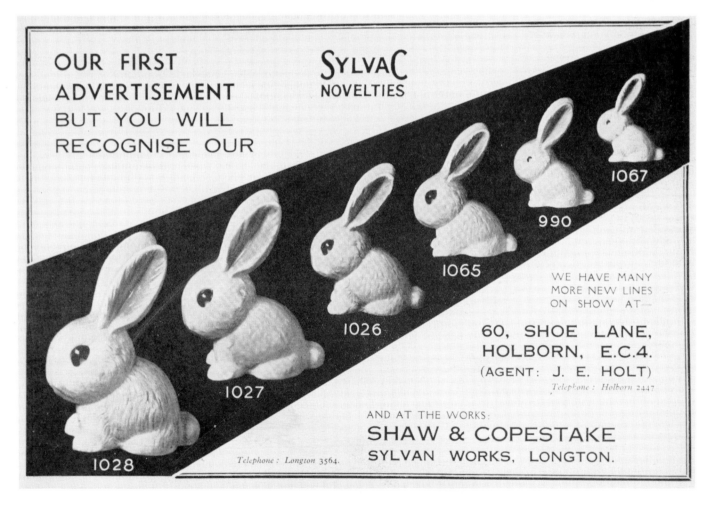

The first SylvaC advertisement appeared in the Pottery Gazette on January 1st 1936.

▲   Opening of the new London Showrooms in 1953. From left to right: Mrs. W.F. Wentworth-Shields, who officially opened the showrooms, Mr. W.F. Wentworth-Shields, Director of the British Pottery Manufacturers' Federation, Mr. Richard Hull, Managing Director, Mr. H.W. Town, in charge of the new showrooms and Mrs May Alcock Company Secretary of Thomas Lawrence (Longton) Ltd.

▼   A section of the new London showroom.

CHAPTER 3

HOW SYLVAC WAS MANUFACTURED

This is a description of the production methods used in the late 1940s in the old Shaw & Copestake factory which was probably built in the 1890's, and the Thomas Lawrence Factory built in 1898, until the opening of the new factory in 1957. Shaw & Copestake were always bringing in new methods of production, even in the old factory, and this was a continuous process. We find the old bottle kilns still being used, but alongside are new gas fired kilns. This chapter has been compiled from information found in the SylvaC and Falcon Bulletin, produced sometime between 1948 and 1951. These Bulletins were issued periodically, and were fully illustrated. I have been able to find the names of some of the workers, and have included these for your interest.

When a new article was suggested for production, the first stage was for the artist designer to sketch the subject to the exact size as required and showing all the detail. This drawing was then discussed by a committee of the heads of the production, decorating and sales department, along with the modeller, whose job it was to reproduce the drawing in either clay or plasticine. This committee discussed all the snags likely to occur when making or decorating the article, and also its feasibility as a saleable line. Once agreement had been reached and the design approved, the modeller reproduced the drawing exactly to scale.

From this original model, the mouldmaker prepared the first mould in plaster of Paris, called the block mould. This was done by marking out on the model the number of parts required for the mould, which would depend on the type of figure.

An intricate mould would be five to ten parts. Sometimes, the head or legs were made separately and stuck on the body in the making process. A mould was then taken of each of the parts of the block mould and this was known as 'the case'. From this case the parts of the working moulds were prepared, which when joined together make a complete working mould ready to be passed into the making departments.

The lines were manufactured in earthenware body, which had four principal ingredients, as follows:

STONE. This was obtained from Cornwall, when broken up and ground acted as a flux to hold the clays together in the body, and gave density to the finished article.

FLINT. The best quality came from France in the form of large pebbles. These, before use, were calcined or roasted and then finely ground. Flint gave the body its stability.

BALL CLAY. Came from Dorset or Devon, and was mined from the ground. It was a brownish tinted clay which gave the earthenware body its plasticity.

CHINA CLAY. Mined in Cornwall. After washing and weathering it was used to give the body its whiteness and helped with its plasticity.

The above ingredients were all mixed together in the correct proportions with water in a blunger to produce rough slip. The rough slip was run through very fine mesh lawns to remove any dirt, and then passed through magnets to remove any iron. This completed the process of preparing the earthenware clay. The surplus water was removed by passing the clay through a filter press, the solid clay was then passed through the 'pug' which made the clay more pliable and easy to handle.

To make a casting slip, a known weight of the made clay was mixed with water, silicate of soda and soda ash. The last two items acted as a medium to keep the clay particles in suspension, more fluid, and assist with the process of casting.

The casting slip was pumped up into the making shops from the slip house and when the moulds were assembled, they were filled with the slip and left to stand for approximately one hour. During this period the plaster mould, being porous, absorbed the water from the slip, where it was touching the mould. Consequently, when the surplus slip was poured out of the mould, it left a thin layer of clay adhering to the side of the mould. After being left to dry for an hour, the mould was opened and the cast clay piece removed. If any parts were made separately, they were stuck on in this wet state, which was a very skilled operation. The article was then left to dry, after which the seams etc., were carefully removed by an

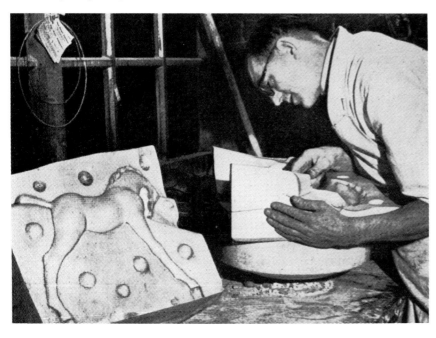

◄ Mouldmaking. Edward Walker, head mould maker at the Thomas Lawrence factory preparing mould in plaster of Paris.

◄ The sliphouse at the old Shaw & Copestake factory. Left, pugging the clay, centre, measuring the flint, right removing the magnet. On the far right is Mr. E.J. Radford works director.

◄ The casting shop at the old Shaw & Copestake factory. Left, filling moulds with casting slip, centre, emptying moulds, right, carrying finished clay to oven. Second from left is Mr. Frank Ridge who left in 1952.

◄ Fettling, in the old Shaw & Copestake factory. Removing surplus clay from seams with knife and sponge.

◄ Making flowers in the old Shaw & Copestake factory. The petals were made separately in the palm of the hand to be pieced together to form a flower. Individual flowers and leaves were then assembled together to form attractive flower groups.

► The continuous oven at the old Shaw & Copestake factory. Placing ware in saggers and carrying to placer. This picture shows the entrance to the continuous gas oven.

◄ The intermittent oven at the Thomas Lawrence factory. Carrying and filling saggers into the intermittent oven. When completely filled this entrance was built up with the fire bricks before commencing to fire. Williams Holmes is on the ladder, he left in the mid 1960s.

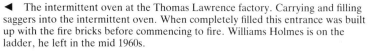

◀ Florence Key in the Thomas Lawrence factory aerographing or spraying the colour decoration on to the ware. Florence retired in the mid 1970s.

◀ Dipping house in the old Shaw & Copestake factory. Left to right, dipping biscuit ware in glaze, carrying ware to the kiln, aerographing colour, cleaning base of ware.

◀ Biscuit warehouse at the Thomas Lawrence factory. Brushing and cleaning the biscuit ware after biscuit oven fire.

◄ Glost oven at the Thomas Lawrence factory. Placing wares in trucks before firing.

◄ Glost oven at the Thomas Lawrence factory. Checking temperature on recorders and placing ware. James Brian clay manager is on the left, he retired in 1971.

◄ Glost oven at the Thomas Lawrence Factory. Drawing truck of fired ware from oven. On the right is E. Roy Taylor clay manager and later to become works director at Shaw & Copestake.

◄ George Wright in the decorating shop at the Thomas Lawrence factory, handpainting the wares. George retired in 1981.

◄ Decorating shop. Handpainting at the old Shaw & Copestake factory.

◄ The Thomas Lawrence warehouse. Back from left, Kate Worsdale, retired in 1973, Nellie Stewart, left in 1952. Front from left, Bill Tunicliffe, Janet Collis and Joan Ayres.

operation known as 'fettling'. The article had now finished its first stage of existence and was a very delicate piece of clay, neatly moulded and made to its own shape.

Completely round articles were machine made by a process called 'jolleying'. For this method, the clay after being 'pugged' was used in its plastic state. The machine rotated the mould, which formed either the inside or outside of the article, the other side being shaped by the application of a metal tool, brought down on to the clay in the mould by operating a lever.

Flower groups were completely hand made, each petal and leaf being made separately. They were formed in the palm of the hand from a roll of specially prepared plastic clay. The petals were pieced to-gether to form a flower and then assembled with the leaves into attractive flower groups.

The next stage was the first fire, known as biscuit firing. This was done in either intermittent bottle shaped ovens, fired with long flame coal, or a continuous gas kiln. The reason the Potteries was situated in Stoke-on-Trent was because of the deposit of long flame coal. Shaw & Copestake were using both methods, the most modern at that time being the continuous gas kiln, which was 82ft. long and rose to a temperature of 1160°C, and operated 168 hours per week. The ware was placed in fireclay containers known as saggers, these were placed in a small truck, each truck holding 12 to 16 saggers. A truck was placed in the oven at the entrance every two hours, and was slowly pushed through, taking 30 hours to reach the exit. Fifteen trucks were in the whole length of the continuous oven. The temperature rose gradually to 1160°C in the centre, and fell towards the exit end.

The intermittent bottle shaped oven was 16ft. in diameter and 18ft. high and held approximately 1,500 saggers. The filled saggers were placed in sixty columns of twenty-five saggers high in the oven, which was fired for 65 to 70 hours to a temperature of 1160°C. The firing took 12 to 15 tons of coal fed to nine fireboxes round the base. Before emptying the oven had to cool off for a period of 36 to 48 hours.

When the ware came out of the biscuit oven, it was hard and porous. After cleaning and brushing, if it was for underglaze decoration, it went straight to the decorating department. For example, animal models had the eyes painted in and the colour shading put on the body. They were then passed to the dipping or glazing department. White or coloured glaze ware went straight from the biscuit warehouse to the dipping department. In this department, the article was dipped into the liquid glaze of the colour required. This was a highly skilled operation as the dipper had to make sure the article only absorbed the correct amount of glaze, regardless of its porosity.

After cleaning the base, it was ready for the next stage of firing, which was done in a continuous electric glost oven, 97ft. long, rising to a temperature of 1060°C. This oven contained 17 trucks, one going into the oven every 96 minutes, taking 25 hours to go from end to end. The ware in this case was placed on siliminite shelves, each truck having five shelves. No two pieces had to touch one another when they were placed, or they would stick together and be a complete loss.

Some lines were ready for sale when they came from the glost oven, others had to go on to the decorating department for further painting, gilding or lithographing, etc., and were again fired to fasten the decoration on to the glaze, in a continuous enamel kiln rising to a temperature of 750°C.

The finished goods were selected and papered in the finishing warehouse, and then assortments were made up to the customers requirements. These assortments were packed in crates and casks and marked for their destination.

The SylvaC and Falcon fancy earthenware was shipped for 70 years to all parts of the world, and they had accredited representatives in all the principal countries.

When the new factory opened in 1957, the process was basically the same, except that all the kilns were either gas or electric. They also introduced a mechanised casting unit, and many small conveyors and mechanised aids. In 1964 they introduced a new packing system called 'Poly-tite', in which ware was packed skin tight.

The old Shaw & Copestake warehouse. First left Margery Addison, shipping clerk, second left Geoffry Abbott progress manager, retired in 1960, third right Roy Davies, despatch manager.

CHAPTER 4

PRODUCTS OF THE FACTORIES

THE SYLVAC FACTORY

The early Shaw & Copestake products consisted of, and here I quote the very first Shaw & Copestake advert in 1904: 'Decorated Vases, Jugs, Flower Pots, Cheese Stands, Trinkets and Toilet Ware, and Fancy Earthenware', some of the vases were very large, being 21″ high. They were very ornate and heavily decorated with gold and a lot of hand painting, during this period the firm were employing about 25 men painters. Some of the designs from 1904 were reproduced in 1981 from an original Catalogue, (unfortunately lost), called, not surprisingly the 1904 Range.

During the First World War the firm used a lot of cellulose decoration, which consisted of painting with cellulose paint straight on to the biscuit ware, and no glaze being applied to the articles. This was a much cheaper finish, and although it did not wear very well, it was possible to use a more attractive range of colours than normal ceramic colours. Production of this type of decoration ceased in the early 1950s.

After the First World War and in the 1920s they produced clock sets in a very attractive style. These can be found in an assortment of colours and decorations. Also jug and toilet sets, in bold colours and decorations. Having dilligently searched for some of the older ware, I now have a fairly good idea of what was available. Some of the colour combinations were very strange, but presumably it was the fashion of the time.

In the late 1920s the first animals appeared, starting with a range of elephants in a black cellulose finish, also a swan and some gnomes for the garden.

In the 1930s a complete change came over the firms productions, a new matt glaze was introduced in blue, green, brown and ivory. This proved to be so popular that other colours were gradually introduced. Mr. Richard Hull junior developed this new finish, in conjunction with a local colour firm called Harrison & Sons (Hanley) Ltd. Some matt glazes continued until 1982. Every conceivable colour was eventually produced in a matt glaze, from black, through to white.

Although other potteries tried to copy this glaze, no one managed to produce it really successfully as it had to be fired at a lower temperature than the majority of kilns were able to achieve. The matt glaze was used on a large variety of Shaw & Copestakes wares, including animals, vases and jugs, tableware, book-ends and ashtrays. It was to contribute largely to their success. The hand-painted and cellulose ware continued to be produced as well. During the 1930s a large number of rabbits, dogs and animals and novelty vases were produced, called in the trade 'Fancies, for a popular class of trade'. They proved to be *very* popular and some lines were continued until 1982. They also produced some art deco vases, but it was the fancies that were becoming popular. Shaw & Copestake did not have their own designer at this time, and used freelance designers.

In 1935 Shaw & Copestake participated in the British Industries Fair for the first time, and from then on it became a regular event. The export side of the business continued to flourish. Other outlets emerged, for the fancies, and they were used as fairground prizes, seaside and holiday souvenirs, the bunnies were even filled with bath salts or cotton wool for the Christmas market. Flying ducks suddenly appeared, always recognisable because SylvaC (or Falcon) flying ducks always fly to the left, whereas most others fly to the right. Were SylvaC responsible for the first Flying Ducks? As the others all appeared around the same time it is impossible to say, and there is no record as to who modelled or designed them.

During the War years, when the Shaw & Copestake factory was requisitioned by the Ministry of Defence, they moved into the Thomas Lawrence factory, which already belonged to them. Both firms continued with full production for export, and the home market was catered for as far as possible within the limits of the permitted quota. In an advert dated July 1942, they state 'SylvaC decorated ware has now been withdrawn for the duration of the War. Order your assorted crates of Jugs, Teapots, Beakers in White Finish'. Both firms were introducing new ranges throughout the war years, Shaw & Copestake produced a spitfire ashtray, Number 1667 and a fireplace ashtray complete with kitten Number 1622 in 1941. By 1945 Shaw & Copestake were back in their own factory and offering a wide range of earthenware fancies in semi-matt mottled glazes, bright-glazed colourings and coloured matt glazes. A particularly nice range brought out in 1949 was the blackberry tea and coffee set, made in primrose and pink.

During the next few years both factories were working at full pressure, using each others designs and marking items Falcon Ware or SylvaC. Thomas Lawrence already had their own designer and modeller, Mr. Reginald Thompson, and he was now designing for both factories, in conjunction with outside modellers.

During the 1950s and 60s, many new lines were introduced, wall plaques and floral brooches amongst them. A new logo was introduced in the 1960s, a Mr. SylvaC modelled by Mr. Thompson, but the brain child of Mr. M. Chapman, the commercial director, and was used for a number of years. It was used on the SylvaC labels, and catalogues and for general advertising. Mr. SylvaC was also made in the form of an ash tray, Number 3542, about 10″ high, which was given to dealers to display on their counters. The only known Mr. SylvaC ashtray still in existence is at the Crown Winsor factory shop.

A lot of advertising ware was made. A Leyland lorry ashtray Number 5404 made in 1977 is an interesting item, only about 1000 were made, for Leyland offices, it was designed by Mr. R. Thompson, and the paintress Vera painted only 10 a day as they were so intricate. A quantity of commemorative ware has been produced, and items especially for Fortnum & Masons, and Harrods.

In 1970 a Hollyberry range was introduced to decorate the Christmas table, and very attractive it looks too, with a dark green glaze and bright red berries. New designs were not quite so prevalent in the 1970s, the impression is of a gradual slowing down.

A few dog & horse head brooches and pendants were also made, a few thimbles and a new Tudor Cottage Ware was available in 1981, but only seven of the planned 30 pieces were ever produced.

By 1982 rumours were rife at the factory, it was obvious to the staff the firm were in trouble, the modellers were the first to realise, as they always work for a year ahead and work was scarce. The packers were on a two or three day week. Other potteries were also in difficulties, due to the economic climate. The Shaw & Copestake workers just hoped and prayed they would be able to survive. But it wasn't possible. When they were all called into the showroom, and told the bad news it still came as a terrible shock. Suddenly the majority of them were out of work. A very small number of staff were kept on by the workers Co-Operative who took over the factory, using the name Longton Ceramics. This enterprise only lasted a short time, and it was taken over by Crown Winsor.

As Crown Winsor purchased the Shaw & Copestake moulds

Pages from the 1960 catalogue, showing novelty and floral ware.

31

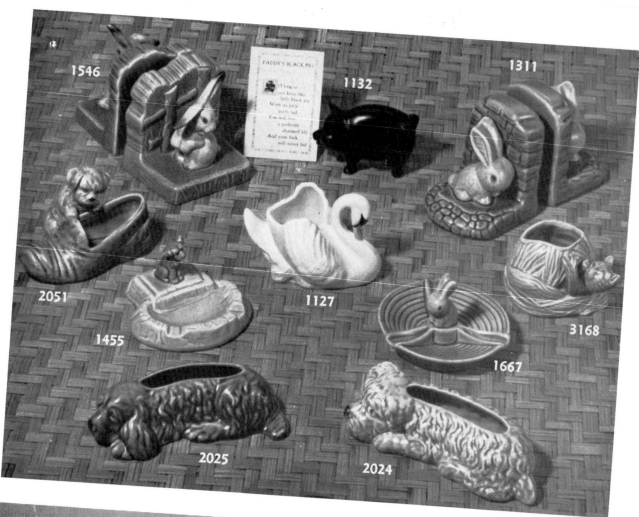

1546   1132   1311
2051   1127   3168
1455   1667
2025   2024

◄▲ Pages from the 1960 catalogue.

THE *SylvaC* DUCK FAMILY

HOLDER 2278
DUCK FAMILY 2397
HOLDER 2277
2398   2396
HOLDER 707
HOLDER 1127

▲ The 1904 range as shown in the 1980 catalogue.

▲ Novelty Money boxes.

▲ "Mine host". Falcon Ware.

▲ "Jeanette". Falcon Ware.

▲ Leyland lorry ashtray 5404. Owned by Vera Leese the paintress.

◄ Mr. SylvaC ashtray, with 'Toby' the dog, 3542. Modelled by Reginald Thompson, and used for advertising purposes. This one was seen in the factory shop. Note Mr. SylvaC has a teapot head, a wall vase body, uses the S and C for arms and legs and is holding a jardiniere. SylvaC is always spelt with a large S and C.

Bison 4732 8″ long   Buffalo 4733 9½″ long.

with the factory, it is not surprising that some of the original designs are still being produced. It is also possible that these will vary from time to time, and they may bring out some other old Shaw & Copestake wares. So far these have not been reproduced in the Matt glazes. They are either a plain white glaze or handpainted. A large number of the dogs are still being produced, and seem as popular as ever. A lot of the original SylvaC ware now has the Crown Winsor mark, which was impressed on the base of the bear the SylvaC mark, which was impressed on the base of the moulds. Naturally any new ware made by Crown Winsor bear their own mark.

The toby jugs and character jugs are also still very popular, but the majority of these were outside modelled by a firm called Longton New Art Pottery Co Ltd, Parkhall Street, Longton, trading under the name of Kelsboro Ware. So some jugs may be found with that name as well as the SylvaC name.

The vast range of products that were available can be seen in the Register of Numbers.

THE FALCON FACTORY

The products of the Falcon Factory were very similar to the Shaw & Copestake Factory. They did not make table ware, but specialised more in toilet ware and trinket sets, along with the

vases and jugs. They advertise Fancies and Novelties in 1928, but I have no idea what they were. Their ware is very nicely decorated with coaching scenes, glorious Devon scenes, cottages & hollyhocks and a flight of swallows. They also made childrens toilet ware.

They had a very strong export market, which continued throughout the War years. During which time they also produced utility lines, jugs teapots etc. From this time, when Shaw & Copestake were using part of the Falcon Works, they were producing a considerable amount of SylvaC Ware.

After the Second World War, they brought out a range of table accessories, and the Cavalier Range, Numbers 300–309 was introduced in 1945, they apparently were producing a range of over 100 lamp bases and old English character studies for the U.S.A. In 1948 they introduced the English rose table accessory range which included a tea and coffee set. In 1950, they produced a lovely set of 'straw hat posies' which was featured in the Sunday Graphic in 1953 with a lady 'wearing' the hat. The range included wall vases, plant pots, and sweet dishes and are really nice collectors pieces Numbers 281/2/3, 299, 314/5. By 1957, they had moved out of Falcon Works, and joined Shaw & Copestake at the Sylvan Works. By which time they were both producing the same items. The Thomas Lawrence (Longton) Ltd., company ceased trading in 1962, and was finally wound up in 1964.

The Cavalier range and some character jugs as shown in the 1960 catalogue.

2208

2084

2083

2154

1820

Flower of the Month
Lucky
BIRTHDAY EAR RINGS

Flower of the Month
Lucky
BIRTHDAY BROOCHES

Birthday Brooches

1821

Birthday Ear-rings

1997

1822

169

▲ Some earings, brooches and floral ware seen in the 1960 catalogue.

▼ Page from small leaflet issued in the 1950s.

SEAGULL WARE M.102

WALL VASE 2079
6¼" High

BOWL 2112
4¼" High   9½" Wide

BASKET 2119
6½" High   6¼" Wide

JUG 2086
6¼" High

CANDY BOX 2111
3" High   5" Wide

JARDINIÈRE 2113
3¼" High   7½" Wide

Two leaflets probably issued in the 1950s. These items were made in the Thomas Lawrence factory.

Some rare items. From left back row: Duck 2396, Welsh lady candle holder 1288, stag 3154, vase 2314, Churchill cigar ashtray no number Falcon Ware, pig and piglet no number Falcon Ware, Paul 3112. Front row from left: gondola 384, mallard 5119, tortoise 136, dish with lizard 431 Falcon Ware.

▲ From left: 1996 dog looking into basket, 3560 dog jumping over wall, 31 dog on slipper, 2045 two square baskets same number different depths, 3132 dog with panniers, 1484 top hat, 586 dog and barrel.

▲ Funnies. From left: Poodle 3428, sheepdog 3423, puppy 3114, tiny 1400, yawning 3433, puppy 3116, dachshund 3426, Yorkshire terrier 3432.

▲ Some of the ashtrays available in the 1940s. From left: 1366 with dog, 1455 with bunny, 1622 fireplace, 1667 with dog, 1454 with cat, 1455 with dog, 1366 with seagull two bunnies and dog, 1181 hare and match holder.

CHAPTER 5

SYLVAC ANIMALS AND PIXIES

SYLVAC DOGS

Shaw & Copestake had already marketed at least 40 dogs before the start of the Second World War. So the potential for dog ornaments had been realised. The first dogs were probably modelled about 1930, and the majority were originally designed by a French modeller. Mr. Hull travelled abroad extensively, in connection with the export trade, and had good contacts in France, where quite a lot of his ideas came from.

The first dogs appearing in the Register are Numbers 1043/4, and 1117, unfortunately I have no description of them. 'Monty the Mongrel' Number 1118, is the first well-known dog, he was sold for many years, and was in the 1935 advert in the Pottery Gazette.

Undoubtedly, the most popular of these Pre-War dogs, were the terriers, Numbers 1378/79/80. They were still being produced at the factory when it went into liquidation, in 1982. Although by then they were obtainable in fawn matt only. Much to my surprise, the middle size was for sale in the factory shop on my last visit (September 1988), but in white shiny gloss only.

Not far behind in the popularity stakes, were the Scottie dogs Numbers 1205–1209, known as 'MAC', they were designed by a Czechoslovakian modeller called Otakar Steinburger, in 1932, who was residing in Peckham. Shaw & Copestake probably sold them shortly after 1932. They have been seen in all colours, and cellulose finish, and I have even seen one in lead. Mr. Steinburger probably sold his design to other firms as well. Some of the other dogs were so similar in design to the Scottie, that I am almost sure Mr. Steinburger modelled several other ranges. This is also borne out by the fact that he registered several designs of dogs at the Patent Office in London on the same day.

So the Pre-War dogs had quite a Continental flavour to them. All the dogs were available in a wide range of colours and glazes.

From 1940, most of the dogs were modelled at the Falcon Pottery, where Shaw & Copestake had joined Thomas Lawrence, due to the Concentration of Industry. No doubt a lot of these dogs were designed by Mr. R. Thompson, the resident Falcon Ware designer and modeller. They were given the low two or three figure numbers.

In the 1950s Shaw & Copestake brought out the 'Dog with Toothache' known on the Factory as 'Toby', modelled by Mr. Thompson, in four sizes, Numbers 2451, 2455, 3093 & 3183, mostly seen in stone matt. They were made until the 1970s, and Toby was also Mr. SylvaC's constant companion. I asked Mr. Thompson why Toby had a bandage round his head, 'because he has toothache of course', was the reply.

From the 1950s many more dogs were modelled, including the caricature dogs of Stephan Czarnota, but mostly in the classical style of Mr. Thompson. Although a number were still finished in the matt glaze, the majority were natural colours. Over 200 dogs were eventually modelled, some of which are still in production. Practically every breed of dog was represented in the selection. There are humerous dogs, shy dogs, sad dogs, serious dogs, naughty dogs, dogs with slippers, holding pipes and climbing out of cheese dishes. Any SylvaC dog is worth collecting regardless of colour, but more collectable with a good SylvaC mark.

The very large dogs were produced in much smaller quantities, due to the space required to fire them, consequently making them quite scarce.

Shaw & Copestake, ever resourceful, used many of the dogs on vases, ashtrays, bookends, posies, bowls and novelty items.

Most dogs were designed by Mr. Reginald Thompson, but also by Stephan Czarnota, John Lawson, George Matthews, and of course Otakar Steinburger.

SYLVAC RABBITS

Possibly the most popular of the SylvaC Ware are the round bunnies, Numbers 1028,1027,1026,1065,990,1067,1386 and 1400, ranging in size from 10″ to 2″. The price quoted in the 1940 catalogue for the 10″ Bunny Number 1028 is 26/- PER DOZEN! These bunnies are largely responsible for a lot of SylvaC collecting, as they seem to bring back the aura of the 1930s. Mr. Richard Hull returned from France one day in great excitement. He had seen our bunny, and knew he was on to something good. Mr. William Shaw, his partner, rather scathingly remarked 'No one is going to buy green rabbits'. However, Mr. Hull did go ahead, and produced one of the most successful lines. They were available in all colours and glazes, green matt being the most popular, and were produced from the 1930s until about 1975. In the 1972 catalogue they were reduced in number from the original eight to five, and were offered in the unusual colours of burnt orange, mustard and purple, glossy, of course. The matt colours discontinued about 1970. The larger bunnies were apparently also used as cottonwool containers, with the cottonwool protruding from the tail, also bathsalt containers, but how the bathsalts were retrieved I do not know.

Harry the Hare, Numbers 1300,1299,1298,1265, were registered at the Patent Office by Shaw & Copestake in 1936. Registered Number 815840. Number 1298 was made until 1970, at which time it was produced in, fawn, green, turquoise and yellow matt. The others finished in the 1940s. They were all made originally in a wide variety of colours and finishes.

Lop Ear the Rabbit also appeared at this time, Registered Number 815839, (1936), Numbers 1302,1303,1304. They continued until 1975, also finishing in burnt orange, mustard and purple. The matt colours being discontinued about 1970. Another set of lop eared rabbits are 1525,1526 and 1511, the difference being they were looking ahead, whereas the earlier lop ears were looking round.

There were also two sets of crouching rabbits available in the 1940s, three with ears up, Numbers 1389,1388 and 1371, and three with ears down Numbers 1523 and 1530 and 1529. I also have a small crouching bunny with one ear up and one down, Number 1497 (1940s). The two bunnies kissing are Number 1534, after which there is a dearth of rabbits until the delightful set of ski-ing rabbits, made at the Falcon Pottery. Numbers are 25–29, and they are depicted, standing, injured and falling, nicely hand-painted in various colours, only between 2¼″ and 3½″ high. The first record of them is 1950 and they were only made for a short time.

Number 2955 a large crouching rabbit was seen in the 1960s for a short time, and Number 2980 an upright rabbit with bow tie, and protruding teeth, appeared in the 1960s, mostly seen in matt yellow.

The next series of rabbits was modelled in 1975, by George Matthews, Numbers 5289,5290 and 5291, they were upright and

TERRIER AND SCOTTIE DOGS

	1380	1379	1378	1209	1208	1207	1206	1205
Approx. height	11"	8"	5"	11"	9"	7½"	6¼"	5"
Price per doz.	34/6	18/6	7/3	33/–	24/6	16/6	11/6	6/6

DOGS

	1262	1261	1245	1259	1412	1118	1369
Approx. height	8"	7¼"	5¾"	2¾"	9"	6¾"	5"
Price per doz.	36/–	27/–	20/–	6/9	36/–	13/6	7/3

	1227	1415	1121	1295	1122	1332	1123
Approx. height	5"	5"	4¾"	5"	3¾"	5½"	3½"
Price per doz.	11/–	14/6	11/–	14/6	11/–	14/6	11/–

Pages of dogs reproduced from a 1940 catalogue.

Two pages from a 1960 catalogue.

41

2451   2455   3183   1246   1247

2331   3179   3167   2473   3177

1414   2421   3182   3175   1415

◄▲ Pages from a 1960 catalogue.

3174   210   1548

176   203   209

18   115   188   177   116   114

◄ Dachshund 177   Alsation 178.
Dachshund 188   Alsation 185.
From a 1950s leaflet.

◄ Corgis 3137 3133 3136
Corgis 3134   3135

▼   Vase 4528 Canine range.

43

RABBITS

	1028	1027	1026	1065	990	1067	1386	1400
Approx. height	9¾″	8¼″	6¼″	6″	5″	4″	3″	2″
Price per doz.	26/-	18/-	12/-	9/6	6/3	5/-	4/6	3/-

HARES AND LOP-EARED RABBITS

	1300	1299	1298	1265	1389	1388	1371	1304	1303	1302
Approx. height	9¼″	7½″	6″	3″	7½″	5½″	3½″	8½″	7″	5½″
Price per doz.	21/-	14/-	7/-	4/3	18/-	12/-	5/9	19/-	11/6	7/-

	1525	1526	1511	1492	1499	1498	1529	1523	1530
App. hgt.	8½″	10½″	13″	5½″	4¼″	3¼″	3¼″	4½″	5½″
Price doz.	13/6	18/6	33/-	13/6	7/-	5/6	6/3	9/6	16/6

(Matt White with Coloured Beak)

Reproduced from a 1940 catalogue.

44

1146	1145	1144	1143	1142	1391	1390	1046
Approx. height 9¾"	8½"	7¾"	6¼"	5¼"	6"	4½"	6"
Price per doz. 24/-	17/-	11/3	9/-	6 3	12/-	6 3	6 6

1427	1374	1428	1414	1373	1431	1447	1422
App. height 4¾"	5"	4¼"	5¼"	4½"	3½"	3½"	4¾"
Price doz. 13/3	7/6	13/3	11/-	7/6	13/3	14/-	18/-
						(Made in 2 Sizes)	

▲   Pages from a 1940 catalogue.

Reproduced from the 1970s catalogue.

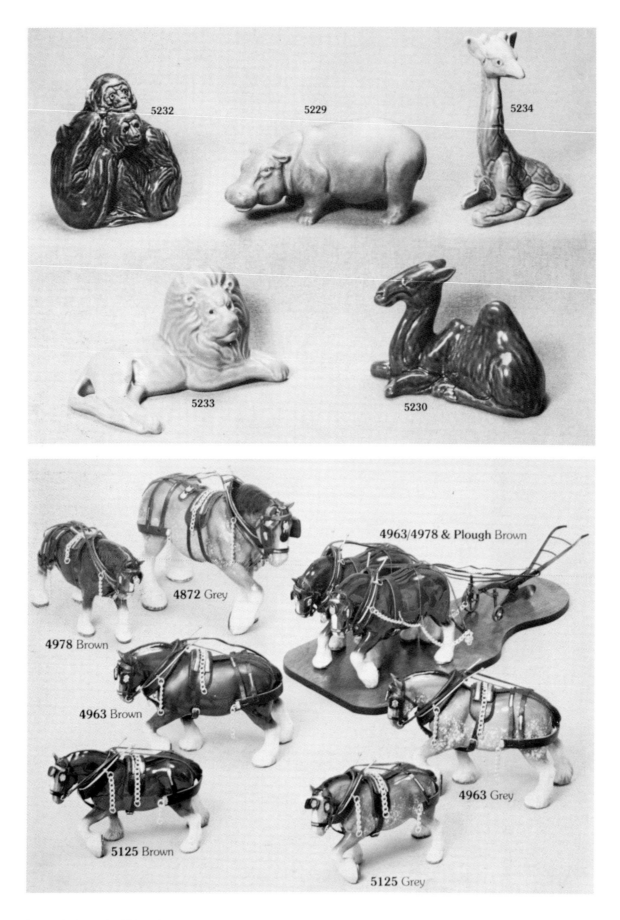

A selection from the 1980 catalogue.

A selection of SylvaC animals and birds.

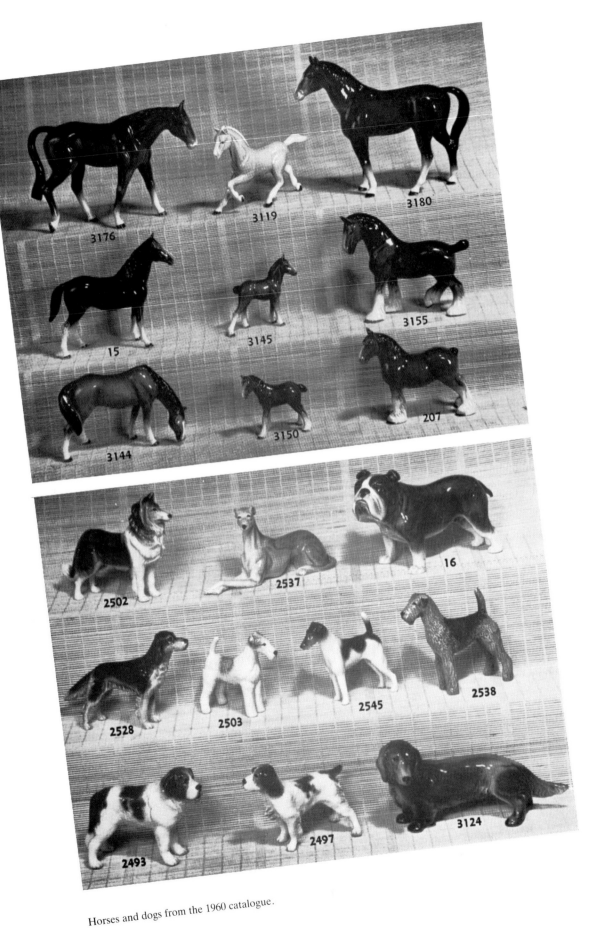

Horses and dogs from the 1960 catalogue.

48

lop eared, and fawn matt, and were available until 1982. In 1981, George Matthews modelled a childrens rabbit money-box, Number 5658, this rabbit has both ears down and is clutching a carrot, and that was the last SylvaC rabbit.

Rabbits of course feature quite a lot on ashtrays, bulb pots, bookends, vases and novelty ware, even wall vases.

The SylvaC bunnies were copied by many potteries, and it is sometimes difficult to tell them apart. As all SylvaC bunnies are numbered on the base (except the tinies), it is advisable to only buy clearly marked bunnies. Never be surprised at the unusual range of colours they can be found in. I hesitated for some time before buying a large cellulose orange hare, Number 1300, as the colour was so strange, but was delighted to discover later he was a genuine Shaw & Copestake hare. I have since discovered other cellulose decorated rabbits but would consider this finish quite rare. There is certainly plenty of scope for collectors of rabbits as the variations in sizes and colours abound, they are probably the most well-known and admired of the SylvaC ranges.

The largest round bunny, Number 1028, 10″, is very sought after and was made until 1975, it is possible there was also a larger one, but I have no definite confirmation of this. There are some gaps in the Register at this point, so it is quite possible. Perhaps a collector has this information.

OTHER SYLVAC ANIMALS and BIRDS

Venturing into the world of animal figures, was an exciting time for Shaw & Copestake. They tentatively tried out the market with a set of elephants, starting at Number 768, available in black or grey, matt, glossy or cellulose finishes, and a swan, Number 795, probably a flower holder. These seemed to do quite well, and were followed with the first of the bunnies Number 990. The rest, as they say, is history. The animals were undoubtably the influence of Mr. Richard Hull junior, who was already showing his flair for judging the market trends. Not that we should in anyway undermine the business accumen of Mr. Hull senior, who had run a very successful business for many years, and I'm sure he was wholeheartedly behind his son in this new field. Possibly they had some animal novelties in the earlier years, kingfisher Number 700, is an example, but there is no definite evidence of this.

Enthusiastically they tried many different animal figures, with mixed results.

Starting with the elephants, from Number 768 to 771 (possibly 772 but not registered) and 815, were elephants striding along with their trunks in the air, they were finished in matt black or grey or cellulose finish. Ranging in size from 4″ to 8½″. The 'elephant with howdah' range, Numbers 773,788,789, 814,826, also striding but with a howdah on its back, was available in five sizes in a cellulose finish.

The first cat was Number 1046, with back arched and tail in the air, it was later joined by Number 1313, a large version, and Number 1400 a very small version. Quite a lot of these cats are still about, all surprisingly with their tails intact. Other cats Numbers 1086–88, sitting, mostly seen in black gloss, were a standard SylvaC line for many years, and Numbers 1086/7, are still in production. Cats are also to be found in baskets, boxes, shoes and boots, on top hats, and in a ball of wool. By the 1980s Shaw & Copestake had quite a large range of cats, of all types, Numbers 5107,5111,5236,5237,5261, & 5262. Three caricature cats, 2794/5 and 2722, and the Stephan Czarnota cats, Numbers 5298/9/300 show quite a different style of modelling. A lovely set of little Siamese kittens Numbers 99–103 is worth looking out for and also the cats with long

necks Numbers 3404 & 3457, and one embossed with flowers Number 3392.

Lucky pig number 1132 in black matt has also been seen advertising bacon, which seems a bit insensitive! His luck obviously held, because he was made until 1982. The new lucky pig, Number 1486, in a sitting position was not so lucky and was only produced in the 1940s.

There was a set of five squirrels, all nibbling an acorn, Numbers 1142/46, obviously not very popular as they finished in the 1940s.

Number 1281, heralded the first lamb, of which there were quite a few different designs, and Number 1293 brought forth the first duck.

The birds really started in earnest with 1328 a woodpecker, 1330 a kingfisher, 1331 a bird reaching into the water, and a set of seagulls 1349/51 and 1357, followed by birds Numbers 1375 and 1376.

The first fox Number 1369 was in a sitting position, whereas fox Number 1424 was crouching. Number 1372, was the first polar bear. The bears were also decorated as pandas.

Shaw & Copestake had quite a strong range of horses, ponies, foals and donkeys, the first of which appeared in the 1930s Number 1334 a rather lovely foal standing. Then Number 1374, a rather chubby little chap, that could be a donkey. He was followed by Number 1422, a horse sitting and 1428, a little donkey that was produced until 1982. There followed over the years many lovely horses, including the huntsman with his hounds, Number 21, re-numbered 4707, and the little girl on her pony, Number 4708.

Going back to Number 1390 and 1391 are the koala bears, there are a few vases and posies with koala bears attached, and these are avidly collected by any visiting Australian, as is kangaroo Number 1493.

Also in the 1930s we have the only frog Number 1399, (which was re-numbered and used as a pomander), apart from the money box frog, Number 5097. Horace the hippopotomus, Number 1425, who I think is enchanting, only made it into the 1940s. Number 1431 is a calf, 1451 a stag, and Number 1458 a rather large leopard chewing his foot. There is even a very handsome lizard Number 1467.

Number 1519 is a rather unusual stag on a rock, followed by three small polar bears/pandas Numbers 1520,1521 and 1522. Number 1527 is a sitting elephant.

The animals, together with other products, were transferred to the Falcon Pottery for the duration of the War. At the Falcon Pottery a very large range of all different types of animals was produced, using the two and three figure numbers.

Another interesting range made at the Falcon Pottery, was designed by Arnold Machin M.A. It was a group of cat, horse standing, tigress, and stag, Numbers 3151–54.

An ever popular group were the three chimpanzees, Numbers 96, 97 and 98, modelled in the late 1940s or early 50s by Mr. R. Thompson.

The Thomas Lawrence Works made most of the animals until the closure of the factory in 1957, when they moved into their new shared premises with Shaw & Copestake.

In the new factory, a few more animals were modelled. There was an otter, a fox, a squirrel, a bull and an osprey. These were all in the Prestige Range, also a rather serious Rhinoceros.

This gives you some idea of the animal figures available during the factories lifetime, there were many more, as will be seen in the register of numbers. The last animals on record are two pandas Number 5578 sitting, and Number 5579 standing, modelled by Mr. George Matthews.

All information regarding production dates of the animals mentioned, can be found in the register of numbers.

◄ From left: Ducks 2396 and 1499, osprey 3339, golden crested grebe 3162, duck 1498, bird 1376. Front from left: mallard 5119, golden eyed duck 5120, shoveller duck 5122.

► Large foal at back Number 107, third row, from left: horse galloping no number, donkey 5131, second from left: donkey 1428, foal 1334, donkey 1374, mule 3384, front: foal 1447.

◄ Monkey 3141, Donkey 183, Cat 184. From a 1950s leaflet.

50

5517/1
5520/1
5519/1
5522/1
5521/1
5518/1

5522
5521
5523
5524/1
5520
5524/1
5519
5525/1
5523/1
5518
5525
5517

Sold only in multiples of 6   *Individual box size 101 × 76 × 22mm (4″ × 3″ × ⅞″) approx.*

Brooches and pendants as shown in the 1981 catalogue.

GNOMES

The Happy Little Men who are a never ending source of delight....

Sylvac

▲ Garden gnomes as shown in a 1950s catalogue.

PIXIES AND GNOMES

It may surprise SylvaC collectors to learn that Shaw & Copestake produced a range of garden gnomes. The first appearing in the 1930s, Number 962, followed by seven others, Numbers 1024, 1092–5, 1097 and 1221. These were cellulose finished, the largest being 14″ high and the smallest 4½″ high. Numbers 1024 and 1221 were made until the late 1950s, but the others were discontinued in the 1940s. It is most unlikely these outside gnomes have survived, as the cellulose finish is not very durable, and I would be most interested to know if any collector has one. A new range was introduced in the 1950's and was available until the 1960's Numbers 74, 75, 81–83, 87, 108, 110, 113. The largest of this range was Number 110 which was 16″ high and the smallest was 4¾″ high, it may be possible some of this later range is still about, but there again I have not been able to trace an example.

The first pixies were Numbers 1420 and 1421, the first is a pixie sitting under a toadstool, with a squirrel, and has the inscription 'Lucky Pixie' around the base, available from the 1930s until 1956. Number 1421 is a pixie in the same sitting position, but perched on a mound with a small toadstool behind him, this also is inscribed 'Lucky Pixie' 1930s until 1940s. They can be found in fawn/green/blue matt.

There are many pixies or gnomes attached to posies or bowls, 1480 and 1481 were the first examples. The round bulb bowl Number 1513 and 1514 is probably the one which evokes most memories, 'My grandmother had one of those', is a remark constantly heard. It is a woodland scene with recesses for gnomes and bunnies, originally in a matt glaze, but later in the M101 decoration, (See Chapter Six – Vases and Jugs).

Number 1513/4 was made from about 1940 until 1965. There followed a heart shaped posy Number 1963 in the 1950s and an oval bowl Number 2049, both with a gnome. Also in the 1950s was the wall vase Number 320 with a gnome on the front, one peeping over the top, and one round the corner, Number 353 is a log with a recess for a gnome and Number 355 a tree house jug with a gnome sitting at the door (sometimes a rabbit is found sitting at the same door).

If you want to start your day with a smile, you can do nothing better than collect the lazy pixies. These little fellows can be seen dozing off on a wheelbarrow 708, beside a toadstool 707, against a log and a basket 2275 and 2276, and a watering can and flowerpot 2277 and 2278. The reason for the lower numbers may mean they are originally old Shaw & Copestake numbers, I know the wheelbarrow was also used with flowers, or made in the Falcon factory at a later date. A larger wheelbarrow number 747 also sports a pixie. These items sometimes have other gnomes or animals on them. They are mostly to be found in the matt glazes, but sometimes in a glossy finish.

A gnome on an upturned toadstool 2158 might be found but is quite rare, and a different gnome beside a yellow bamboo cane 2799 is another collectable item. Another pixie again is seen on bowls 2295 an acorn, 2289 a square container with a grass effect, 2339 and 2346 both with a grass and toadstool background.

Many people collect the pixies and gnomes, they are worth collecting for entertainment value alone. The pixie on the horseshoe vase, Number 4297, guarantees to bring you good luck from Ireland. But perhaps I do him an injustice, could it possibly be a Leprachaun?

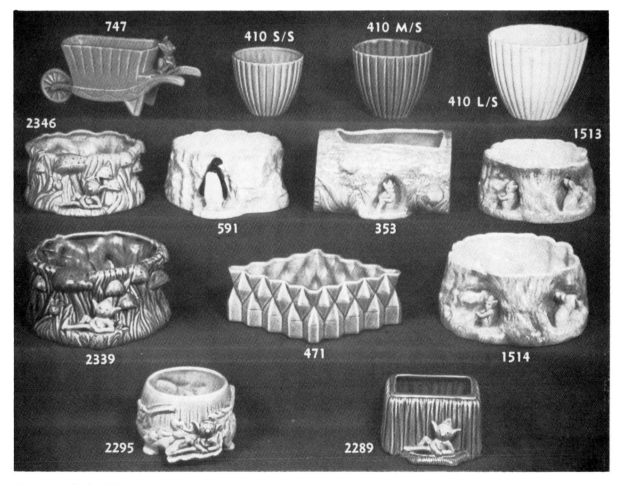

From a page in the 1960 catalogue.

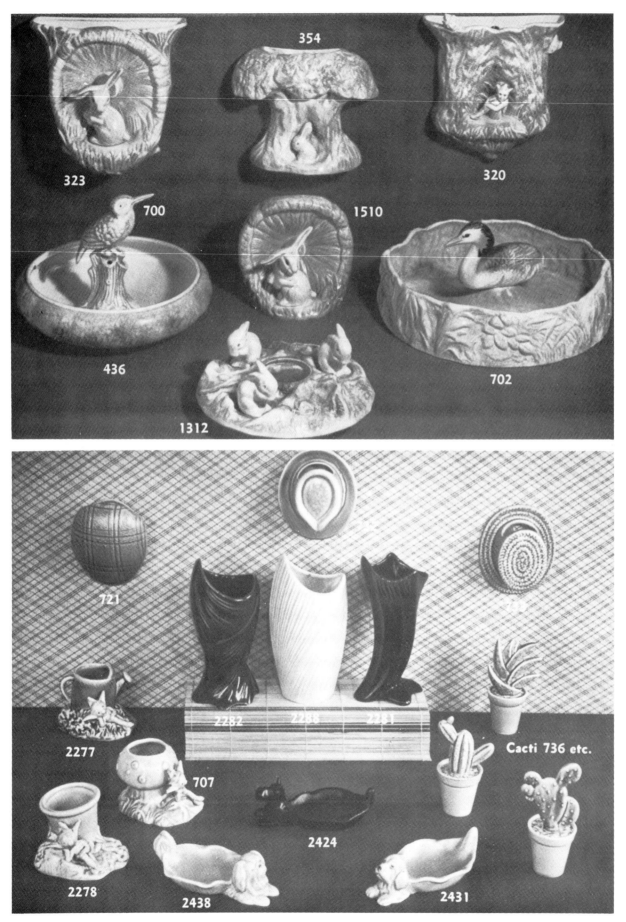

Pages from a 1959 and 1960 catalogue.

54

CHAPTER 6

POPULAR SYLVAC WARE

WALL PLAQUES AND WALL VASES

The best known of the wall plaques, is probably the set of four flying ducks, Numbers 1360, 1403, 1402 and 1401. The tiny 1403 came later, as the number was first used in the 1940s for a posy in the shape of a seal. The first Pottery Gazette advert for the ducks was in 1939, but they may have been available a few years before. SylvaC ducks always fly to the left, whereas other ducks more often go to the right. They were produced in green, blue and fawn matt glaze, as well as hand painted. They are also to be found with the Falcon Ware mark, and it is thought they were mostly made in the Thomas Lawrence factory.

There are three seagull wall plaques, also flying to the left, Numbers 1543–45, seen in a white matt glaze, and three swallows flying to the right Numbers 3156–58 in a dark blue glossy finish. All these birds are beautifully hand decorated in natural colours, and are really worth collecting.

Almost each range of wares had a wall vase, so there are plenty to collect. Some were decorated with hand painted flowers, others had budgies perched on them like Number 1956 which incidently has also been seen with a swallow attached. The budgies are green or blue. A blue tit on a coconut, Number 687, handpainted in natural colours, is one of the blue tit range.

There is a very unusual range of hats, a boater 733, a cap 721 a trilby 732, and a girls straw hat, no number.

Quite a feature of a SylvaC Collection would be the bunny and mushroom wall vase, Number 323, and also the bunny and tree 354, and gnomes in the tree 320. Three dog head wall plaques, spaniel Number 88, scottie Number 89 and terrier Number 90 are also available in a handpainted finish. The dogs heads were given other numbers at one time (Numbers 25,26 & 27), these numbers conflict with the ski-ing bunny numbers, no definite explanation has emerged as to the reason for this.

Two very unusual wall plaques, designed by Mr. R. Thompson, were Numbers 327 and 329, 327 was a teenage boy's head and 329 a teenage girl's head. These were beautifully coloured, and are very rare.

In 1977 Mr. R. Thompson designed sets of martingales. They were ceramic discs which fitted into leather straps for hanging on the wall, available in a variety of decorations, such as horses, ships, French paintings, hunting scenes, dogs and Cries of London, Numbers, 5582/3.

The Cavalier Range also has a wall plaque plate, Number 5327.

ASHTRAYS AND BOOKENDS

Shaw & Copestake made a large number of ashtrays. The most popular being the ashtrays Numbers 1181, 1366, 1454, 1455, and 1622. The adornments on these ashtrays varied a lot, but were usually rabbits, dogs, cats, birds, sometimes aeroplanes and cars. No doubt there are many I have not seen. They make a very interesting collection as you have two SylvaC items for the price of one. The later ranges, The Woodland Range and Riverside Range etc, all had ashtrays, with a small animal attached, and some of these continued until the 1980s, so there is enormous scope for a collection.

There were also many advertising ashtrays, such as the Mr. SylvaC with Toby the dog, 3542, the Leyland lorry 5404, Peter Rumsey Abergavenny 3467, Pipers Whisky ashtray Number 5436, and Guiness ashtray Number 5437. Then there are the novelty ashtrays such as the golf ball Number 4125.

The book-ends are more scarce. There were two different styles to start with, Numbers 1311, a brick wall effect, and Number 1546 a fence background. Sitting in front of which would be a bunny, dog, flowers or other item. Then came the horse at the stable door 2521, and the fish on a wave Number 2522, both very nicely finished items. I also note bookend Number 2826 in the Register, but have not yet seen this one.

SYLVAC VASES & JUGS

Like a lot of the Stoke-on-Trent potteries, vases and jugs were the mainstay of the factory. They were produced continually from the start of the pottery at the turn of the century, to its end in 1982, changing styles to keep up or ahead of the latest trends. Experimenting with colours, designs and glazes, sometimes coming up with a real winner, others doomed to immediate failure. One winner that comes to mind is the acorn vase with the squirrel handle. It seemed to keep its appeal from the 1930s, through to the 1980s. It was first designed in 1935, (Numbers 1115 & 1195), then remodelled with a spout in the 1950s (Numbers 1958/9), and remodelled once again without the spout in the 1960s (Number 4068). The same applied to the vase with the stork handle, which was also modelled three times. Both these vases were also produced in miniature.

The hollyhock vase, the gnomes climbing into the mushroom vase, and the rabbits climbing into the furze vase, were not quite so popular, they were also remodelled, but didn't quite make it into the 80s.

Other vases in this style that dropped by the wayside earlier were the dragon handle vase 1116, and the stags head vase 1167, which didn't even make it into the 1940s. The monkey and coconut vase 1190, birds nest vase 1305 and budgie tail vase 1370, fared slightly better, making it into the 1940s. Real collectors items these early drop outs.

The animal vases were always an important feature of Shaw & Copestakes products, and they continued to bring out new combinations right up till 1977. The very first animal vase must have been the acorn vase, 1115, and the last was in the Harvest Time Range, Numbers 5243–5250 showing a little mouse nestling amongst the corn. In between those two ranges were the Woodland Range, with a squirrel or fawn, the Riverside Range with the swan, and the Giant Panda Range, with a panda that looks so surprised, and a bit put out at being there.

The smaller vases with an animal attached, such as the chimney pot, with either cat, owl or stork Number 2425 and the palm tree with hippo, giraffe or elephant Number 2430, were very amusing. Have you seen the dog dressed for tennis, and the city gent dog attached to vase Number 2660? Surely worth collecting for novelty value alone.

The Hyacinth leaf range Numbers 2452/3 etc, must be the most common SylvaC vase. This range was modelled by Mr. R. Thompson, in the 1950s and continued until 1982.

Every conceivable shape was tried out, some vases have shape names instead of numbers. When you consider the Falcon Pottery were also churning out masses of vases, it makes one wonder where they all went. But we have to remember the large export business that was built up over the years.

Jugs also seemed very popular, the large jugs that went with the toilet sets, and the sets of three jugs in different sizes. Some of which had the most lovely designs, others too gaudy for

	1274	1138	1115	1195	1196	1318	1370	1305	1190
App. hgt.	8½″	10″	8½″	7½″	8½″	8¾″	7½″	8″	7″
Price doz.	33/-	28/6	28/6	22/6	33/-	33/-	22/6	33/-	33/-
			(Made in 2 Sizes)						

	1416 (Cellulose Finish)	1451	1246	1312	1285	1284	1296	1423	1397
App. height	5″	5″	4½″		5¼″	3¾″	4″	2¾″	
Price doz.	12/6	14/-	9/6	30/-	16/3	11/6	12/-	7/-	13/-
					(Made in 2 Sizes)				

	1487	1481	1513	1514	1480	1479	1484
App. height	4½″	Diam. 8″	Diam. 7″	Diam. 8″	Diam. 5½″	Length 9″	Height 3¼″
Price per doz.	13/6	23/-	M.85 36/-	45/-	16/6	15/-	14/-
			Matt 33/-	42/-			
			(Made in 2 Sizes)				

From the 1940 catalogue.

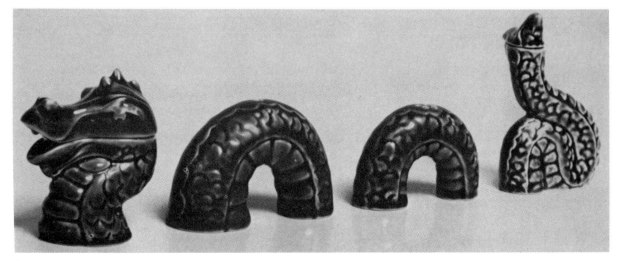

Sea monster cruet set 5468.

Jugs and Bowls

JUG 1969

JUG 406

WALL VASE SWALLOW

WALL VASE BUDGERIGAR

JUG 1959 MADE IN TWO SIZES

JUG 455

JUG 1960

BOWL 468 MADE IN TWO SIZES

BOWL 1514 MADE IN TWO SIZES

JUG 355

▲ Page from a 1950s catalogue, showing unusual wall vase with swallow Number 1956.

3930

◄ Bull Number 3930, part of the Prestige range.

Bell 5535
120mm (4¾") *high*

L/S Tea Pot 4809 (4/5 cup)
146mm (5¾") *high*

Two piece Cruet 4832
90mm (3½") *high*

Coffee Pot 5537
228mm (9") *high*

Beaker 4817
115mm (4½") *high*

Breakfast/Salad Plate 4811
203mm (8") *across*

Cheese Dish 4815
178mm (7") *long*

Honey (or Preserve) Jar 4812
114mm (4½") *high*

Four piece Cruet 4832
228mm (9") *long*

The Croft range of table ware.

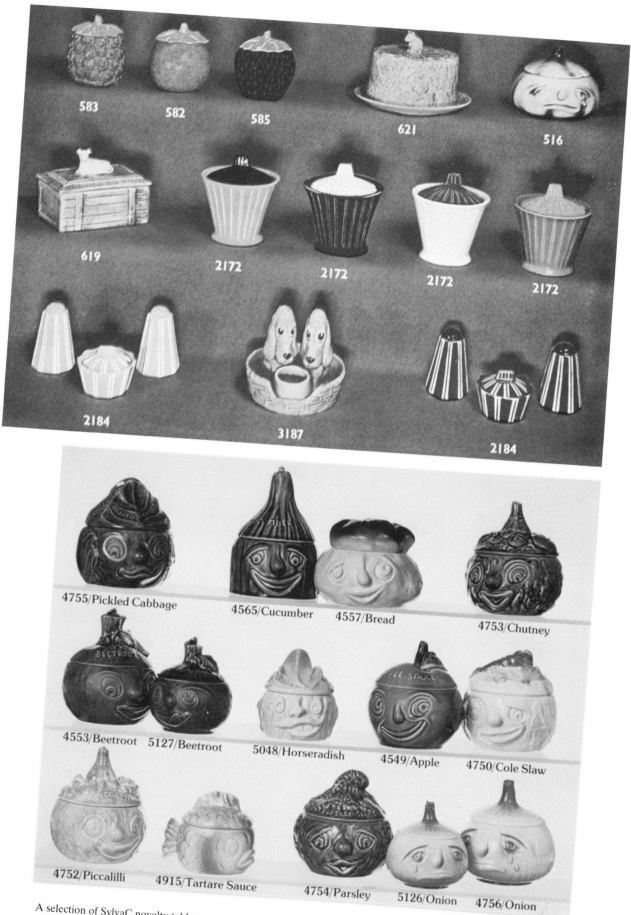

583   582   585   621   516

619   2172   2172   2172   2172

2184   3187   2184

4755/Pickled Cabbage   4565/Cucumber   4557/Bread   4753/Chutney

4553/Beetroot   5127/Beetroot   5048/Horseradish   4549/Apple   4750/Cole Slaw

4752/Piccalilli   4915/Tartare Sauce   4754/Parsley   5126/Onion   4756/Onion

A selection of SylvaC novelty tableware.

WITH SOME POTS, THE ORIGINALITY IS ON THE OUTSIDE.

Frank Cooper's Original Oxford Marmalade
was created over 100 years ago for people who wanted something
highly distinctive and delicious.
It has a style all of its own, a pleasing individuality, just like
these conserve pots.
At a conservative estimate, in a hundred years no one's
come up with anything more original.

THE TASTE OF INDIVIDUAL CHARACTER.

Frank Cooper Limited, 84 High Street, Oxford OX1 4BG

▲ The dogs head honey-pot was used recently in the FRANK COOPER'S Marmalade advertisement. Reproduced by kind permission of CPC (UK) Ltd. The FRANK COOPER'S OXFORD label is a registered trade mark of CPC (UK) Ltd., Esher, Surrey KT10 9PN.

◄ A display of the dogs head range, reproduced from a SylvaC catalogue. Numbers as follows: ... 1850, cruet 1715, toast rack 1990, butter 1818, ... 1849.

60

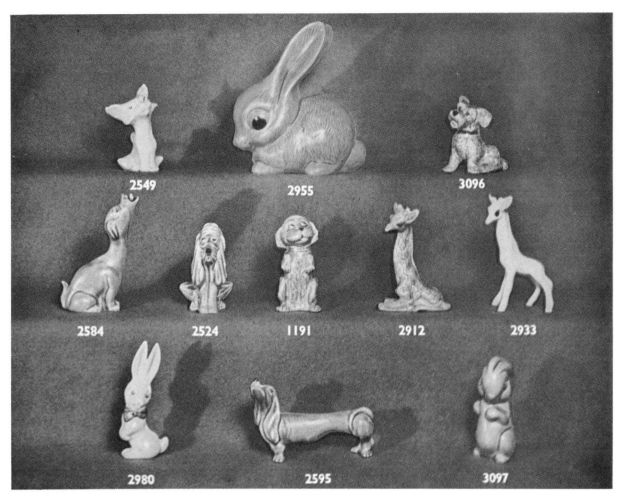

▲   Some unusual SylvaC animals.

Various novelty containers. Back row from left: 567 duck and barrel, 2425 chimneys with owl, stork and cat, 568 bowl with fawn.
Front row from left: 2025 spaniel, 1457 tree stumps with bunnies, 2024 sealyham.

▼ The sea provided much inspiration for SylvaC ware. These are just a few of the ranges. Back row from left: New shell 3524, coral 3907, Nautilus 2449. Front row: Dolphin 5188, Marina 4161, New shell 3532, boats 1394 and 1393.

▲ Pisces range table ware.

▲ Cordon Brun range.

Teddy Nursery range.

▲ Zooline Nursery Range.

Novelty vases. Back row from left: 4297 pixie Ireland, 4227 scottie dog Scotland, 3711 harp Ireland, 4236 horseshoe Cheddar. Front row from left: 2656, 2658, 2655 all with lamb, 2600 with three different dogs.

words. It seems they loved any shade of mauve or purple, blended with any other colour that took their fancy.

All this changed in the early 1930s, when green, orange and fawn became fashionable. This progressed to the mottled look, a blend of greens and fawns decoration number M101, pale green and blue number M102, pink and green number M112, dark blue, green & fawn M106, shades of crimson M135, shades of blue M134, shades of fawn M105.

The cellulose ware was also given decoration numbers, and were very attractive and brightly coloured. This style of decorating finished in the mid 1950s. It was no longer available in the 1959 Catalogue.

TOBY AND CHARACTER JUGS

There is a vast range of Toby and Character jugs. Mostly modelled in the 1960s by Longton New Art Pottery Co., Ltd., Parkhall Street, Longton, trading under the name of Kelsboro Ware. Shaw & Copestake purchased all the moulds from them. They were also produced with the Kelsboro Ware trademark, and are still produced with the Crown Winsor mark. Although they are very fine pieces, its a matter of opinion as to whether they are genuine SylvaC models. Shaw & Copestake and Thomas Lawrence did model their own character jugs, namely Punch (un-numbered) produced during the 1940s, 50s and 60s, Henry V111 also originally un-numbered until 1960s when it was numbered 4488 and, the Cavalier 306-re-numbered 4487 (1945–1965). Other original character jugs re-numbered are Number 4489 Yeoman of the Guard, Number 4491 William Shakespeare, Number 4492 George Bernard Shaw, Number 4486 Dick Turpin. These were re-numbered or given a new number to fit in with the sequence of numbers issued to the character jugs. Some of the really early ones can be found in the matt glazes, and the later models are carefully hand painted. The character and Toby jug numbers start at number 4400 in the Register of Numbers.

SYLVAC TABLE WARE AND TEA SETS

Shaw & Copestake have always made a considerable amount of table ware, by which I mean jam pots, butter dishes, sugar bowls, teapots, jugs, cake plates, cruet sets, and everything to compliment the table setting. Also sometimes called table fancies. The most collectable of which must surely be the dogs head set. Would you believe, a little dogs head poking up from the butter dish, honey pot, cheese dish, cruet set, and toast rack. A really delightful set and available in either green/fawn or fawn/green. Numbers ranging from 1818 to 1990. (The honey pot was used recently in an advert for Frank Cooper's Marmalade.) 'There are many novelties of this type including the cow butter dish, 619, mouse cheese dish 621, and cat & mouse cheese dish 4525, also several cow cream jugs.

Of course the SylvaC honey pots are a legend, and are collected by many people. The range is quite extensive, the most popular being the strawberry, orange, pineapple,and blackberry, 582/5. But not many people know there is another range of fruit, with faces, Numbers 4895–4899 designed by George Matthews in the 1970s. There is a range of basket style containers with fruit decorating the lid, Number 4865, they all have the same number but with different lids. They used the same fruit lids for the leaf honey pots. Then there are the sports honies, made up of a golf ball, football, rugby ball, and bowls, Numbers 4712/5. Quite an amusing honey pot is the bee honey, looking very pleased with himself, he has obviously just eaten all the honey, 5383, designed by Mr. George Matthews in 1977. This is just a small example of what is available.

What can I say about the novelty pickle jars, and sauce bowls? There are at least fourteen of them, all with very bemused expressions, Numbers from 4549–5127 (not consecutive). I should hurry if you want to collect them, the prices are increasing all the time. George Matthews who designed most of these, has a lot to answer for.

There are not all that many SylvaC tea sets or coffee sets. By far the nicest was the blackberry tea set, made about 1949, and available in primrose or pink, numbers around 1862. Also very attractive is the butterfly range, the only piece I have seen is the honey pot, but there were other pieces as well. The numbers are a bit scattered, but start about 3554, they were designed by Mr. R. Thompson in the 1960s. There was also the Wyka Range, Totem Range, the Hollyberry Range for Christmas, and the Croft Cottage Range. The Avon tableware was one of the widest ranges, and was available with several different patterns, the most popular of which was Limegrove. The Cordon Brun Range was also quite extensive, including an 18 piece tea set and 15 piece coffee set. There was also the Medway Range, and a few items in the Brazil Range. There was a Pisces Range, of fish shaped tableware.

It was fitting that one of the last SylvaC designs was the range of Tudor Cottage table ware. Thirty items had been planned, but only seven were produced. Unfortunately there were no plates, cups or saucers to complete the set, but Mr. George Matthews really excelled himself with this design. It was made in 1981, and is still in production. How nice that the last SylvaC range was of such high quality.

SMALL POSIES NOVELTY CONTAINERS AND MINIATURE VASES

Shaw & Copestake made many small posies, in a variety of shapes colours and designs. Many of these were attached to an animal or decorated with flowers. Some were pure novelty items, like the straw hat shapes, which in fact look very nice on the wall, there are two baskets, a hat pot, and posy bar in this range. One of the most popular posies was the curved posy Number 1479, which had either a small bunny or dog perched on one end, a similar design can be found with a lady draped over one end Number 1327. The round posy with three bunnies, Number 1312, is often to be seen, as is the round posy with the gnome in the centre Number 1480/1. There is also a heart shaped posy with gnome, the gnomes were sometimes replaced by animals. The squirrel eating from a bowl Number 1494 was also produced for quite a time.

All these small novelty posies are very fascinating, there are so many combinations. The dog on the slipper Number 31, and dog and shoe Number 2051, are really delightful, as are the dog posies Numbers 2024/5, the terrier and spaniel.

An interesting discrepancy has been found with posy Number 2054, which is an oblong basket, with a small dog. They come in two depths 1¾" and 2¼". There is also a round basket Number 1996, seen with a dog standing, or a little dog trying to climb in. Number 568 is a small bowl, with grass effect with either a fawn or rabbit. Number 3560 has a dog jumping over a wall, and Number 586 is a dog in a barrel. Number 586 is not numbered on the base, only stamped with a SylvaC mark.

Another set of novelty containers are Numbers 2798-owl on a tree trunk, 2799-gnome on a bamboo tree, 2800-fox with a pine-cone, 2807-two monkeys and a coconut, all under three inches high. The kitten in a ball of wool, Number 3163 is either loved or hated. But should be part of the SylvaC collection, as should the kittens in a boot, Number 4977.

Small posies are also made as part of another range, as in the Woodland Range, Numbers 4231 and 4239, and the House in the Glen Range, Number 4890.

There are many miniature vases the most popular was Number 475-with the stork handle and 1993-with the squirrel handle. Another set being 4783–87, all 3" or under. There is also a miniature tankard Number 4810.

The anenome posies came in three sizes, Numbers 123,126 and 127, and there is a very small container called sheaf, Number 1909 seen on its own or with hand decorated flowers.

This just gives you an example of a few of the items available, there are many more to be found.

TANKARDS, MUGS AND BEAKERS

There is a large range of tankards, mugs and beakers to be found with the SylvaC mark. From the standard coffee mug, to the novelty sports tankards. Some tankards have been m mark a special occasion, such as the Nottingham Football Club Centenary Year-1965, Number 3488. were souvenirs, as 3546 for Jersey. There was an A Chivalry set of six tankards, all Number 4245 dep different Earls and Princes. There are ten sports tankards, soccer to sailing from Number 4719 to 4728 and six no tankards featuring a skull Number 4570, a drinking Number 4574, a riding boot Number 4584 and a fish in t sizes Numbers 4566,4567 and 4387. There is also D'Ye John Peel Number 1614.

Most of the table ware ranges also included a bea Number 1600 in the Dahlia range, Number 4633-Hollybe range, and Number 4801-Medway Range. There are also ma individual coffee beakers in various designs.

Some SylvaC novelties as shown in the 1960 catalogue.

CHAPTER 7

TRADEMARKS AND LABELS

It is probable that Shaw & Copestake started a numbering system of some sort right from the inception of their Factory. But a large amount was unmarked with just the shape name. The 1904 advert in the Pottery Gazette shows a sketch of a vase Numbered 273 also named Holborn. Holborn being the shape name. I have in my possession two very ornate vases of the pre-first World War period, the number of which is 371, they also have the daisy mark,(without the SylvaC name), which apparently was not used until about 1925. The 1929 Pottery Gazette Directory and Diary show the daisy mark without SylvaC, being used, and the 1937 Pottery Gazette Directory and Diary, shows both daisy marks being used, with and without the SylvaC name. Unfortunately, with no early Shaw & Copestake records available these dates cannot be wholly accurate, but will give you a general guide.

I have some un-numbered jugs with the name SILVO on the base. Obviously the shape name, but perhaps the first step towards SylvaC?

Most of the pre-second World War items do not have SylvaC impressed on the base. These moulds were obviously made before the SylvaC name was extensively used, but the mould numbers are very distinctive, and some of the wares have a SylvaC label attached. They started to impress the SylvaC name on the bases from about 1937, but it was very haphazard, and not all items were marked. They also used a rubber stamp on the base of unmarked ware. There doesn't appear to have been any definite system used, and many different labels and marks can be found, as can be seen from the examples shown. Although it may be possible to tell when a label or mark was FIRST introduced, Collectors must remember the haphazardness of the SylvaC system. Old labels seem to emerge on later models, and it is not a good idea to date by label. SylvaC labels even become mistakenly attached to non-SylvaC items. I have also been working on the theory that the SylvaC Ware in the slanting flowing style seen stamped on

many of the wares, was used by the Falcon Pottery to mark the SylvaC items, but it hasn't been possible to complete this particular investigation.

In an attempt to date the SylvaC trade mark, I have spent some time at the Patent Office in London, where trade marks are registered. There was no trace of the SylvaC trade mark being registered before 1938.

You will notice the style of numbering differs on the ware made in the Falcon Factory, being embossed rather than impressed. Some of the later items also had a different style of numbering, using smaller figures.

FALCON WARE

There are several different Falcon Ware marks. One with LG in the centre (Lawrence and Grundy), used in the 1930s. The falcon, the artists palette and the urn, with T. Lawrence above it, and Falcon Ware below it, were all probably 1940s.

In the 1950s Mr. Reginald Thompson designed the slanting flowing lines of SylvaC Ware and Falcon Ware, and back stamps were made. I have never seen any Falcon Ware labels, all the marks have been printed, stamped, or impressed on the base of the item. The very early Falcon Ware does not seem to be numbered. Most of it is named. Although the individual decorations were given numbers.

You have probably wondered at the significance of the additional letters or numbers sometimes found on the bases. It was probably the initial or mark of the mould maker.

J.H. Weatherby & Sons (Ltd) Falcon Pottery, Hanley also used a FALCON WARE mark, and I believe there are other Falcon Potteries.

A few SylvaC and Falcon Ware items did not have numbers and I have listed these at the back of the Register.

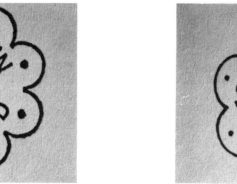

1925–1937   1935–1940.

About 1920s.

1930s.

1930s.

1940s–1950s.

1940s–1950s.

1940s–1950s.

SYLVAC
STAFFORDSHIRE
HAND
PAINTED
MADE IN ENGLAND
TOBY

1950s.

1940s–1950s.

1960s–1980s.

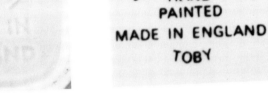

SYLVAC
WARE
MADE IN
ENGLAND

1950s.

1940s–1950s.

1960s–1970s.

1940s.

1950s–1960s.

Label from 1960s.

Label from 1960s.

Label from 1970s.

From 1970s.

From 1980s.

Crown Winsor 1982+

Falcon 1920–1930s.

Falcon 1920s–1930s.

Falcon 1930s–1940s.

Falcon 1940s.

Falcon 1940s–1950s.

1940s–1960s.

1950s–1960s.

1950s–1960s.

1950s–1960s.

Please note, in the absence of any records of the marking system used at the factories, these dates can be no more than a very general guide.

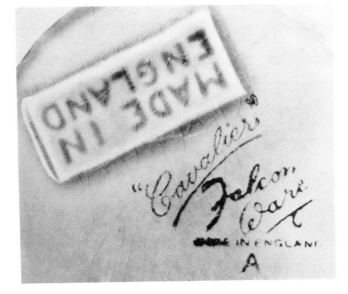

1950s–1960s.

CHAPTER 8

POTTERY PERSONALITIES

MR. WILLIAM SHAW. FOUNDER OF SHAW & COPESTAKE

MR. WILLIAM SHAW was born in 1874, and founded SHAW & COPESTAKE about 1894. Mr. Copestake, his first partner, only stayed a few months, and a new partnership was formed with Mr. Richard Hull, senior. Mr. William Shaw who was only in his early 20's when he started the business, retired from Shaw & Copestake in May 1942, having successfuly run the business in partnership with the two Mr. Hulls for more than 40 years. He passed away on December 31st, 1950, at the age of 76. It is not yet known if Mr. William Shaw came from a family of pottery manufacturers. As there were several Shaws in the area also manufacturing earthenware, it is likely there was some connection. Mr. William Shaw also had a son connected with the business.

MR. COPESTAKE

It is thought that Mr. Copestake only stayed in partnership with Mr. Shaw for a few months, possibly six. He then seems to vanish without trace. But there are other Copestakes in the same business in that area, the most well known being Dewes & Copestake. They were in business in 1896, and based in Caroline Street, Longton, Stoke-on-Trent, it is possible there was a connection. However although Mr. Copestake disappeared off the scene so quickly, his name carried on until 1982.

MR. RICHARD HULL SENIOR-PARTNER IN SHAW & COPESTAKE

MR. RICHARD HULL SENIOR joined Shaw & Copestake shortly after it was founded. He was born in Frisby, Leicestershire on 11th August 1865, his parents were farmers. He came to the Potteries whilst very young, and began working in the pottery industry with a Mr. Joseph Ball, who was a manufacturer of china in Anchor Place, Longton, Stoke-on-Trent. Later he went to Canada, where for about six years he was in the employment of Gowans, Kent & Co, Crockery & Glass Importers, Toronto. On his return to the Potteries he joined Mr. Shaw at Shaw & Copestake, taking over Mr. Copestakes partnership, and was responsible for building up the large export business that continued successfully until the late 1970s.

During the First World War he was a volunteer guard and a special constable. He was a great sportsman, loved football, golf and shooting. He was a director of the Blythe Bridge Bowling and Tennis Club, a member of the Dunrobin Bowling Club, Meir Golf Club, Stockton Brook Golf Club, and also the Totteridge Club in South Herts. A wonderful character, who continued to participate in the business until his death on the 29th September 1935 at the age of 70. It is rather ironic that despite his love of sport and the open air he died of tuberculosis.

MR. RICHARD HULL JUNIOR-CHAIRMAN & MANAGING DIRECTOR

MR. RICHARD HULL JUNIOR joined his father, Richard Hull senior at Shaw & Copestake in 1924. at the age of 18, and devoted his whole life to the running of the pottery. He was very proud of the fact that he started at the bottom of the business, and worked his way up. When his father died in 1935 Richard junior became Mr. Shaws partner and there began a successful, partnership until Mr. Shaws retirement in 1942. The business became a Limited Company in 1936. Although having no artistic talent himself, there is no doubt that Mr. Richard Hull knew exactly which wares were required by the market, and he was very clever at picking the designs that were successful. He was keen to promote the animal models and novelties and travelled all over the world looking for ideas. One of his greatest successes were the green matt rabbits, and they are still the most well known of SylvaC Ware. It was also his idea to use the SylvaC name, devised from the letters S for Shaw and C for Copestake, and incorporating the name of the factory, which was Sylvan. He continued to work at extending the export market, and was able to combine his love of travel with promoting the wares.

Mr. Hull was a founder member of The Ornamental Pottery Association, served on various Committees of the British Ceramic Manufacturers Federation, and was also a member of the organising panel for the pottery and glass section of the Blackpool Gift Fair. During which time he met many members of the Royal Family. Mr. Richard Hull junior died in 1977 at the age of 71, after several years of ill-health.

In the 1930s Mr. Richard Hull married Miss Eileen Grundy, daughter of Mr. John Grundy, Managing Director of Thomas Lawrence, Falcon Pottery. Which he eventually took over due to the untimely death of Mr. John Grundy.

Mrs. Eileen Hull, has been kind enough to assist in my research, and given me vital background information to enable me to build up a picture of her family. Although not connected with the day-to-day running of the pottery, Mrs. Hull was a sounding board for Mr. Hulls latest ideas for new wares. Mrs. Hull was the mainstay of the pottery canteen during the War, and ran it with great efficiency for the duration of the War, providing over 70 workers with a cooked meal every lunchtime.

MR. E.J. DENNIS DIRECTOR FROM 1942

MR. E.J. DENNIS was a life long friend of the Hull family. After the untimely death of Mr. John Grundy of Thomas Lawrence (Longton) Ltd, Mr. Dennis took over Mr. Grundy's shares, to become a member of the board of directors with Mr. Hull, in 1938. He subsequently became a director of Shaw & Copestake in 1942, and despite being very involved with his own family business, took an enormous interest in the Falcon and Sylvan Works. He was always ready with a suggestion for the latest inovations in the pottery industry, and together with Mr. Hull, took great pride in the building of the new Sylvan Works, making sure the factory had all the most up-to-date equipment.

MR. E.J. RADFORD DIRECTOR FROM 1947

MR. E.J. RADFORD became a director of Shaw & Copestake in 1947. He took a particular interest in the building of the new factory, which started in 1955. Mr. Radford passed away in 1974.

◄ Mr. William Shaw, founder of Shaw & Copestake.

▼ Staff Group c1960. Standing left to right: William Lake-Assistant Clay Manager, Malcolm Chapman-Commercial Director, Roy Davies-Dispatch Manager, Ivan Hallam-Representative Northern Area, Reginald Thompson-Senior Modeller/Designer, Gerrard Salt-Decorating Manager, Ronald Wright-Assistant Decorating Manager, James Brian-Clay Manager. Seated left to right: Eric J. Dennis-Director, Richard Hull-Chairman and Managing Director, E. John (Jack) Radford-Works Director.

MR. M.D. CHAPMAN DIRECTOR FROM 1962

MR. M.D. CHAPMAN an accountant, joined Shaw & Copestake in 1955 assisting Mr. Richard Hull on the commercial side of the business, he was appointed a director in 1962. Mr. Chapman took an enormous interest in all aspects of the pottery, even suggesting designs. It was his idea to introduce a Mr. SylvaC, which was used for advertising purposes for a number of years. Mr. Chapman having a wonderful memory has been of considerable help in compiling information for this book. He has been able to put me in touch with many members of staff and directors, and is obviously very proud of his association with Shaw & Copestake. He was a personal friend of Mr. Hull junior, and fortunately has been able to remember all the vital information Mr. Hull passed on to him during their conversations. Thank goodness he was interested enough at the time to absorb all this information, and has passed it on for posterity.

After the liquidation of Shaw & Copestake, Mr. Chapman set up his own business, IMPORTING ceramics to Stoke-on-Trent, and appears to have found a surprisingly successful niche for what would seem to be an unlikely venture.

MR. E.R. TAYLOR WORKS DIRECTOR FROM 1974

Mr. E.R. Taylor became a director of Shaw & Copestake in 1974 and remained with the company until 1982. He had previously been employed at the Thomas Lawrence Pottery as clay manager from 1948 until 1957. After spending a short time in Canada, he managed a small pottery in Wallasey, Cheshire. In 1961, he returned to Stoke-on-Trent, to start his own pottery. In 1971, faced with a compulsory purchase order on his premises, he accepted the position of works manager at Shaw & Copestake Ltd. Fortunately, Mr. Taylor has been able to identify lots of the photographs taken at the potteries.

MR THOMAS LAWRENCE (Falcon Ware)

MR. THOMAS LAWRENCE founded his pottery, in Wharf Street, Stoke-on-Trent, about 1888. There is a wonderful paragraph in the Pottery Gazette May 2nd 1898 as follows: 'Thomas Lawrence, late of Wharf Street, Stoke-on-Trent, has removed to a commodius Pottery, which he has specially erected in Waterloo Street, Longton'. He was interested in photography, and before the turn of the century had attempted to decorate a vase with a photograph of his nephew John Grundy. Mr. Lawrence retired to Colwyn Bay, but still visited the pottery every week, staying the night with his nephew John Grundy, who eventually became managing director of the Falcon Works.

MR. JOHN GRUNDY (Falcon Ware)

Mr. John Grundy, was managing director of Thomas Lawrence, Falcon Works, from about 1920. He was the nephew of Thomas Lawrence, who founded the business.

Thomas Lawrence became a limited company in September 1938. Sadly just three days after the limited company was formed Mr. John Grundy died. Mr. Grundy was to have been governing director and chairman of the new company. Mr. Richard Hull, his son-in-law, and Mr. E.J. Dennis stepped in, and Mr. Dennis took over Mr. Grundys shares in the business. Mr. Grundy was a very talented artist, and was mostly to be found in the decorating shop, working on the latest design. He was happiest when he had a paintbrush in his hand, and was much respected by his workforce. He knew every one of his employees by their first name. His remaining family take great pride in the paintings and drawings still in existence. He loved to hand paint the vases and several examples of his work still exist.

He was also very proud of the fact that he paid 2d. per week insurance to the local Cottage Hospital for each of his employees, so they could be well looked after if they were taken ill.

Although of an artistic nature, he was an equally astute business man, and it was a flourishing company that Mr. Richard Hull and Mr. E.J. Dennis took over in 1938.

Richard Hull Senior.

Thomas Lawrence.

Richard Hull Junior.

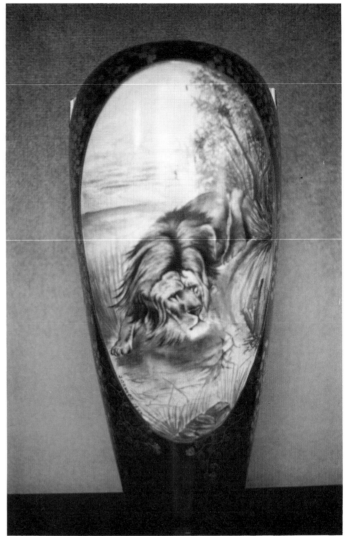

▲ An early attempt by Mr. Thomas Lawrence to decorate pottery by photography. The photograph is of Mr. John Grundy, his nephew.

▲ A vase handpainted by Mr. John Grundy in 1897 at the Thomas Lawrence factory.

◄ Leopard 1458 9½″ high, and Spaniel 1462 11″ high. As shown in the 1940 catalogue.

CHAPTER 9

DESIGNERS/MODELLERS

MR. REGINALD THOMPSON B.E.M

Mr. Thompson joined Thomas Lawrence (Longton) Ltd, in 1917, at the age of 14. He was employed as a painter, painting at the benches and extending lithos. As his outstanding artistic talent became apparent, he was awarded a scholarship to the Hanley School of Art, where he completed the course for pottery, decorators and designers, with distinction. After completion of the course he applied for the position of decorating manager at the Thomas Lawrence Works. Mr. John Grundy, the managing director, gave him a six months trial, and he subsequently became the youngest decorating manager in the Potteries at the age of 19, in 1922.

After the amalgamation of Shaw & Copestake Ltd and Thomas Lawrence (Longton) Ltd., in 1938, Mr. Thompsons designs were used at both factories, and he became chief designer. He finally retired in 1978 having completed the staggering total of 62 years loyal service, and was awarded the British Empire Medal in recognition of his services to the pottery industry.

You will be able to see in the Register of Numbers Mr. Thompsons numerous and varied designs and models. He made a very important contribution to the success of the factories. When the new factory was built and the two potteries merged together, Mr. Thompson found he was not only designing, but managing the decorating department, training the paintresses, as well as modelling. It was soon realised this was too much for one person and after discussion with Mr. Richard Hull some of the responsibility was delegated to other employees. Mr. Thompson then specialised in designing, modelling, training, and quality control. Some of his models were inspired by his love of gardening, particularly the Wishing Well, Dovecote, and Blue Tit ranges. His much loved cairn terrier, Wendy, 3447, was modelled in 1963, and is still in production, and even the stray cat he befriended, 5236, now has a place in SylvaC history. Some of his finest work can be seen in the Prestige range, and the Cavalier range. He also made several figures for the Falcon factory, unfortunately un-numbered, but marked Falcon Ware. One was called Jeanette, and was a young lady with flowers, one was a girl on a swing, another was called Bretton Girl.

It is difficult to mention all his work but the MR. SYLVAC ashtray was particularly well done. Mr. Thompson had a good rapport with Mr. Richard Hull junior, the managing director, and between them they would work out the various models, with perhaps Mr. Hull giving him the initial idea, and Mr. Thompson being able to produce exactly what was needed. Mr. Thompson had his own special brand of humour which can be seen in the pixie range, the tennis playing dog Number 2660 and the kitten in a ball of wool, Number 3168.

Mr. Thompson was a very quiet unasuming gentleman, who perhaps did not receive the recognition due to him. A man of many talents, artist as well as modeller he was sorely missed by everyone when he retired in 1978. He continued working for Shaw & Copestake Ltd until the age of 75, and then only due to illness did he finally retire. His whole life had been spent in the Potteries, he never took a holiday, and only once ventured abroad to Italy, accompanying Mr. Richard Hull on a business trip. Mr. Thompson died in April 1988 at the age of 85. Fortunately I was able to meet him several times, and have the conversations on video tape. It was particularly interesting to learn of the terrible working conditions prevalent at the time he started work in 1917, and the gradual improvement until the time of his retirement in 1978. When he first started work he would use the Potteries Electric Tramway, which played a large part in linking the five towns together. Mr. Thompson was a wonderfully talented man and it was a privilege to know him. It is fitting that so much of his work is now being collected and appreciated. It was a great joy to him, in the last months of his life to know of the interest being taken in his work. He loved to reminisce about his life at the Falcon and Sylvan Works.

MR. STEPHAN CZARNOTA

Stephan Czarnota joined Shaw & Copestake Ltd., possibly in the late 1950s or early 1960s, and came originally from Hungary. He left Shaw & Copestake about 1966, to work freelance. During his time he modelled a large variety of wares. He was particularly good at the caricature models, and will be remembered for the range of long faced dogs Numbers 2938, 2950 and 2951 modelled in the early 1960s. (This information from Mr. M. Chapman, as the Mould Makers Register does not give modellers names until about 1963.) Also the Funnies range of dogs 3422–3433. He particularly enjoyed the humerous side of modelling, but also produced some classical dogs and animals, and many vases and flower pots.

MR JOHN LAWSON

John Lawson joined Shaw & Copestake as a trainee modeller, working with Mr. Thompson and Stephan Czarnota in the 1960s but left before 1966 to emigrate to America. He seems to have modelled a considerable amount of ware in that time, including animals, vases, and also the Pebble Range of vases and bowls, of which a considerable amount is still to be seen. His initials are also by the Prestige piece of the otter with fish, Number 3459. But Mr. Reginald Thompsons daughter Jeanette, remembers her father bringing this model home to paint, and rather assumed her father had also modelled it. It may have been a combined effort, which I believe was the case with other models. His models can be identified in the Register of Numbers. He was replaced by Mr. George Matthews.

MR. GEORGE MATTHEWS

George Matthews joined Shaw & Copestake in 1966, and stayed until liquidation of the company in 1982. He trained at the Newcastle School of Art, his first job in the pottery industry, was with the Boston Pottery, Sandiford, where he was taken on as a modeller. But as this was such a small pottery, and modelling was not required on a continual basis he found that he was asked to help in other departments, such as the mould making section, setting kilns, carrying ware etc. It was with this good grounding of all aspects of the pottery industry that he was taken on as Mr. Reginald Thompsons right hand man. George Matthews displays an amazing talent for all types of modelling, including animals, tableware and vases. He joined Shaw & Copestake at the height of their success, and his talents certainly meant this continued for many years. It is difficult to pick out any special models as they were all of such high quality, but perhaps the bust of Sir Winston Churchill, Number 5165, modelled in 1974, and the Tudor Cottage Ware Numbers 5670–5676 modelled in 1981 are worth a special mention.

◄ Reginald Thompson in the Thomas Lawrence factory c1949, supervising the painting of hat bands. In the background other workers are lithographing nursery ware. Left foreground is Gladys Hill.

► George Matthews working on the bust of Churchill, Number 5156, in 1974. The workshop as you can see was in an old part of the building, and was originally used by Cyples Colour Works before being incorporated into Shaw & Copestakes factory.

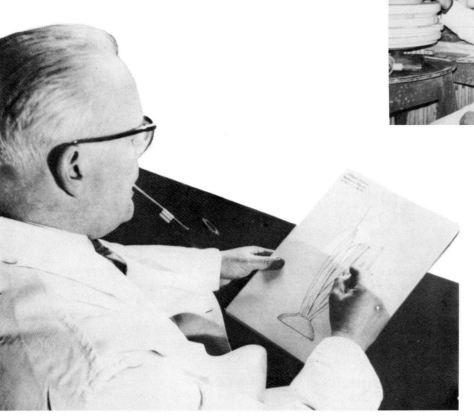

◄ Reginald Thompson sketching the Hyacinth Leaf range. This range was introduced about 1959 or 1960, but the photograph was taken after 1962 which suggests it was specially posed for a brochure.

George also had a very special relationship with Mr. Reginald Thompson, and visited him frequently during the last months of his life, a gesture that was so appreciated by the Thompson family.

After George Matthews was made redundant in 1982, he started his own business. He now makes the most beautiful resin based models of woodland and animals scenes under the trade name of Sandringham. Who knows, you may see a resemblance to some SylvaC animals in the Sandringham models.

FREELANCE MODELLERS

OTAKAR STEINBURGER–Was a freelance modeller and designer in the early 1930s, he came originally from Czechoslovakia, but lived in Peckham, London. He modelled 'Mac' the scottie dog range, Numbers 1205–1209, and possibly dogs Numbers 1261/2 and 1245, which seem to be in a similar style. I was able to look up the registered number of the scottie dogs, at the Patent Office in Holborn, London, and I noticed that on the same date in 1932, Mr. Steinburger also registered many other designs, of dogs and other inventions. So I do feel that some of the early dogs were his designs.

MR. CHEADLE did quite a lot of work for Thomas Lawrence or Shaw & Copestake before the War, of which there is no record. The first recorded model is Number 3311, bowl with bird. Mr. Cheadle also designed some of the Feather Range in the 1960s, but there is very little of his work recorded. Mr. Thompson thought Mr. Cheadle may have modelled the tiny figures of Pete, Pam and Paul, Numbers 3111/2/3, and also the ski-ing rabbits, Numbers 25–29.

MR. WOOLLAM also designed or modelled from the 1930s, but once again there is no record of his work, only a few items in the Feather Range in the 1960s, and a cup and saucer in the Magnolia Range Number 3547.

MR. ARNOLD MACHIN M.A. designed and modelled a futuristic range of animals Numbers 3151–54. These included a cat, horse, tigress and stag, and were made at the Falcon Pottery. Mr. Machin also advised on the type of decoration most suitable for his designs.

MR. RICHARD DENNIS, son of the director Mr. E.J. Dennis also designed one or two items. One of which was a mug Number 4682, with owl embossed.

Some other initials are also given in the Register. These were sometimes the mould makers initial, and it is not known if they modelled the items. Some initials have been untraceable, and it is possible they were errors made by the person entering the information.

Stephan Czarnota modelling alsation Number 3170.

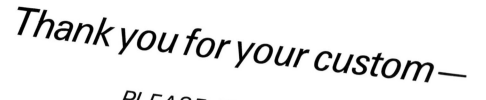

Advertising leaflet used until closure of Shaw & Copestake.

78

◄ Modus 80 animals.

▼ Assyria range. Vase 4573, plate 4690, fern pot 4678, small vase 4693, bowl 4699.

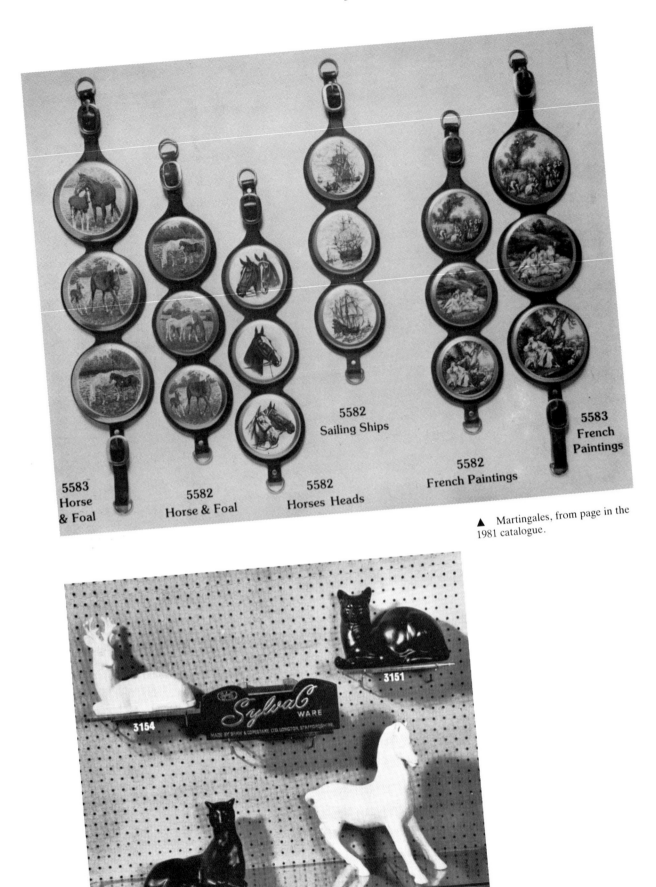

5583
Horse
& Foal

5582
Horse & Foal

5582
Horses Heads

5582
Sailing Ships

5582
French Paintings

5583
French
Paintings

▲ Martingales, from page in the
1981 catalogue.

3154

3151

3153

3152

◄ Black and white matt animals
designed by Arnold Machin M.A.,
can also be found in other colours
and finishes.

Old Shaw & Copestake vases from about 1910. From left Number 509, Number 371, Number 432, Centre Vase Number 578. All with very ornate decoration, and bearing the early daisy mark.

Shaw & Copestake jugs, probably 1920. Blue jug has daisy mark and is hand painted with a boat on a lake scene. Others are marked Silvo and are attractively decorated.

82

(*top left*) Clock set about 1920s. Clock Number 605 and vases Number 606. They all have the daisy mark.

(*bottom left*) Clock set about 1920s. Clock Number 605 and vases Number 606. With swan decoration, all have the daisy mark.

(*above*) The jugs are both Number 573. The jug on the left has the daisy mark with SylvaC in the centre. The clocks are number 605, decorated with roses and a Japanese lady. The dressing table items are hand painted with the boat on the lake scene and have the early daisy mark.

(*below*) Wild duck range in cellulose finish with embossed design. From left vases Numbers 650 and 785, clock Number 649, (the clock face is not original), vases Numbers 1858 and 650, in the front, trinket box 804.

Dragon handle jug Number 1116. Note the flames on the bottom left.

Very rare Art Deco jug Number 1147.

A collection of SylvaC cats. Numbers from left top row are: 2549, 5298, 5300, 5107 large siamese, 184, 1046. Bottom row: 1485, 1296, the two white kittens in the centre are not numbered, 3168, 4977, small siamese in front: 102.

On the left Collon Number 2 vase, decorated with a boat. On the right Number 679 from the Evening Fantasy Range.

A 1939 setting for SylvaC ornaments. Note the rare matt coloured flying ducks, the dancing lady Number 920 and in the hearth lizard Number 1467.

A fine example of horse and rider Number 4707 (formerly Falcon Number 21), with hounds Number 4709.

(*far left top*) Novelty bowls. Top row from left: Numbers 569, 1513, and 587 (rabbit hutch). Middle row from left: Numbers 548, 355 and 689. Bottom row from left: Numbers 572, 353, 2049.

(*top left*) Top row: Wyka range tableware. Middle row: Dovecote range tableware. Bottom row: Blackberry range tableware.

(*far bottom left*) SylvaC honeypots. Note: Strawberry with face, second from left top shelf. Honey bee, fourth from left middle shelf and Butterfly range, third left bottom shelf.

(*bottom left*) Top row Numbers: 2295, 1514, 282 (Falcon Ware). Middle row: Numbers 591, 1510, 550. Bottom row Numbers: 468, 473, 2512.

(*top right*) Two ashtrays Number 1366, with seagull Number 1357 and dog number 1433.

(*middle right*) Lop Ear the rabbit in three sizes Numbers 1304, 1303 and 1302.

(*below*) Back row from left: Giant Panda range money box Number 5576, Riverside range vase Number 4377, Harvest range vase Number 5246, Woodland range vase Number 4233. Front row from left: Woodland range tray Number 4293, House in the Glen range 4890, Squirrel range posy Number 2468, Woodland range posy trough Number 4231, Riverside range vase Number 4393.

Character and Toby jugs. Numbers from left top row: 4431, 4401, 4460, 4439. Numbers from left bottom row: Punch no Number, Henry VIII originally un-numbered given 4488, 4440, 4411, Cavalier 306 re-numbered 4487.

Tankards, from the left top row: Number 2375, 1775 and 3278. Middle row: 4721, 4727, 4245, 4725 and 4719. Bottom row: 1614, 2343 and 4570.

PART TWO

THE REGISTER OF NUMBERS

EXPLAINING THE REGISTER OF NUMBERS

The Register of Numbers has been compiled from catalogues, The Pottery Gazette and Diary, the mould makers register, and collectors of SylvaC. The catalogues I have date from 1940 to the last Shaw & Copestake catalogue of 1982.

Sometimes there are two items to one number, presumably the number was changed or re-used. I have given both descriptions if this is the case. Occasionally the measurement is given without indicating whether it is height, length or diameter, unfortunately this information is not available. It could also be the case height or length of the mould. I'm sorry if the description sometimes seems obtuse, but I have faithfully copied the information available for that particular item. I haven't attempted to date the production times by the year, as this information is not known in all cases. I think it best to give approximate guide lines, unless I am absolutely certain of the year.

There is very little information available regarding the designers or modellers of the early wares. Otakar Steinburger, Mr. Cheadle and Mr. Woollam are the only Pre-War names known. Reginald Thompson probably designed most of the Post-War pieces, but they may also have used his Pre-War Falcon Ware designs. The Falcon Ware numbers are at the begining of the Register, and the only dates I can give them are the year of the catalogue or Gazette I have first seen them in.

Sometimes they are referred to as a 'New Item', then I can be sure of the first production date.

Intermingled with these early numbers are a few old Shaw & Copestake numbers which I have found on items at Antique Fairs. After reaching the 700s the picture is a little clearer, and I can be more sure of the dates.

There may be some gaps in the Register, this is usually because numbers were saved to continue with the range if necessary, but were not used. Other gaps are due to the fact they are not in the catalogues or mould makers register, and I have to find the number when searching the antique fairs. This list is the most comprehensive list available at this time.

As inches have been used in the original catalogues I have kept to this measurement throughout the Register. Descriptions and spellings sometimes vary such as Posie/Posy, this is how they were described and I thought it nice to keep to the original descriptions. It has taken many months of painstaking checking and cross checking and searching to compile this register, and I do hope you will find it useful when collecting SylvaC.

In order to make it as easy a possible to look up the item I have put the number first, followed by item and description, then size and approximate production dates.

To save space in the Register I have used the following abbreviations:

h...height	l...length	a...across
d...diameter	ch...case height	cl...case length
cs...case/clay size	Ct...catalogue	PG...Pottery Gazette
Sl...shape list	Bl...SylvaC Bulletin	HP...hand painted
No snip...no spout	Shrink...make smaller	OM...outside modelled
L/S...large size	M/S...medium size	S/S...small size
S-i-P...still in production at this date.		Ass.Cols...Assorted Colours

Mould Makers, Designers or Modellers initials

RW...Ronald Wright		HH...Harry Huson (Mould Maker)
EB...Eric Baker (Mould Maker)		TH...Tom Hudson (Mould Maker)
RT...Reginald Thompson	JL...John Lawson	SC...Stephan Czarnota
GM...George Matthews	C...Mr. Cheadle	W...Mr. Woollam
JB...J. Brian	RD...Richard Dennis	JR..J. Radford

REGISTER OF NUMBERS

The following two and three figure numbers are mainly Falcon Ware numbers with a few old Shaw & Copestake numbers. It has not been possible to date them accurately, some could be early Falcon Ware numbers. But they are mostly dating from the 1940s. The dates have been compiled from the various documents indicated. These items will be found with SylvaC or Falcon Ware Marks. Space has been provided at the end of the column for collectors to tick off items in their collections.

NUMBER	ITEM	DESCRIPTION	SIZE	Approximate PRODUCTION DATES	TICK
1	Deer				
2–14	No information				
15	Horse	Standing. Brown HP	6¾"h Seen in Ct	1950s–1982	
16	Dog	Bulldog. Standing HP	5¼"h Seen in Ct	1950s–S-in-P	
17	Bison	Standing. Brown HP	Seen in Ct	1950	
18	Dog	Spaniel. Sitting Fawn Matt & HP	5"h Seen in PG	1945–S-in-P	
19	Dog	Saluki. Sitting	Seen in PG	1952	
20	Dog				
21	Horse	With huntsman. Re-numbered 4707 in '70s.	9"l 8½"h	Prob till late '70s	
22–23	No information				
24	Bird	Wall Plaque			
25	Rabbit	Ski-ing Standing Fawn & Green Matt and HP	3½"h Seen PG	1950–Short Run	
26	Rabbit	Ski-ing Injured Fawn & Green Matt and HP	3"h Seen PG	1950–Short Run	
27	Rabbit	Ski-ing Fallen Fawn & Green Matt and HP	2¼"h Seen PG	1950–Short Run	
28	Rabbit	Ski-ing Fallen Fawn & Green Matt and HP	3¼"h Seen PG	1950–Short Run	
29	Rabbit	Ski-ing Fallen Fawn & Green Matt and HP	3"h Seen PG	1950-Short Run	
30	No information				
31	Slipper	Dog lying on front Green & Fawn Mt	6"l Seen Ct	1940s-50s	
32	No information				
33	Lizard				
34	Dog				
35–38	No information				
39	Figure	Red Riding Hood			
40	Rhino				
41	Elephant				
42	Cat				
43	Duck				
44	Rabbit	Jug	5"h		
45	Cat or Dog	Jug	5"h		
46	Dog	Jug	5"h		
47	Dog	Bulldog			
48	Rhino				
49	Lion				
50	Camel				
51–52	No information				
53	Wolf-Bison	Possibly two animals together			
54	Eagle				
55	Pony				
56	Lamp-Buffalo	Possibly buffalo on base			
57	Dog				
58	Lamp				
59	Pelican				
60	Horse				
61	No information				
62	Lion				
63	Giraffe				
64–65	No information				
66	Sea-lion				
67	Dog	Cairn Terrier standing Hand painted	4"h Seen Ct	1950s	
68	Elephant	Standing Grey Hand painted	9"h Ct & PG	Late 50s–1983	
69	Bear				
70	No information				
71	Lamp-Eagle	Possibly Eagle on base			
72	Dog	Scottie Standing	5¼"h Seen PG	1950s	
73	Dog	Sitting Grn & Fn Matt & HP	4¼"h Seen PG	1950s–1960	
74	Gnome	For Garden. Sitting. Cellulose	6¾"h Seen B1	1950–1960	
75	Gnome	For Garden. Sitting. Cellulose	6"h	1950–1960	

76	Dog			
77–80	No information			
81	Gnome	For Garden. Reclining. Cellulose	8″l Seen Ct & Bl	1950s–60
82	Gnome	For Garden. Reclining. Cellulose	8″l Seen Ct & Bl	1950s–60
83	Gnome	For Garden. Playing Banjo. Cellulose	8″h Seen Ct & Bl	1950s–60
84	No information			
85	Tiger			
86	No information			
87	Gnome	For Garden. Standing. Cellulose	7¼″h Ct & Bl	1950s–1960
88	Wall Plaque	Spaniels Head Hand Painted	3½″h PG	1950
89	Wall Plaque	Scotties Head Black Hand Painted	4″h PG	1945
90	Wall Plaque	Terriers Head Hand Painted	4″h PG	1950
91	No information			
92	Elephant	Standing. Green Matt or Grey HP	4″h Seen Bl	1950–1982
93	Lion	Lying HP	6½″l 2¼″h	Short run
94	Bull			
95	Horse			
96	Chimpanzee	Crouching Brown Handpainted	7″h Seen Bl	1950–1982
97	Chimpanzee	Crouching Brown Handpainted	4¼″h Seen Bl	1950–1982
98	Chimpanzee	Crouching Brown Handpainted	4″h Seen Bl	1950–1982
99	Cat	Siamese Brown or Black HP	5″h	1950–1970
100	Kitten	Siamese Sitting Brown or Black HP	S/S Seen Bl	1950–1970
101	Kitten	Siamese Standing Brown or Black HP	S/S Seen Bl	1950–1970
102	Kitten	Siamese Playing Brown or Black HP	S/S Seen Bl	1950–1970
103	Kitten	Siamese Lying Brown or Black HP	S/S Seen Bl	1950–1970
104	Cat	In Basket		
105	Mouse			
106	Mouse	See 4990		
107	Foal		L/S	
108	Foal	Standing Hand Painted Brown	M/S Seen Ct	1950s
108	Gnome	For Garden. Reclining. Cellulose	10″h 14½″l Ct	1950–1960
109	Foal		S/S	
109	Giraffe			
110	Gnome	For Garden. Sitting. Cellulose	16″h Seen Bl	1950–1960
111	Girl			
112/3	Boys			
113	Gnome	For Garden. Reclining. Cellulose	11″h 16″l Seen Bl	1950–1960
114	Dog	Spaniel Lying. Fawn Matt & HP	7″h Seen PG	1950s–1975
115	Dog	Spaniel Sitting. Fawn Matt & HP	3″h Seen PG	1950s–1975
116	Dog	Spaniel Lying. Fawn Matt & HP	3¼″l	1950s–1975
117–118	No information			
119	Cottage			
120	No information			
121	Candlestick			
122	Bowl			
123	Dish	Anenome Posy. Ass. Cols. HP	8¾″dia Seen Bl	1950–1960
124/5	Horses			
126	Dish	Anenome Posy. Ass. Cols. HP. & Floral	7½″dia Seen Bl	1950–1960
127	Dish	Anenome Posy. Ass. Cols. HP.	10¼″dia Seen Bl	1950–1960
128	Wall Vase			
129	Posy	Hat Shape. Ass. Cols. HP. & Floral	4½″dia Seen Bl	1950–1960
130–32	Penguins			
133	Hippo			
134	Bear			
135	Horse			
136	Tortoise	Container. Shell as lid. HP	5½″l 2¼″h	Short run
137	Bird			
138	Swallow			
139	Wall plaque			
140	Horse			
141	Foal			
142	No information			
143/4	Fl. holders			
145	Dog	Scottie. Also with coat. Standing	3⅝″h Seen Ct	1950s–S-in-P
146	Dog	Scottie. Standing	2⅜″h Seen Ct	1950s–1965
147	Dog	Scottie. Standing	2¾″h Seen Ct	1950s–1965
148	Dog	Scottie. Sitting	2¾″h Seen Ct	1950s–1965
149	Dog	Dog and Chair		
150	Rabbit	Holder		
151	Posy	Small with Flowers & Bunny	Seen Ct	1950s

152	Posy	Small Swan with Flowers	Seen Ct	1950s
153	Wall Vase			
154	Ashtray			
155	Dog	Bulldog Standing. Matt & HP	3¼"h Seen Ct	1950–1965
156	Wall Vase			
157	Dog			
158	No information			
159	Elephant			
160	Dog			
161	Dog	Dog and Bowl		
162	Dog	Terrier Lying Head on Paws HP	1¾"h 7½"l Seen Ct	1950s
163	Dog			
164	Cat			
165	Top Hat	With Kitten. Matt Colours	3"h	
166	Dogs	Two Sealyhams. Matt	3⅛"h Seen Ct	1950s
167	Horse			
168	No information			
169	Dish	Shell Shape with Flowers Ass. Cols.	S/S Seen Ct	1950s
170	Dog	Poodle Sitting. Matt	5¼"h Seen Ct	1950s–1970
171	Container			
172–175	Bears			
176	Dog	Boxer Standing HP	4¾"h Seen Ct	1950s–1975
177	Dog	Dachshund Standing Matt & HP	3"h PG & Ct	1950s–1975
178	Dog	Alsation Lying front paws crossed	4½"h Seen Ct	1950s
179	Dog			
180	Container			
181	Top Hat			
182	Boat			
183	Donkey	Sitting Laughing Matt	5½"h Seen Ct	1950s
184	Cat	Sitting Boxing Matt	4¾"h Seen Ct	1950s
185	Dog	Alsation Matt Sitting	1¾"h Seen Ct	1950s
185	Mermaid	(Mould Makers Register)		
186	No information			
187	Dog			
188	Dog	Dachshund Matt & HP Sitting	1¾"h Seen Ct	1950s–1975
189–191	No information			
192	Vase	Falcon Slim Shape		
193–195	No information			
196	Jar	Ginger jar with cover	9½"h	1950–1983
196	Shoe	(Mould Makers Register)		
197	Jar	Ginger jar with cover	10¾"h Seen Ct	1950–1983
198	Pot	For plant Misty Morn & Rosslyn	5¾"h Seen Ct	1950–S-i-P
199	Pot	For plant Misty Morn & Rosslyn	7"h Seen Ct	1950–S-i-P
200	No information			
201	Tray			
202	Candlestick			
203	Dog	Setter Running HP	4¼"h Seen PG	1950s–1965
204	Dog			
205 & 206	Foal			
207	Horse	Horse Standing HP	6"h Seen Ct	1950s–1960
208	Horse			
209	Dog	Boxer Sitting HP	5½"h Seen Ct	1950s–1970
210	Dog	Daschund on Hind Legs HP	6½"h Seen Ct	1950s–1975
211 & 212	Dog			
213	Foal			
214	Pony	Shetland Brown Standing HP	5"h Seen Ct	1950s–1983
215	Dog			
216	Jug			
217	Dog			
218	Jug	Sanora Range		
219	Jug			
220	Vase	Misty Morn Range	Very Large	
221	Vase	Rosslyn & Misty Morn Range	15"h Seen PG	1951–1965
222	Jug	Sanora Range	7¼"h Seen PG	1941–1970
223	Vase	Misty Morn Range	7½"h Seen Ct	1950s–1983
224	No information			
225	Vase	Sanora Range	Seen CT	1950s–1960
226	Vase	Sanora & Misty Morn Range	6½"h Seen Ct	1950s–1970
227	No information			

228	Vase	Falcon Ware Shapes		
229	Vase			
230	Vase	With Handles Falcon Ware Shapes		
231/232	No information			
233	Vase	With Decorative Handles Falcon Ware Shapes		
234/235	No information			
236	Vase	Sanora & Dovedale Range	8″h Seen S1	1950s–1970
237	Vase	Falcon Ware Shapes		
238	Vase	Small Round. Falcon Ware Shapes		
239	Vase	Falcon Ware Shapes		
240	Vase	Falcon Ware Shapes		
241–244	No information			
245	Jug	Sanora range	3½″h Seen Ct	1950–1960
246	Vase	Sanora range	Seen Ct	1950–1960
247/248	No information			
249	Jug	Misty Morn Range	6¾″h Seen Ct	1950s–1983
250/251	No information			
252	Bowl	Sanora, Dovedale & Rosslyn Ranges	12″dia Seen Ct	1950s–1970
253	Bowl	Dovedale range		1950s–1960
254–255	No information			
256	Dish	Leaf shape green & cream	10½″dia	
257	No information			
258	Vase	Rosslyn Range	10″h Seen Ct	1950s–1960
259	Jug	Sanora, Misty Morn & Rosslyn Ranges	10″h Seen Ct	1950s–1983
260	Jug	Rosslyn & Misty Morn Ranges	8″h Seen Ct	1950s–1960
261–264	No information			
265	Vase			
266–271	No information			
272	Jug	Rosslyn & Misty Morn Range	12″h Seen Ct	1950s–1960
273	Jug	Dovedale Range	12″h Seen Ct	1950s–1960
273	Vase	Old Shaw & Copestake Holborn	16″h Seen Ct	1904
274–277	No information			
278/9	Posy	Posy Rings		
280	Hat	Flower Holder Cream Blue Ribbon	6″dia Seen Ct	1949–1960s
281	Hat	Pot Cream Ass. Col. Ribbon	L/s Seen Ct	1949–1960s
282	Hat	Pot Cream Ass. col. Ribbon	M/s Seen Ct	1949–1960s
283	Hat	Pot Cream Ass. col. Ribbon	S/s Seen Ct	1949–1960s
284–286	No information			
287	Bowl	With feet	10″dia Shape List	
288/289	No information			
290	Bowl	Sugar-Leaf design		
290	Ashtray	Cig. Box. County Scene		
291	Vase			
292	Jug	Dovedale Range	8″h Seen PG	1949–1960
293	Jug	Dovedale Range	10″h Seen PG	1949–1960
294	Box	Candy, Cavalier or Country Scene	5½″l Seen PG	1949–1960
295	No information			
296	Mug			
297	Tray	Twin. Hydrangea Pink/Primrose HP	Seen PG	1951
298	No information			
299	Basket	Nut Bowl Hat. Cream/Col. Ribbon	7½″dia Seen PG	1949–1960
300	Jug	Cavalier Range	5″h Seen PG	1945–1960
301	Jug	Cavalier Range	4″h Seen PG	1945–1960
302/303	No information			
304	Jug	Cavalier/Country Scene	3″h Seen PG	1945–1960
305	Jug	Cavalier/Country Scene	2¼″h Seen PG	1945–1960
306	Jug	Cavalier Toby. Matt/HP 4487 New no.	4¾″h	1945–1965
307	Jug	Cavalier/Country Scene	4¼″h Seen PG	1945–1960
308	Beaker			
309	Jug	Cavalier/Country Scene	6″h Seen PG	1945–1960
310	Sugar			
311	Hat	Straw Hat	Seen PG	1949
312	Jug	Toby Beefeater	Seen Ct	1950–1960
313	Jar	Cavalier	Seen PG	1945
314	Basket	Cake Basket, cream/col Ribbon	Seen PG	1949–1960
315	Posie	Posie Bar	Seen PG	1949–1960
316	Vase			
317	No information			
318	Vase			

319	Wall Vase			
320	Wall Vase	Green/Brown with 3 gnomes	7½"h Seen Ct	1950s–1960
321	Wall Vase			
322	Jardiniere			
323	Wall Vase	Mushroom with Lop ear bunny Gr/Brn	7¼"h Seen Bl	1950s–1960
324	No information			
325	Teapot	Country Scene		
326	Bowl	Sugar. Country Scene		
327	Plaque	Teenage Boys head		
328	Pot	Honey. Country Scene		
329	Plaque	Teenage Girls head		
330	No information			
331	Teapot	Hydrangea Range	Seen PG	1951–1960s
332	Honey Pot	Hydrangea Range	Seen PG	1951–1960s
333	No information			
334	Jug	Hydrangea Range 4 sizes	Seen PG	1951–1960s
335	Tray	Country Scene		
336	No information			
337	Tray	3 sections Hydrangea Pink/Primrose	Seen PG	1950s–1960s
338	Jug	Hydrangea Small size	Seen PG	1950s–1960s
339	Sugar	Hydrangea Small size		
340	Tray	Country Scene		
341	Tray	Country Scene		
342	Cheese	Dish. Hydrangea Range Pink/Primrose	Seen PG	1950s–1960s
343	Bowl	Fruit. Hydrangea Range Pink/Primrose	Seen PG	1950s–1960s
344	Jug	Hydrangea Range	Seen PG	1951–1960s
345	Coffee	Coffee-pot Hydrangea Range	Seen PG	1951–1960s
346–347	No information			
348	Vase			
349	Vase	Handbag. Matt Fawn	5½"h	1950s
350	Jug	Hydrangea Range	Seen PG	1951–1960s
351	Jug	Hydrangea Range	Large Seen PG	1951–1960s
352	Mug	Hydrangea Range	Seen PG	1951–1960s
353	Bowl	Bulb. Log with gnome Grn/Brn	8½"l	1950–1965
354	Wall Vase	Tree with Small bunny Grn/Brn	6"h	1950–1960
355	Jug	Tree house with gnome Grn/Brn	6¾"h	1950–1960
356–357	No information			
358	Jug			
359	No information			
360	Jug	Matt. Ass. Colours	5¾"	1950s
361–362	No information			
363 & 364	Jug			
365	Dish	Sweets. Hydrangea Pink/Primrose	Seen PG	1950s
366	Saucer	Fruit. Hydrangea Pink/Primrose	Seen PG	1950s
367	No information			
368	Bowl	Bulb. Embossed with leaves. Ass. Cols	Seen Ct	1960
369	Pot	Fern. Embossed with leaves. Ass. Cols	7"h Seen Ct	1960–1983
370	Vase			
371	Vase	Old S & C Mauve & Gold	10"h	1910–30?
371	Jug	Matt. As 368	7¼"h	1950s
372 & 373	Tankard			
374	Tankard	Old Bull & Bush	Seen PG	1950s
375	No information			
376	Vase	Sanora Range HP	3½"h Seen Ct	1960–1965
377	Bowl	Drinking, Sanora Range	Seen Ct	1950s–1960s
378	Bowl	Drinking, Sanora Range	Seen Ct	1950s–1960s
379	Bowl	Drinking, Sanora Range	Seen Ct	1950s–1960s
380	Vase	Rosslyn Range	8"h Seen Ct	1960s
381	Wall Vase			
382	Wall Vase	As a Ribbon	Seen Ct	1960s
383	Vase	With Handle on top Sanora Range	Seen Ct	1960s
384	Vase			
385	Vase		8¼"h Seen Sl	
386	Jug	Straight. Plain	8"h Seen Sl	
387	Vase	As 385 with side handles	8¼"h Seen Sl	
388	No information			
389	Vase	Twin horns. white	L/s	
390	Dish	With cover		
391	Box	Cigarette		

392	Bowl			
393–395	Jugs		3″h Seen Sl	
396	Bowl			
397	Jug			
398	Jug	Min. Rose Cream & Green	3″h	
399	Tray	Sanora Range HP	Seen Ct	1960s
400	Jug	Miniature Jug Vase	3″h Seen Ct	1960–1983
401	Jug	Miniature Jug Vase	3″h Seen Ct	1960s
402	Jug			
403	Pot	Coffee		
404	Teapot			
405	Tray			
406	Jug	Dorothy Bag Matt Ass. Cols	7″h Seen Ct	1950s–1983
407	Jug			
408	Basket			
409	Bowl	Jardiniere. White Matt	10″l Seen Sl	1950s–1970
410	Pot	Ass. Cols. L/s–M/s & s/s	Seen Ct	1950s–1965
411	Pot	Ass. Cols.	Seen Ct	1960s
412	No information			
413	Bowl	Fruit. Vine-Range HP	12¼″l Seen Ct	1950s–1983
414	Basket	Vine Range HP	10″l Seen Ct	1950s–1983
415	Bowl	With handles. Satin Glaze	11¼″l Seen Ct	1950s
416	Tray/Posy	Leaf Shaped	7½″l	
417	No information			
418	Bowl	Ass. Colours	Seen Ct	1950s & 60s
419	Pot	Flower. Ass. Colours	Seen Ct	1950s & 60s
420	Jug			
421/422	No information			
423	Jug			
424	Toastrack			
425	No information			
426/427	Jugs	Made in two sizes 9¼″h and 6″h	Seen Sl	1950s & 60s
428	Jardiniere			
429	Log			
430	No information			
431	Tray	Rouge Decoration	7¼″l Seen Ct	1950s & 60s
432	Jug			
432	Vase	Old Shaw & Copestake Vase		1915?
433	Vase	White also with Budgerigar	8¾″h Seen PG	1950s
434	Vase	White Matt satin glaze	9″h Seen Ct	1950–1965
435	Vase	White. Also with Budgerigar	8¾″h Seen PG	1950–1965
436	Bowl	Floating with Kingfisher No. 700	9½″dia Seen Ct	1960s
437	Bowl			
438	No information			
439/440	Vases			
441	Jug			
442–444	No information			
445	Jardiniere	With handles	13″l	
446	Tray			
447	Bowl			
448	No information			
449	Pot	Fern		
450–452	No information			
453	Jug	Dorothy Bag Green Matt	3½″h	Short Run
454	Posy			
455	Jug	Dovecote	L/s Seen Ct	1950s–1960
456	Jug			
457	Jug Handle			
458	Pot	Honey		
459	No information			
460	Tray			
461	Jug	Sanora Range and mottled	7″h Seen Ct	1950s & 60s
462	No information			
463	Jug	Satin Glaze Decoration	5¾″h Seen Ct	1950s & 60s
464	Jug	With 3 Spouts & Sanora Range	5″h Seen Ct	1950s & 60s
465	Jug	Vine Range HP	8″h Seen Ct	1950–1983
466/467	Jardinieres			
468	Bowl	Round with Frogs & Lizards	L/s Seen Ct	1950s/60s
469	Bowl	Round with Frogs & Lizards	8″dia	1950s/60s

470	No information			
471	Bowl	Diamond shape	10¼"l Seen Ct	1950s & 60s
472	Wall Vase	Vine Range HP	8"h Seen Ct	1950s–1965
473	Bowl	Round with owl	7½"dia	Short Run
474	Jardiniere	With Handles		
475	Vase	Min jug vase with stork handle	3"h Seen Ct	1950s–1983
476	Vase	Min jug vase. Hollyhock	3"h Seen Ct	1950s & 60s
477	Hat	Top hat with cat on rim		Short Run
478	Jug	Vine Range HP	6"h Seen Ct	1950s–1983
479	Bowl	Sydney Range with 2 handles		1950s & 60s
480	Jug	Diamond as 471		1950s & 60s
481	Posy Bar	Diamond as 471 & 480		1950s & 60s
482	Tray			
483	Vase			
484	Bowl	Triangular with 3 spouts	10½"dia	1950s & 60s
485	Bowl	With spout but no handle	5½"h	1950s & 60s
486	Jug	Tall & thin with handle	10½"h	1950s & 60s
487	Jug	Curved with handle	7¾"h	1950–1965
488	Bowl	Triangular	4"h	1950s & 60s
489	Jug	Sauce or gravy boat	12¾"l	1950–1969
490	Jug	Tall Jug. Australian flowers Sydney Range		1950s & 60s
491	Jug	Sauce or gravy boat	5½"h	1950s & 60s
492	No information			
493	Bowl	Low with two handles	11½"l	1950s & 60s
493	Shaving Mug			
494	Holder	Flower. Twin. Top handle	3¼"h	1950s & 60s
495	Settee	No other information		
496	Vase			
497	Dish	Fruit. Dovecote Range	13"dia	1950s–60s
498	Bowl			
499	Jug			
500	Bowl	Fruit. Sydney Range		1950s & 60s
501	Jug	Australian flowers–Sydney Range	M/s	1950s & 60s
502	No information			
503	Jardiniere			
504	Bowl			
505	Bowl			
506	Dish	Butter. Plain		
507	Lamp			
508	Bowl			
509	Vase	Old S & C with handles. Black with Pink Roses	10"h	1920?
509	Basket	Shell Range with handle. White	6¾"h Seen Ct	1956–1970
510	Jug	Shell Range White	9¼"h Seen Ct	1956–1960
511	Jug	Shell Range Matt White	6¼"h Seen Ct	1956–1960
512	Jardiniere	Shell Range	14"l Seen PG	1956–1975
513	Jardiniere	Shell Range	9¼"l Seen PG	1956–1975
514	Jardiniere	Shell Range	6½"l Seen PG	1956–1975
515	Vase			
516	Bowl	For Onion Sauce	5½"dia Seen PG	1956–S-in-P
517	Vase			
518	Jug	Narrow. Sanora Range	Seen Ct	1950s & 60s
519/520	No information			
521	Hat			
522	No information			
523	Wall Vase			
524	Wall Vase	Sydney Range	Seen Ct	1950s & 60s
525	Tray			
526	Tray Leaf	Flat with small posie	8½"l	
527	Tray Cone	Flat with small posie	8½"l	
528	Tray	Flat with small posie		
529	Butter	Dish. Dovecote Range. Round	5"dia	1950s–60s
530	Cheese	Dish. Dovecote	4½"h	1950s–60s
531	Basket	Fruit. Dovecote	11¼"dia	1950s–60s
532	Teapot	Dovecote	L/s	1950s–60s
533	Sugar	Bowl. Dovecote	3"dia Seen Ct	1950s–60s
534	Jug	Cream. Dovecote	3¼"h Seen Ct	1950s–60s
535	Pot	Honey. Dovecote	4"h Seen Ct	1950s–60s
536	Dish	Cucumber. Dovecote	12½"dia Seen Ct	1950s–60s

537–539	No information			
540	Dish	Lettuce. Dovecote	8½"dia Seen Ct	1950s–60s
541	Bowl	Salad. Dovecote	9½"dia Seen Ct	1950s–60s
542	Cup & Plate	Combined (T.V. Set) Dovecote	Seen Ct	1950s–60s
543	No information			
544	Jug	White with blue or green Budgie	9"h Seen Ct	1950s–1965
545	Basket	White with blue or green Budgie with top handle	8½"h Seen Ct	1950s–1965
546	Jardiniere	White with blue or green Budgie	6½"h Seen Ct	1950s–1965
547	Bowl	Shallow, with blue or green Budgie	13"h Seen PG	1950s–1965
548	Jardiniere	White with Budgie	9½"l Seen PG	1950s–1965
549	Vase	Duotone	Seen Ct	1950s–1960s
550	Bulb Pot	As Iceberg with large penguin	L/s	
551	Jug			
552	Urn			
553	Urn			
554–556	No information			
557	Jug	Slymcraft and Steppes Range	7"h Seen Ct	1950s–1983
558/559	No information			
560	Jug	Fawn Matt with green duck	6½"h Seen Ct	1950s
561	Jug	Various Ranges & finishes	4¼"h Seen Ct	1950s
562	Jug	Slymcraft Range	6½"h Seen Ct	1950s & 60s
563	No information			
564–566	Vases			
567	Bowl	Novelty. Fawn Matt Barrel Green Duck	2½"h Seen Ct	1950s & 60s
568	Bowl	Fawn Matt with green bunny or Bambi	2½"h Seen Ct	1950s
569	Bowl	As 567	4¼"h Seen Ct	1950s & 60s
570	Jug	Narrow. Rouge Decoration	11"h Seen Ct	1950s & 60s
571	Jug	Steppes Range & Rouge Decoration	9"h Seen Ct	1950s & 60s
572	Jug	As Ice with penguin	8"h	
573	Vase			
573	Jugs	Two. Pink with Pink Roses & Gold	7¾" & 6¾"	1920–?
574	No information			
575	Vase			
576	Cup & Saucer			
577	Teapot	Dovecote Range	S/s Seen Ct	1950s & 60s
578	Vase	Old Shaw and Copestake	6¾"h	1920-?
579/580	Vases			
581	Basket			
582	Honey	As Orange with green lid	3½"h Seen Ct	1950s–1983
583	Honey	As Pineapple with green lid	3½"h Seen Ct	1950s–1983
584	Honey	As Grape with green lid	3½"h Seen Ct	1950s–60s
585	Honey	As Strawberry with green lid	3½"h Seen Ct	1950s–1983
586	Bowl	Novelty. Fawn barrel with green dog	3"h Seen Ct	1950s–60s
587	Hutch	With Rabbit	8"l 4"h	
588	Jug	Squirrel on Cone		
589	Bowl	Various Ranges & colours	4"dia Seen Ct	1950s & 60s
590	Bowl			
591	Bowl	Round with penguin	4"h Seen Ct	1950s & 60s
592	Bowl			
593	No information			
594	Penguin			
595	No information			
596	Jug			
597	Bowl			
598	Bowl	For Bulb	Seen Ct	1959–1960s
599	Vase	Duotone Range		
600–602	Vases			
603	Urn	Lion handles. White matt/green shading	L/s Seen Ct	1950s–60s
604	Urn	Lion		
605	Bowl			
605	Clock	Highly decorated. Old S & C Daisy mark	9¼"h	1920s–30s
606	Two Vases	To match Clock set. Colours & Designs may vary	7¼"h	1920s–30s
606	Jug			
607	Vase			
608	Scorpion			
609	Bowl	For Punch		
610–613	No information			

614	Bowl	Shell		
615	Jardiniere	Sea Shell. White Matt Green shading	5¾"l Seen PG	1956–1970
616	Jardiniere	Sea Shell. White Matt Green shading	9½"l Seen PG	1956–1970
617	Pot	For plant. White Matt Green shading	Seen PG	1956–1960
618	Jardiniere	For plant. White Matt Green shading	7¾"l Seen PG	1956–1970
619	Butter	Dish. Amber. With cow on lid	5"l Seen Ct	1950s–S-i-P
620	Pot	For Butter		
621	Cheese	Dish. Stilton Col. Mouse on lid	6¾"dia Seen PG	1950s–S-i-P
622	Vase			
623	No information			
624–626	Vases			
627	Vase			
628	Vase	Classic Range. White Matt.	8"h Seen Ct	1960s–1983
629	Vase	Classic Range. White Matt.	9"h Seen Ct	1960s–1970
630	Vase	Classic Range. White Matt.	6"h Seen Ct	1960s–1975
631	Bowl	Classic Range. White Matt.	6"dia Seen Ct	1960s–1975
632	Vase	Classic Range. White Matt.	10"h Seen Ct	1960s–1970
633	No information			
634/635	Bowl			
636	Bowl	Shallow. Curved.	10¾"l Seen Ct	1950s–1965
637	No information			
638/639	Bowl	Duotone. Shallow	Seen Ct	1950s & 60s
640	No information			
641	Vase			
642/643	No information			
644	Vase			
645	Wall Vase	Classic Range. White Matt	9"h Seen Ct	1960s–1970
646	Pot	Classic Range. White Matt	5"h Seen Ct	1960s–1970
647	Pot	Classic Range. White Matt	4"h Seen Ct	1960s–1970
648	Jardiniere	Classic Range. White Matt	10"h Seen Ct	1960s–1970
649	Bowl	Classic Range. White Matt	8½"dia Seen Ct	1960s–1970
649	Clock	With Wild Duck Decoration S & C	10"h	1920s & 30s
650	Vases	To match above Clock S & C	7½"h	1920s & 30s
650	Vase	Twin. Steppes Range	Seen Ct	1950s–1960
651/652	Vases			
653	Wall Vase			
654	Tray			
655	Pot			
656	Vase	Green or fawn matt finish	Seen Ct	1950s & 60s
657	Bowl			
658	Vase			
659	Wall Vase			
660–662	No information			
663	Bowl			
664/665	No information			
666/667	Candle Stick			
668	Wall Vase & Handle			
669/670	Candle Stick			
671	No information			
672	Candy Box			
673	Dish	Shallow. Various decorations	Seen Ct	1950s & 60s
674–676	Vases		5"h Seen Ct	1950s–1983
677	Vase			
678/679	Vases		6"h Seen Ct	1950s–1970s
680/681	No information			
682/683	Vases		6"h Seen Ct	1950s–70s
684	Vase		5"h Seen Ct	1950s–1983
685/686	No information			
687	Wall Vase	Coconut with Blue Tit	6½"h Seen Ct	1950s–1965
688	Vase	Treetrunk with Blue Tit	7"h Seen Ct	1950s–1983
689	Jardiniere	Treetrunk with Blue Tit	11"h Seen Ct	1950s–1983
690–694	No information			
695	Bowl			
696	No information			
697	Vase	Black Hand	Seen Ct	1950s & 60s
698/699	Pots			
700	Kingfisher	To go with Bowl 436 & 726	6½"h	1920s–1965
701	Bowl	With Swallow		

702	Bowl	With Golden Crested Grebe (No. 3162)	Seen Ct	1950s–1960s
703	Barrel or Barrow			
704	Jug			
704	Pot	Old S & C with Garden Scene	4¾"h	1920s
705/706	Bowl			
707	Holder	Novelty Mushroom with pixie	3"h Seen Ct	1950s–1970
		With gnome or Mother Rabbit		1950s–1975
708	Holder	Novelty wheelbarrow with flowers	5"l Seen Ct	1950s–1960
		With Pixie		1950s–1970
		With gnome		1950s–1975
709	No information			
710	Vase	Like a Fish. Black or White matt	Seen Ct	1950s & 60s
711/712	Vase	Various decorations	Seen Ct	1950s & 60s
713	Wall Vase	Various decorations	Seen Ct	1950s & 60s
714	Bowl	Various decorations	Seen Ct	1950s & 60s
715	No information			
716	Jug	Various decorations	Seen Ct	1950s & 60s
717	Tray			
718	Wall Vase	White or Black Matt	12½"dia Seen Ct	1950s–1965
719	Tray			
720	Hat			
721	Wall Vase	In Shape of cap. Green Matt Checked	4"h Seen Ct	1950s & 60s
722/3	Hats			
724	Posie	Nautilus Range. As Seashell. White & Green	9"dia Seen Ct	1950s–1965
725	Vase	Fish, standing on head. White or Black Matt	Seen Ct	1950–1960
726	Wall Vase	Nautilus Range White & Green	8"h Seen Ct	1950s–1965
726	Bowl	Old S & C to go with 700 Cellulose finish		1920s
727	Dish	Small. Various designs		1950s–1960
728	No information			
729/731	Vase			
732	Wall Vase	Trilby Hat. Green Matt	4"h Seen Ct	1950s–1960
733	Wall Vase	Straw Boater	4"h Seen Ct	1950s–1960
734	Vase		8"h Seen Ct	1950s–1975
735–738	Pots	Cacti Range Novelty	about 4" Seen Ct	1950s–1960s
739	Vase		8¼"h Seen Ct	1950s–1965
740	Vase			
741	Vase		8¼"h Seen Ct	1950s–1965
742	Pot	Floral or Cactus	about 4" Seen Ct	1950s–1960
743	No information			
744–746	Vases		5"h Seen Ct	1950s–1970
747	Holder	Novelty Barrow with pixie	10"l Seen Ct	1950s–1975
748	Vase	As 739 Large size	L/s Seen Ct	1950s–1960
749	Vase		6"h	1950s–1970
750	Vase			
751	Vase		6"h Seen Ct	1950s–1970
751	Dog	Shaw & Constable (Mould Makers Register)		
752	Vase		10¼"h Seen Ct	1950s–1970
753	Vase	Nautilus Range White & Green	9½"h Seen Ct	1950s–1965
754	Jug			
755	Vase			
756	Jardiniere	Nautilus Range	9½"h Seen Ct	1950s–1960s
757/758	No information			
759	Pot	Shell Range		
760–767	No information			

THE FOLLOWING NUMBERS ARE ALL SHAW & COPESTAKE NUMBERS DATING FROM 1930 BUT CAN ALSO BE FOUND WITH THE FALCON WARE MARK. THE NUMBERS HAVE BEEN COLLECTED FROM THE POTTERY GAZETTE, CATALOGUES, MOULD MAKERS REGISTER, AND SYLVAC COLLECTORS.

768	Elephant	Black Glaze, Matt, Grey & Cellulose	4"h	1930–1983
769	Elephant	Black Glaze, Matt, Grey & Cellulose	4"h	1930–1983
770	Elephant	Black Glaze, Matt, Grey & Cellulose	7¼"h	1930–1983
771	Elephant	Black Glaze, Matt, Grey & Cellulose	8½"h	1930–1983
772	No information			
773	Elephant with			
	Howdah	Cellulose Finish		1930–1940
774–777	No information			
778	Basket			
779–784	No information			
785	Vase	Wild Duck Range. Cellulose Finish	5¼"h	1930–?
786–787	No information			

788/789	Elephants with Howdah	Cellulose Finish Black		1930–40s
790–794	No information			
795	Swan			
796/7	No information			
798	Elephant with Howdah	Black Cellulose		1930–40s
799–803	No information			
804	Dish with lid.	Wild Duck Range. Reg No 769029 (1931) Diamond Shaped. Cellulose Finish	3″h	1931–?
805–813	No information			
814	Elephant & Howdah	Black Cellulose		1930s–1940s
815	Elephant	Black Glaze & Cellulose	4½″h	1930s–1983
816–825	No information			
826	Elephant with Howdah	Black Cellulose		1930s–1940s
827–848	No information			
849	Cheese dish			
850–879	No information			
880	Lamp?			
881–883	Vase			
884	Vase	Mottled Green & Beige		
885–890	No information			
891	Dutch Clog			
892–897	No information			
898	Jardiniere	Pink Green & Grey Mottled	10″l × 5¼″h	1930s–1970
899–919	No information			
920	Figure?	Dancing lady. Green or Blue Matt	8½″h	1930s
921–925	No information			
926	Pot			
927–934	No information			
935	Jug			
936–953	No information			
954	Cream Jug			
955	Sugar Bowl			
956	Cream Jug			
957–960	No information			
961	Shoe	With china flowers. Ass. Colours		1930s–1960s
962	Gnome	For garden. Cellulose painted	5″h	1930s–1950s
963–989	No information			
990	Bunny	Round. Ass. Colours	5″h	1930s–1975
991	No information			
992	Shoe	Puss in Boots, Black		1930s–40s
993–1001	No information			
1002	Vase			
1003–7	No information			
1008	Vase			
1009–21	No information			
1022	Figure	Black boy with banjo	5″h	1930s–1940s
1023	No information			
1024	Gnome	Sitting	4½″h	1930s–1950s
1025	No information			
1026	Bunny	Round. Assorted Colours	7½″h	1930s–1970
1027	Bunny	Round. Assorted Colours	8½″h	1930s–1940s
1028	Bunny	Round. Assorted Colours	10″h	1930s–1975
1029–31	No information			
1032	Possibly Egg Cups & Stand			
1033–38	No information			
1039	Vase			1930s
1040–42	No information			
1043/4	Dogs			1930s
1045	No information			
1046	Cat	With back arched, tail erect. Matt. As 1313	6″h	1930s–1960
1047–60	No information			
1061	Vase			1930s
1062/3	No information			
1064	Bunny	Round with holder, striker or posy	4″h	1936–1956
1065	Bunny	Round Assorted Colours	6″h	1936–1975

1066	Rabbit			1930s
1067	Bunny	Round Assorted Colours	4"h	1936–1975
1068/69	No information			
1070	Vase/Jug	Seen Pottery Gazette 1937		1930s–
1071–85	No information			
1086	Cat	Black Glossy. Sitting	5¼"h	1930s–S-in-P
1087	Cat	Black Glossy. Sitting	7"h	1930s–S-in-P
1088	Cat	Black Glossy. Sitting	9"	1930s–1940s
1089	No information			
1090	Mug	To Match 1091 Green or Blue Matt	3½"h	1930s–
1091	Jug	To Match Mugs above	8"h	1930s–
1092	Gnome	Standing. For garden	8¼"h	1930s–1940s
1093	Gnome	Standing. For garden	9½"h	1930s–1940s
1094	Gnome	Standing. For garden	14"h	1930s–1940s
1095	Gnome & Pot	For Garden	8¼"h	1930s–1940s
1096	No information			
1097	Gnome & Pot	For Garden	9½"h	1930s–1940s
1098	No information			
1099	Cat	Cat & Basket		1930s
1100–11	No information			
1112	Vase			1930s
1113	Bowl			1930s
1114	No information			
1115	Vase	Acorn Vase with squirrel handle	8½"h	1930s–1950s
1116	Jug	With Dragon Handle. Matt or HP	8½"h	1930s
1117	Dog			1930s
1118	Dog	Sitting. Monty the Mongrel, Blue or Green With Brown touches	6"h Seen PG	1935–1940s
1119	Dog	Sitting, with Bow. Blue or Green/HP	4"h	1930s–1956
1120	Dog			
1121	Dog	Terrier standing, Brown & Green/HP	4½"h	1930s–1956
1122	Dog	Standing Sealyham? Matt or HP	3½"h	1930s–1956
1123	Dog	Standing	3½"h	1930s–1940s
1124–26	No information			
1127	Swan	Posy Holder	5½"l	1930s–1982
1128–31	No information			
1132	Pig	Money-Box. Black Matt	4"l	1930s–1982
1133	No information			
1134	Jug	With Shamrock Pattern, Cream/Green and Pink & Green. Witch Pot. See 4186	2½"h	1930s–?
1135	Pot	Witch Pot. See 4188	3¾"h	1930s–1940s
1136	Bowl			1930s
1137	No information			
1138	Vase	With Stork Handle. No Snip. Matt	10"h	1936–1950s
1139	No information			
1140	Sugar	Bowl as 1134 See 4185	2½"h	1930s–?
1141	No information			
1142	Squirrel	Sitting. Cream/Brown Matt	5½"h	1930s–?
1143	Squirrel	Sitting. Green Matt	7"h	1935–?
1144	Squirrel	Sitting. Matt Glaze	7¾"h	1930s–1940s
1145	Squirrel	Sitting. Matt Glaze	8½"h	1930s–1940s
1146	Squirrel	Sitting. Fawn Matt	9½"h	1935–?
1147	Jug	Squat. Art Deco. Green/Orange	6"h	1930s
1148	No information			
1149	Vase	Cellulose Decorated	7½"	1930s–1960
1150	Vase/Jug	Seen in 1937 PG		1930s–?
1151–53	No information			
1154	Boy	Whistling		1930s
1155–60	No information			
1161	Girl	Shy		1930s
1162	Cat		L/s–S/s	1930s
1163	No information			
1164	Cat			1930s
1165–6	No information			
1167	Vase	Hunting Vase with Stag Heads Handle Matt	8¾"h	1936-Short Run
1168–69	No information			
1170	Black Girl	With Banjo? To match 1022	5"	1930s–40s
1171/2	No information			
1173	Vase	Seen Pottery Gazette 1937	8"	1937–?

1174	No information			
1175	Jug	Flat Shape 1939 Pottery Gazette	6¼"h	1930s–1960s
1176	Vase/Jug	Seen PG 1939		1930s
1177–80	No information			
1181	Ashtray	Green with Fawn Hare & Striker no. 1270. Probably with other additions	6½"l	1930s
1182	Rabbit	As used on 1312	2½"h	1930s
1183	Cruet	1937 PG	5"a. 2½"h	1930s
1184	Jam Pot	1937 PG		1930s
1185	No information			
1186	Tray			1930s
1187–88	No information			
1189	Vase/Jug	Seen PG 1937		1930s
1190	Vase	Two monkeys climbing into Coconut	7"h	1930s–40s
1191	Dog	Begging. Joey on collar		1936–1965
1192	No information			
1193	Dog	Begging. Joey on Collar		1930–?
1194	No information			
1195	Vase	Acorn with Squirrel Handle. Matt Col	7½"h	1936–1950
1196	Vase	Mushroom. Two gnomes for handle. Matt Cols. Registered number 809115 (1936)	8½"h	1936–1950
1197	No information			
1198		Cress Dish and Stand to match 1183/4	11¼"h	1930s
1199	No information			
1200	Rabbit			1930s
1201	Vase/Jug	1937 Pottery Gazette		1930s
1202	Dog	Alsation		1930s
1203/4	No information			
1205	Dog	'MAC'. Sitting. Reg. No. 778504. (1932) As. Cls	5"h	1930s–1970
1206	Dog	As 1205	6¼"h	1930s–1940s
1207	Dog	As 1205	7¾"h	1930s–1970
1208	Dog	As 1205	9"h	1930s Short Run
1209	Dog	As 1205	11"h	1930–1970
1210	No information			
1211	Bowl	Tub. Black & shamrock	1¾"h	1930s–1940s
1212	No information			
1213	Honey Pot			1930s
1214	Vase/Jug			1930s
1215	No information			
1216	Jar	Ginger Jar or Biscuit Barrel Ribbed Design	7"h	1930s
1217–20	No information			
1221	Gnome	For Garden With Barrow	8"h 6"l	1930s–1950s
1222–26	No information			
1227	Dog	Standing	5"h	1930s–1940s
1228–36	No information			
1237		Could be bridal pair?		
1238	Elephant	Standing on one leg, dressed. In PG 1937	No more information	
1238	Bird	Information from Mould Makers Register		
1239–43	No information			
1244	Dog	Tall. Sitting. With Collar. In PG 1937	No more information	
1245	Dog	Scottie	5¾"h	1930s–1940s
1246	Dog	Glum. Sitting. Reg. No. 813261 (1936)	4¼"h	1936–1970
1247	Dog	Glum. Sitting. Reg. No. 813261 (1936)	5¾"h	1936–1970
1248	Posy Ring		8"dia	1930s–1940s
1249	No information			
1250	Posy Ring	Plain Colour Glaze	6"dia	1930s–1960s
1251	Posy	Diamond shaped	7"l	1930s
1252	No information			
1253	Jug	Various Decorations	6"h	1930s–1960s
1254	Vase			1930s
1255/56	No information			
1257	Vase			1930s
1258	No information			
1259	Dog	Small Scottie. Dark Brown	2¾"h	1930s–1940s
1260	No information			
1261	Dog	Scottie standing	7¼"h	1930s–1940s
1262	Dog	Scottie standing	8"h	1930s–1940s

1263/4	No information			
1265	Rabbit	Hare	Very small	1930s–1940s
1266	Ash Tray			1930s
1267–9	No information			
1270	Hare	With holder	3″h	1930s–1956
1271	Vase	For Spills	5″h	1930s–1960s
1272	Basket			1930s
1273	Jug	Rope Range. 1937 PG	L/s	1930s Short Run
1274	Vase	Hollyhock Range without snip	8½″h	1930s–1950s
1275–77	No information			
1278	Bowl	Sea-shell Range, White Matt. Grn Shading		1930s–1970
1279	Trough		12½″ × 1½″	1930s
1280	No information			
1281	Lamb			1930s
1282/3	Pots	Plant Pots. Shell. Range. White Matt	9″ & 6″dia	1930s–1970
1284	Lamb	Standing. Matt & HP	4″h	1930s–1968
1285	Lamb		5″h	1930s
1286	No information			
1287	Cat			1930s
1288	Candle Holder	Welsh Lady. Green Matt. with handle	3″h	1930s
1289	Jug	With Mans face, blue matt. Character Jug?	S/s	1930s
1290–92	No information			
1293	Duck			1930s
1294	No information			
1295	Dog	Griffin. Sitting. Matt or HP. Seen PG	5″h	1930s–1956
1296	Kittens	In a Basket. Matt colours, Seen PG 1937	4″h	1930s Short Run
1297	No information			
1298	Hare	'Harry' Reg.No.815840.Oct 1936.Matt Cols	5¾″h	1936–1970
1299	Hare	'Harry' Reg.No.815840.Oct 1936.Matt Cols	7½″h	1936–1940s
1300	Hare	'Harry' Bright Orange Cellulose Painted	9½″h	1936–1940s
1301	Jug			1930s
1302	Rabbit	'Lop Ear'. Reg. No. 815839. Ass. Cols	5½″h	1936–1975
1303	Rabbit	'Lop Ear'. Reg. No. 81539. Ass. Cols	7″h	1936–1975
1304	Rabbit	'Lop Ear'. Reg. No. 815839. Ass. Cols.	8¼″h	1936–1975
1305	Vase	Birds Nest. Bird for handle. Matt Glaze	8″h	1930s–1940s
1306	Vase	Rope Range		1937 Short Run
1307	Vase	Rope Range. Matt Colours	8½″	1937–1970
1308	Vase	Rope Range	S/s	1937 Short Run
1309	Vase	Rope Range	M/s	1937 Short Run
1310	Jug	Rope Range	M/s	1937 Short Run
1311	Book-End	With Various sized bunnies or Floral. Matt colours	5″h	1937–1970
1312	Posy	Round. Three Rabbits. Small hole in centre, on small stand. Matt or mottled	8¼″dia	1937–1960
1313	Cat	With tail erect as 1046	Very large	1930s–40s
1314	Posy	Plain Colour Glaze	3¾″l	1937–1960s
1315	Posy	Plain Colour Glaze	6″l	1937–1960s
1316/7	Posies	Plain Colour Glaze	8″ & 12″l	1937–1960
1318	Vase	Rabbits climbing into Furze No Snip	8¾″h	1937–1950
1319	No information			
1320	Shoe	Ash tray. Black	2″	1937–1960s
1321	No information			
1322	Toast rack		6½″l	1930s
1323	Bulb Pot?			
1324	Posy	Boomerang shape	10″l	1930s
1325	Bulb Pot?			
1326	Posy Holder	With Figure on front. Matt glaze	3½″h	1930s–1940s
1327	Posy Bar	With Figure on end. Matt glaze	8¾″l	1930s–1940s
1328	Bird	Woodpecker. Matt glaze	4″h	1930s–1940s
1329	No information			
1330	Kingfisher	Matt Glaze	4″h	1930s–1940s
1331	Bird	With tail up, head down. Matt glaze	6¼″h	1930s–1940s
1332	Dog	Caricature Daschund Standing Head turned tail in air. 1940 PG Matt	5¼″h 5″l	1939–1940s
1333	Cat	Crouching Matt glaze	4″h	1930s–1940s
1334	Foal	Standing. Matt or HP	4″h	1939–1970
1335	No information			
1336	Posy Holder	With figure	7¼″h	1930s–1940s
1337	Posy Holder	With Flower Seller	6½″h	1930s–1940s

1338/9	No information			
1340	Yacht	As 1393 & 1394	12½″	1930s–1940s
1341	No information			
1342	Jug	Round. Three sectioned handle	6¾″h	1930s–1960s
1343	No information			
1344	Jug	Various Decorations	9″h	1930s–1970
1345	Vase	Vase. Two small handles. Various Dec.	9″h	1930s–1965
1346	Vase	Various Dec. Two Scrolls on each side	10½″h	1930s–1982
1347	Vase			1930s
1348	No information			
1349	Seagull	Matt Glaze	3″h	1930s–1940s
1350	Seagull	Matt Glaze	4″h	1930s–1940s
1351	Seagull	Matt Glaze	5″h	1930s–1940s
1352	Posy Holder	Matt glaze	6″h	1930s–1940s
1353	Posy Holder	Matt Glaze	6″h	1930s–1940s
1354	No information			
1355	Vase	Round. Autumn Range. HP on White Matt		1930s–1960
1356	Jug	Round. Autumn Range. HP on White Matt		1930s–1960
1357	Seagull	Matt Glaze	2¼″h	1930s–1940s
1358	Pot			1930s
1359	Jug	As 1355 and 1356	L/s	1930s–1960
1360	Duck	Flying. As 1402,1401,1403. Matt or HP	12″l	1939–1975
1361	No information			
1362	Shaker	For Flour or Sugar Green or Fawn Matt	5″h	1930s
1363	Jug			1930s
1364	Mug			1930s
1365	Jam Pot	Same design as 1362 Green or Fawn Matt	4¼″h	1930s
1366	Ash tray	Green or Fawn Matt with Various animals at one end	5¾″l	1930s–1950s
1366	Bird	This information from Mould Makers Register		
1367	Jug	Angular. Various Decorations	6″h	1930s–1960s
1368	Bowl	With lid. as 1362. Green Matt	4¼″dia 3¼″h	1930s
1369	Fox	Sitting	5″h	1930s–40s
1370	Vase	Decorated as Budgie with Tail for Handle	7½″h	1930s–1940s
1371	Rabbit	Crouching. Matt coloured	3½″h	1930s–1940s
1372	Polar Bear		2¾″h	1930s
1373	Lamb	Standing. Matt Colours	4″l	1930s–1940s
1374	Donkey	Matt Colours	4″l	1930s–1940s
1375	Bird	Hen?	3½″h	1930s
1376	Bird	Matt Green. Round & Fat	3″h	1930s–1940s
1377	No information			
1378	Dog	Terrier. Sitting. Matt or HP	5″h	1939–1982
1379	Dog	Terrier. Sitting. Matt or HP	8″h	1939–1982
1380	Dog	Terrier. Sitting. Matt or HP	11″h	1939–1982
1381	No information			
1382	Dog	Spaniel. Sitting as 1462 & 1461	8″h	1930s–1940s
1383	No information			
1384	Wall Vase			1930s
1385	No information			
1386	Rabbit	Round. Ass. Colours	3¼″	1930s–1975
1387	No information			
1388	Hare	Crouching	5½″h	1930s–40s
1389	Hare	Crouching	7½″h	1930s–40s
1390	Koala Bear	On a Log. Matt colours	4½″h	1930s Short Run
1391	Koala Bear	On a Log. Matt colours	6″h	1930s Short Run
1392	No information			
1393	Yacht	As No. 1340. Matt Colours. Posies	5¾″h	1938–1950s
1394	Yacht	As No. 1340. Matt Colours. Posies Reg. No. 826482 (1938)	8½″h	1938–1960s
1395	Wall Vase	Ridged. With or without flowers	6¼″h	1930s–1960s
1396	No information			
1397	Posy	Horse shoe shape. Plain Col. Glaze	6″dia	1930s–1960s
1398	Dog			1930s
1399	Frog	Matt Colours	2½″h	1930s–1956
1400	Tinies	Combined number for very small animals, including Bunny,Mouse,Dog,Cat,Duck	1½″h	1930s–?
1401	Duck	Flying. Wall plaque. HP. See no. 1360	6½″l	1939–1975
1402	Duck	Flying. Wall plaque. HP. See no. 1360	9½″l	1939–1975

1403	Posy	In shape of Seal		1939–1950s
1403	Duck	Flying. Wall plaque. HP. See no. 1360	5"l	1950s–1975
1404	Jug	Various decorations	6½"h	1930s–1960s
1405/6	No information			
1407	Vase	Serpent like decorations	8½"h	1930s–1960s
1408	No information			
1409/10	Jugs	Various decorations	5¼"h & 8"h	1930s–1960s
1411	No information			
1412	Dog	Airdale Terrier	9"h	1930s–40s
1413	Triple Vase	Like tree trunks		1930s–40s
1414	Dog	Griffin. Sitting	5"h	1930s–1970
1415	Dog	Griffin? Standing	5"h	1930s–1970
1416	Vase	Tree trunk with Koala Bear	5"h	1930s–40s
1417	Jug			1930s
1418	Jug	Various Decorations	8¼"h	1930s–1960s
1419				
1420	Pixie	Sitting under Toadstool with Squirrel Lucky Pixie on Base. Matt Colours	3"h	1930s–1956
1421	Pixie	Sitting on mound. Lucky Pixie. Matt Cols	3"h	1930s–1940s
1422	Horse	Sitting, as 1447	4¾"h	1930s–40s
1423	Bear	Brown. Standing. Matt colours	3"h	1930s–1960s
1424	Fox	Crouching on ground. Matt colours	2¼"h & 6¼"l	1930s–1960
1425	Hippo	Standing. Matt colours	3"h	1930s & 40s
1426	Bear/Panada	Standing. Matt colours	3¼"h	1930s–1956
1427	Lamb	Looking at tail	4¾"h	1930s–40s
1428	Donkey	Standing. Matt or HP	4¼"h	1930s–1982
1429	Duck	As 1499 Large Size	5½"h	1930s–40s
1430	No information			
1431	Calf	Standing	3½"h	1930s
1432	Cat	3 in one		
1433	Dog	With Paw in sling. Matt or HP	3½"h	1930s–1970
1434	Cat	Lying Down		1930s
1435	Jug	For Cider. Barrel shaped	8 to 10"	1930s
1436	Mug	For Cider. Barrel shaped		1930s
1437	Jam Pot	Barrel Range		1930s
1438	Butter/Cheese Dish	Round. Barrel Range		1930s
1439	Cruet	Three pieces on Stand. Barrel Range	4½"a. 1¾"h	1930s
1440	Butter or sweet dish	Barrel Range	4"a	1940s
1441	Cigarette Barrel	Green/Blue/Fawn Matt		1940s
1442	Match Holder	Barrel Range		1930s
1443	Sauce Bottle Holder/Vase	Barrel Range		1930s–40s
1444	No information			
1445	Sauce/Gravy boat	Barrel Range	5¼"l	1930s
1446	Biscuit Jar	Barrel Range		1930s
1447	Foal	Sitting. Matt or HP	4"h	1930s–1960
1448	Bowl			1930s
1449	No information			
1450	Dog			1930s
1451	Stag	Standing. Matt colours	5⅜"h	1930s–1960
1452	Jug	Character. Mr. Pickwick	6"h	1930s–1960s
1453	Jug	Character. Mr. Micawber	6"h	1930s–1960s
1454	Ashtray	Round. With Kitten or other. Matt cols	5¼"l	1930s–40s
1455	Ashtray	As Pond. With bunny or other. Matt cols	4¾"dia	1930s–1965
1456	No information			
1457	Holder	Two tree stumps, with two bunnies	3"h	1930s–40s
1458	Leopard	Chewing Foot	9½"h	1940s
1459	Serviette Ring	With 1265 Hare		1940s
1460	No information			
1461	Dog	'Sammy' the Spaniel. Sitting. Matt Cols	6"h	1930s–40s
1462	Dog	'Sammy' the Spaniel. Sitting. Matt cols and HP	11"h	1930s–1970
1463–66	No information			
1467	Lizard	Matt colours	6"l	1930s–40s
1468–9	No information			
1470	Cruet	Pepper & Salt		1930s
1471–8	No information			

1479	Posy	Curved with dog or bunny one end Matt		1930s–40s
1480	Posy	Round with gnome in middle. Matt cols	5¾"dia	1930s–1960
1481	Posy	Round with gnome in middle. Matt cols	8¾"dia	1930s–1960
1482/3	No information			
1484	Top Hat	With Dog & Kitten. Matt Colours	4"h	1940–1960
1485	Candle Stick	With flowers in centre. Pastel Cols. HP	4"h	1940–1960
1486	Lucky Pig	Sitting		1940s
1487	Posy Log	With Koala Bear	4½"h	1940s
1488	Posy			1940s
1489	Vase			1940s
1490/1	Vase	Various decorations	4¾"h	1940–1960s
1492	Duck	As 1498 and 1499	5½"h	1940s
1493	Kangeroo			1940s
1494	Squirrel	Eating from bowl. Matt colours	4"h	1940–1960s
1495	Vase			1940s
1496	Basket			1940s
1497	Rabbit	Crouching. One ear up. Matt colours	3"l	1940s
1498	Duck	As 1492	3¼"h	1940s
1499	Duck	Registered no. 833893. (1939/40)	4¼"h	1940s
1500	Panda			1940s
1501	No information			
1502	Dog			1940s
1503	No information			
1504	Dog	With paw in basket. Matt colours	3½"h	1940s
1505	Lamb	Six different	Very Small	1940s
1506	Panda	Sitting	5½"h	1940s
1507	No information			
1508	Foal	Standing. Matt or HP	5"h	1940s–1960s
1509	Rabbit	Lop Ear Matt colours	3¾"h	1940s–1960
1510	Vase	As mushroom with Lop Ear Rabbit	5½"h	1940s–1960
1511	Bunny	Sitting up. One ear down	13"h	1940s
1512	Dog	Crouching	3"h	1940s
1513	Bowl	Round with gnomes and bunnies	7"dia	1940s–1965
1514	Bowl	Round with gnomes and bunnies	8½"dia	1940–1965
1515/16	No information			
1517	Ashtray	With squirrel	4¾"h	1940s
1518	Squirrel	Eating nut. Matt colours	3½"h	1940s
1519	Stag on Rock		4¾"h	1940s
1520	Bear/Panada	Sitting	2⅛"h	1940–1956
1521	Bear/Panada	On back	1½"h	1940–1956
1522	Bear/Panada	Standing	1¾"	1940–1956
1523	Rabbit	Crouching. Cellulose finish. Crm & Brwn	4½"h	1940s
1524	Dog	With paw in sling. Matt finish	6"h	1940s
1525	Bunny	One ear down as 1511	8½"h	1940s
1526	Bunny	As 1511	10½"h	1940s
1527	Elephant	Sitting	3½"h	1940s
1528	Dog	Scratching	app. 3½"h	1940s
1529	Rabbit	As 1523. Matt colours	3½"h	1940s
1530	Rabbit	Crouching as 1523	5½"h	1940s
1531	Ashtray	Banjo Shape	5¾"l	1940s
1532	Ashtray	With kissing bunnies	3¼"h	1940s
1533	Dog	Setter	13¼"h	1940s
1534	Bunnies kissing		2½"h	1940s
1535/7	No information			
1538	Vase	Various decorations	3½"h	1940s–1960s
1539	No information			
1540	Posie	With 1519 stag	5½"h	1940s
1541	Bowl	Round	3"dia	1940s–1960s
1542	Bowl	Round	4"dia	1940s–1960s
1543	Seagull	Flying. Wall Plaque. Matt White	4½"l	1940s–1960s
1544	Seagull	Flying. Wall Plaque. Matt White	7¼"l	1940s–1960
1545	Seagull	Flying. Wall Plaque. Matt White	8½"l	1940s–1960s
1546	Bookends	With Lop Ear Rabbit. Matt Colours	4½"h	1940s–1965
1547	Vase			1940s
1547	Ashtray	Mandolin shape	5¾"l	1940s
1548	Dog	Collie. Standing	8"l	1940s–1975
1549	Vase			1940s
1550	Vase	Corner?		
1551	Cream Jug	Mottled matt	3"h	1940s

1552	Beaker	Mottled matt	3″h	1940s
1553	Cream Jug	Mottled matt	3″h	1940s
1554–60	No information			
1561	Ashtray or nightlight stand		4¼″dia	1940s
1562–64	Vases	White-Matt	8″h,10″h,11¾″h	1940s–1982
1565	No information			
1566	Posie	As galleon on waves	4¾″h	1940s
1567/8	No information			
1569	Vase			1940s
1570	Vase	Various Decorations	7″h	1940s–1960
1571	Vase	Various Colours	8½″h	1940s–1970
1572	Cruet	Dahlia Range. Ass. Cols		1940s
1573	Ashtray as armchair		2¾″h	1940s
1574–77	No information			
1578	Vase	Round & ridged	8″h	1940s–1960s
1579	Mug	Dahlia Range Ass. Cols	3½″h	1940s
1580	Jugs	Set. Dahlia Range Ass. Cols	6¼″,5¼″,4¼″	1940s
1581	Honey pot	Dahlia Range as 1580 Ass. Cols	4½″h	1940s
1582	Butter dish	Round. Dahlia Range Ass. Cols	4½″dia	1940s
1583	Sugar	Round. No lid. Dahlia Range Ass. Cols	3¼″dia	1940s
1584	Cream Jug	Dahlia Range Ass. Cols	3¼″h	1940s
1585	Teapot	Dahlia Range	6¼″h	1940s
1586	Cheese Dish	Dahlia Range Assorted Colours	7¼″l	1940s
1587	Biscuit Jar	With Cane Handle. Dahlia Range Ass. Cols	6½″h	1940s
1588	No information			
1589	Butter dish	Single Portion with/without lid	4″dia	1940s
1590	Holder	Two Hugging bunnies. Posy or Striker or Floral. Ass. Cols.	2½″h	1940s–1960
1591	Butter dish	Butter Ration Dish With or with out lid		1940
1592/3	No information			
1594	Ashtray	With Bunny or Dog		
1595	Jug	Dahlia Range	8″h	1940s
1596–99	No information			
1600	Beaker	Dahlia Range	4¼″h	1940s
1601–10	No information			
1611	Wall Vase			1940s
1612	Jug/Vase			1940s
1613	No information			
1614	Mug	D'ye Ken John Peel-Hunting Scene	4″h	1940s
1615	Vase			1940s
1616/7	No information			
1618	Jug/Vase			1940s
1619	No information			
1620	Vase	Duo-tone Range	M/s	1940s–1960
1621	No information			
1622	Ashtray	Chimney. Also with kitten		1940s
1623	Jug	Ass. Cols	6″h	1940s–1960s
1624	Jug		6″h	
1625	Jug	Ass. Cols	6″h	1940s–1960s
1626	No information			
1627/8	Vases			1940s
1629–34	No information			
1635	Jardiniere			1940s
1636	No information			
1637	Vase			1940s
1638–40	No information			
1641	Jug/Vase			1940s
1642–45	No information			
1646	Puppy	Playing. Matt Colours	5″l	1940s
1647–52	No information			
1653	Bowl	Embossed	9¾″l 5½″h	1940s–1960s
1654	Dish	With handles, for sweets	5″l 2″h	1940s–1960s
1655	Jug/Vase		8″h	1940s
1656	No information			
1657	Basket			1940s
1658	No information			
1659	Lamb	Standing. Head turned. Matt cols	3¾″h	1940s–60s
1660	Toastrack			1940s
1661	Lamb	As 1659. Reg. No. 838603 (1941)	L/s	1940s

1662–66	No information			
1667	Ashtray	Round. With dog, rabbit, floral or Spitfire	5″dia	1940s–1965
1668–77	No information			
1678	Duck			
1679	Duck	Ski-ing. Matt colours	5″l 2½″h	1940s–50s
1680	Skis			1940s
1681–3	Ducks			1940s
1684	No information			
1685	Jug	Embossed. Various colours	7″	1940s–1965
1686	Vase			1940s
1687–92	No information			
1693	Teapot	Blue		1940s
1694	No information			
1695	Bowl	For sugar. Pink with handles	3″h	1940s
1696/7	No information			
1698	Jug	Green leaf design	3″h	1940s
1699–700	No information			
1701	Jug/Vase			1940s
1702	No information			
1703	Teapot			1940s
1704	No information			
1705	Jug			1940s
1706–09	No information			
1710	Jug	Green	10″h	1940s
1711/2	No information			
1713	Dish	Blue		1940s
1714	Bowl			1940s
1715	Cruet	Tray with dogs head cruet set	7½″l	1940s–1960s
1716–19	No information			
1720	Cruet handle			1940s
1721/22	No information			
1723	Lamp			1940s
1724	No information			
1725	Cruet			1940s
1726	No information			
1727	Teapot			1940s
1728	Jug	Barrel shape. To match 1715		1940s–1960s
1729	Jug			1940s
1730	No information			
1731	Vase			1940s
1732	Vase	Rosslyn & Misty Morn range	9″h	1940s–1960
1733	Tray			1940s
1734–36	No information			
1737	Jug			1940s
1738	Bowl	With three legs. For fruit	8″dia	1940s
1739–43	No information			
1744	Vase			1940s
1745	Jug	Embossed & ridged	6″h	1940s–1960
1746	Jug	Mottled Satin Glaze. Embossed flower	6″h	1940s–1960s
1747	Cheese dish			1940s
1748	Tray			1940s
1749	Teapot			1940s
1750	No information			
1751	Jug/Vase			1940s
1752	Basket			1940s
1753	No information			
1754	Sugar bowl			1940s
1755	Basket			1940s
1756	Jug			1940s
1757	Vase	Embossed wavy lines. Various cols.	6″h	1940s–1960
1758	Vase	Ridged decoration	6″h	1940s–1960
1759	No information			
1760	Bowl	With cover		1940s
1761/2	No information			
1763	Vase			1940s
1764	No information			
1765	Sugar Bowl	To match 1750		1940s–1960s
1766	No information			
1767	Tray			1940s

1768	No information			
1769	Butter dish			1940s
1770	Sugar bowl			1940s
1771	Beaker			1940s
1772	No information			
1773	Basket			1940s
1774	Bowl	Cavalier Range Hand Painted		1940s–1960s
1775	Tankard	Cavalier Range Hand Painted	5"h	1940s–1960s
1776	Cheese dish	Primrose range		
1777	Basket	Basket design	3½"h	1940s–1960s
1778/9	Jug			
1780	Basket	Embossed flowers. Ass. Cols	5½"h	1940s–1960s
1781	No information			
1782	Jug	To match 1780	6½"h	1940s–1960s
1783	Bowl	To match 1780	4"h 6½"l	1940s–1960s
1784	Vase	Mottled Satin Glaze	6¼"h	1940s–1960s
1785	No information			
1786	Vase	Mottled Satin Glaze	4½"h	1940s–1960s
1787	Vase	With horizontal and vertical lines. Handles	4¼"h	1940s–1960
1788–9	No information			
1790	Jug			
1791	Dish	For Sweets. Embossed	6¼"l 2¼"h	1940s–1960
1792/3	No information			
1794	Jug	Squashed look. Various cols.	7"h 7"l	1940s–1960
1795	Jug	Plain. Various colours	6"h	1940s–1960s
1796	Basket	As circle. Various colours	6¼"h 4½"l	1940s–1960
1797	No information			
1798	Tray			1940s
1799/800	No information			
1801	Jug	Cavalier Design		1940s–1960s
1802	No information			
1803	Vase	1940s		
1804–6	No information			
1807	Vase	Dovedale & Rosslyn Range	9¾"h	1940s–1965
1808	Vase	Dovedale Range or mottled satin finish		1940s–1965
1809–12	No information			
1813	Sugar bowl			1940s
1814	Cream Jug			1940s
1815	Jugs	Three sizes		1940s
1816	No information			
1817	Vase			1940s
1818	Butter Dish	With Dogs Head lid as 1715		1940s–1960s
1819	Basket	Also with hand painted flowers	4"h	1940s–1960s
1820	Trinket Box	With hand painted flowers on lid. Ass. Cols		1940s–60s
1821	Powder Bowl	With hand painted flowers on lid. Ass. Cols		1940s–60s
1822	Dish	Small with flowers. Ass. Cols		1940–60s
1823	Bowl	Also containing 8 HP flowers		1940s–1960s
1824	Jug	Mottled Satin Glaze	8¾"h	1940s–1960s
1825	No information			
1826	Bowl	Diamond shape. With grid	7"l 5"h	1940s–1960s
1827	Bulb Bowl	As 1780	5½"l 3½"h	1940s–1960s
1828	No information			
1829	Basket	With sloping handle, for sweets	9"l	1940s–1960s
1830	Bulb Bowl	Plain. Ass. Cols	8½"l	1940s–1960s
1831	Vase	Handles as leaves	6½"h	1940s–60s
1832–37	Vases	With ornamental handles	8½"h	1940s–60s
1838–47	No information			
1848	Bowl	Also with 5 hand painted flowers ass. cols.		1940s–60s
1849	Jam pot	With dogs head lid to match1715 Matt	5¼"h	1940s–1960s
1850	Cheese Dish	With dogs head lid to match 1715 Matt	6½"h	1940s–1960
1851	Basket	Wild duck decoration Matt/HP or Cell. finish		1948–50s
1852	Bowl	Wild Duck Range. HP on White Matt	8"l	1948–60s
1853	Vase	Wild Duck Range. HP on White Matt	6½"h	1948–60s
1854	Jug	Wild Duck Range. HP on White Matt	8½"h	1948–60s
1855	Vase	Wild Duck Range. HP on White Matt	5"h	1948–60s
1856	No information			
1857	Vase	As 1852 with ornamental handles	8½"h	1948–60s
1858	Vase	As 1852 with ornamental handles	8½"h	1948–60s
1859	Bowl	As 1852 with ornamental handles – Diamond shape	5"h	1948–60s

1860	Bowl	As 1852 with ornamental handles – Diamond shape	9½"l	1948–60s
1861	No information			
1862	Dish	Blackberry Range. Pink or Primrose HP	10¾"l	1949–50s
1863	No information			
1864	Dish	Blackberry Range	8½"dia	1949–50s
1865	No information			
1866	Jug	Blackberry Range. Pink or Primrose HP		1949–50s
1867	Jam Pot	Blackberry Range. Pink or Primrose HP	4½"h	1949–50s
1868	Dish with lid	Blackberry Range. Pink or Primrose HP	3"h	1949–50s
1869	Jug	Blackberry Range. Pink or Primrose HP	2¾"	1949–50s
1870	Jam Pot	Blackberry Range. Pink or Primrose HP	3½"h	1949–50s
1871	Sugar	Blackberry Range. Pink or Primrose HP	2"h	1949–50s
1872	No information			
1873	Toastrack	Blackberry Range as 1866	5¼"l	1949–50s
1874	No information			
1875	Jug Set	One of which is 4½"h		1949–50s
1876	Jug	Blackberry Range. Pink or Primrose HP	5½"h	1949–50s
1877	Mug	For shaving		1949–50s
1878–82	No information			
1883	Vase			1949–50s
1884	Teapot			1940–50s
1885/6	No information			
1887	Toastrack	Leaf shaped. Section for butter		1949–50s
1888	Honey Pot			1949–50s
1889	Teapot	Like a cabbage	S/s	1949–50s
1890–91	No information			
1892	Posy	Ring. Also with HP flowers	S/s	1949–60s
1893	Posy Ring			1940s–50s
1894	Dish	For sweets. HP flowers	S/s	1949–60s
1895–97	No information			
1898	Dish	For sweets. Decorated with flowers	S/s	1949–60s
1899	Posy	of hand painted flowers with bow	S/s	1949–60s
1900	No information			
1901	Pot			1940s–50s
1902	No information			
1903	Container	Diamond Shape. Flowers on lid	2¼"h	1940s–50s
1904	Jug			1940s–50s
1905/6	No information			
1907	Tray			1940s–50s
1908	No information			
1909	Posy	of hand painted flowers with bow	S/s	1949–60s
1910	Dish	For sweets with handle. Flower shape HP. Ass. Cols	4½"dia	1949–60s
1911–14	No information			
1915	Jar			
1916	Jar	For biscuits		1940s–50s
1917	No information			
1918	Biscuit Barrel			1940s–50s
1919	Dish	For sweets. One flower HP Ass. Cols	6¾"dia	1949–60s
1920	Dish	For sweets. One flower HP Ass. Cols	5"dia	1949–60
1921	Dish	For sweets. One flower HP Ass. Cols	7½"dia	1949–60
1922	Vase			1940s–50s
1923	Flower Pot			1940s–50s
1924/5	No information			
1926	Jug			1940s–50s
1927/8	No information			
1929	Teapot			1940s–50s
1930	Bowl	Containing HP flowers		1949–60
1931	Box			1940s–50s
1932	No information			
1933	Dish	Flower shape with handle as 1910	5½"dia	1949–60s
1934	Dish	Flower shape with handle Ass. Cols	6½"dia	1949–60s
1935	Tray	As log		1940s–50s
1936	Mug			1940s–50s
1937	Jam Pot	Hobnail design	4½"h	1940s–50s
1938	Jug			1940s–50s
1939	Sugar Bowl	Hobnail design		1940s–50s
1940/41	No information			

1942	Teapot			1940s–50s
1943	Jug Set			1940s–50s
1944	No information			
1945	Cider Jug			1940s–50s
1946	Cheese Dish	Hobnail Design		1940s–50s
1947	Twin tray			1940s–50s
1948	Rabbit Container			1940s–50s
1949–52	No information			
1953	Teapot			1940s–50s
1954	Bowl	With HP flowers		1950–1960s
1955	Dish	As flower Ass. Cols	4½″dia	1950–1960s
1956	Wall Vase	White matt with green/blue budgie/swallow	8″h	1950–1960s
1957	Bowl	With HP flowers	S/s	1950–1960s
1958	Jug	With squirrel handle. Matt/Gloss	7¼″h	1950–1960
1959	Jug	With squirrel handle. Matt/Gloss	8½″h	1950–1965
1960	Jug	With stork handle. Matt/Gloss	10″h	1950–1965
1961	Holder			1950s
1962	Jug	Hollyhock. Matt/Gloss	8½″h	1950–1982
1963	Posy	Heartshape with Pixie	8½″l	1950s–1960s
1964	Posy	Crescent shape	6″dia	1950s–1960s
1965–67	Posies	Straight	4″ 6″ & 8″l	1950s–1960s
1968	Dish	Bon-bon Ass. Cols. With handle	5″dia	1950s–1960s
1969	Jug	Mushroom with gnomes as handle. Matt/Gloss	8½″h	1950s–1975
1970	Jug	Squat	5¼″h	1950s–1960s
1971	Jug	Squat	5¼″h	1950s–1960
1972	Wall Vase			1950s
1973	No information			
1974	Honey Pot			1950s
1975	Box			1950s
1976	Tray			1950s
1977	No information			
1978	Jug	Two rabbits climbing into furze	10″h	1950s–1965
1979–81	No information			
1982–84	Fern Pots			1950s
1985–89	Jugs			1950s
1990	Toastrack	Dogs head range. Green & Fawn Matt	6¾″h	1950s–1960s
1991	Basket			1950s
1992	Posy	Round	6″dia	1950s–60s
1993	Jug	Min Jug with squirrel	3″h	1950s–1983
1994	Tray			1950s
1995	Jug			1950s
1996	Container	As basket, with dog. Matt See 3567	2″h	1950s–60s
1996		Mould Makers Register also gives GIRL under this number		
1997	Bowl	Heart shaped lid decorated with HP flowers	4½″dia	1950s–60s
1998	Barrel Holder			1950s
1999	Posy Bowl			1950s
2000	No information			
2001	Dish	Shell shape with HP flowers. Ass. Cols		1950s–60s
2002	Bowl			1950s
2003	Tray			1950s
2004	Bulb Bowl			1950s
2005	Tray			1950s
2006	Jardinere	Also with HP flowers	S/s	1950s–60s
2007	Jug			1950s
2008–20	No information			
2021	Tray			1950s
2022	Bowl	Heart shaped as 1997. Ass. Cols	3½″dia	1950s–60s
2023	Posy Bar			1950s
2024	Posy	Sealyham dog	7″l	1950s–1965
2025	Posy	Spaniel dog	7″l	1950s–1965
2026	No information			
2027	Bowl	Ivyleaf range. Reg. No. 874069 (1954)	6″l	1950s–60s
2028	Bowl			1950s
2029	Vase			1950s
2030	Basket			1950s
2031	No information			
2032	Tray & Flower Holder	Ivyleaf range. Reg. No. 874070 (1954)	8″l	1950s–60s

2033	Trough	As 2027	7½"l	1950s–60s
2034	No information			
2035	Bulb Bowl	As 2027	9½"l	1950s–60s
2036	Jug	As 2027	8¼"h	1950s–60s
2037	Jug	As 2027 Reg. No. 874072 (1954)	6"h	1950s–60s
2038	Tray			1950s
2039	Dish	With Handle As 2027	3½"h	1950s–60s
2040	Tray			1950s
2041	Bowl			1950s
2042	Basket			1950s
2043	Fern Pot	As 2027	4"h	1950s–60s
2044	Jardiniere	As 2027	7"l	1950s–60s
2045	Jug	As 2027	2⅞"h	1950s–60s
2046	Honey	As 2027	4½"h	1950s–60s
2047	Fern Pot	As 2027	5"h	1950s–60s
2048	Mushroom Bowl			1950s
2049	Bowl	With recess for gnome or other	9"dia 4¼"h	1950s–60s
2050	Wall Vase	As 2027	7½"h	1950s–60s
2051	Slipper	With dog standing Matt/Gloss	3½"h	1950s–1982
2052	Wall Vase	As 2050	5"h	1950s–60s
2053	No information			
2054	Bowl	As Basket with platform for dog or other	5"dia 1⅜"h	1950s–60s
2055–59	No information			
2060	Boot Bulb Bowl	Black Glaze	4¼"h 8¼"l	1950s–60s
2061	Bulb Bowl	Acorn with squirrel handles	11½"l 4½"h	1950s–60s
2062	Bulb Bowl	Tree stump with dogs		1950s
2063	No information			
2064	Flat Dish	Ivyleaf Range		1950s
2065	No information			
2066	Cat			1950s
2067	No information			
2068	Salad Dish	Ivyleaf Range		1950s
2069–74	No information			
2075	Bowl	As 2061	6"l 2½"h	1950s–60s
2076–78	No information			
2079	Wall Vase	With Seagull or Flowers	6½"h	1950s–60s
2080	Tray			1950s
2081/2	Vases			1950s
2083/4	Wall Vases	With HP flowers. Ass. Cols	6"h	1950s–60s
2085	Basket			1950s
2086	Jug	Seagull Ware	6¼"h	1950s–60s
2087	Jug			1950s
2088	Cheese Dish	Ivyleaf Range		1950s–60s
2089	Dish With lid	Ivyleaf Range		1950s
2090	No information			
2091/2	Wall Vases		S/s	1950s
2093–96	Jugs			1950s
2097–8	Bowl			1950s
2099–00	Pots			1950s
2101	Posy	Round		1950s
2102	Posy			1950s
2103	Vase			1950s
2104	Jug			1950s
2105–6	Honey			1950s
2107	Tray			1950s
2108	Basket			1950s
2109	Tray			1950s
2110	Wall Vase			1950s
2111	Candy Box	Seagull Ware	3"h 5"w	1950s–60s
2112	Bowl	Seagull Ware	4¼"h 9½"w	1950s–60s
2113	Jardiniere	Seagull Ware	3¾"h 7½"w	1950s–60s
2114	Bulb Bowl	Autumn Range		1950s–60s
2115	Flower Pot	Autumn Range		1950s–60s
2116	Jardiniere	Autumn Range		1950s–60s
2117	Jardiniere			1950s
2118	Jug/Vase			1950s
2119	Basket	Seagull Ware	6½"h 6½"w	1950s–60s
2120	Cat			1950s
2121	No information			

2122	Bowl	With handles. Also with HP flowers	S/s	1950s–60s
2123	No information			
2124	Vase	Ivyware Range		
2125	Vase			1950s
2126/7	No information			
2128	Dish	Shell shaped with HP flowers		1950s–60s
2129	Pot	Rope Range		1950s–60s
2130	Pot			1950s
2131	Trough	Rope Range. White with green edge	8″l	1950s–60s
2132	Pot	Rope Range	9″l	1950s–60s
2133	Jardiniere			1950s
2134–5	Bowl			1950s
2136	Vase	Duo-tone		1950s–60s
2137	Vase	Various decorations		1950s–60s
2138	Dish	Shallow. Various decorations		1950s–60s
2139	Vase	Various decorations		1950s–60s
2140	Wall Vase	Various decorations	8½″dia	1950s–60s
2141	Bowl			1950s
2142	Dish	Shallow. Various Decorations	7½″l	1950s–60s
2143	Bowl	Various decorations		1950s–60s
2144	Vase	Various decorations		1950s–60s
2145–6	Bowls			1950s
2147	Vase	Various decorations		1950s
2148	Bowl			1950s
2149–50	No information			
2151	Wall Vase	Rope Range	8¾″h	1950s–60s
2152	Bulb bowl	Autumn Range		1950s–60s
2153	Bowl			1950s
2154	No information			
2155	Holder			1950s
2156	Wall Vase	Autumn Range. HP in Natural Autumn Tints on White Matt background		1950s–60s
2157	No information			
2158	Pixie	Sitting on upturned toadstool		1950s–60s
2159	Jardiniere	Autumn Range as 2156	14″h	1950s–60s
2160	Plant Pot	Rope Range White Mt with Green Shading inside	6″l	1950s–1965
2161	Vase	Rope Range White Mt with Green Shading inside	3″h	1950s–1965
2162	Jardinere	Rope Range White Mt with Green shading inside	7″l	1950s–1965
2163	Vase	Rope Range White Mt with Green shading inside	7″h	1950s–1965
2164	Vase			All following 1950s
2165	Cream Jug	With Thistle design	2½″h	
2166	Bowl	For Sugar with Thistle design	2½″h	
2167	Jardiniere			
2168	Candlestick			
2169	Tray			
2170	Tray			
2171	Plant pot	Raphique Range Assorted Colours		1950s–1965
2172	Honey	Raphique Range Assorted Colours		1950s–1965
2173	Plant Pot	Small Handle	5″h	1950s
2174	Candlestick			1950s
2175	Vase			1950s
2176	Vase	Raphique Range Assorted Colours		1950s–60s
2177	Honeypot	Raphique Range Assorted Colours		1950s–60s
2178	Posie trough	Raphique Range Assorted Colours	8¼″l	1950s–60s
2179	Butterdish			1950s
2180	Jardiniere	Raphique Range Assorted Colours		1950s–60s
2181	Wall Vase	Raphique Range Assorted Colours		1950s–60s
2182	Bulb Bowl	Raphique Range Assorted Colours		1950s–60s
2183	Pot			1950s
2184	Cruet Set	Raphique Range Assorted Colours		1950s–60s
2185	Cream Jug	Raphique Range Assorted Colours		1950s–60s
2186	Cruet			1950s
2187	Posie Trough	Rope Range	15″l	1950s–60s
2188	Teapot	Raphique Range Assorted Colours		1950s–60s
2189	Vase	Raphique Range Assorted Colours		1950s–60s

2190	Sugar Bowl	Raphique Range Assorted Colours		1950s–60s
2191	Bowl	Raphique Range Assorted Colours		1950s–60s
2192	Vase	Raphique Range Assorted Colours		1950s–60s
2193	Wall Vase			All following 1950s
2194	Pot			
2195	Wall Vase			
2196	Cheese Dish			
2197	Butter Dish			
2198/9	Vases			
2200	Sugar			
2201	Cream Jug			
2202	Tray			
2203	Tray			
2204	Pot			
2205	Vase			
2206	Candlestick			
2207	No information			
2208	Wall Pocket	With flowers		
2209	Plant Pot	Cactus Range Green/Fawn Matt		
2210	Cream Jug			
2211	Toast Rack			
2212	No information			
2213	Bowl			
2214	Tray			
2215	Trough			
2216	Bowl			
2217	Pot			
2218	No information			
2219	Vase			
2220	No information			
2221	Lamp			
2222	Wall Vase			
2223	Sweet Dish	Lace Range. With flowers. Ass. Cols	5¼"a	1950s–60s
2224	No information			
2225	Sweet Dish	With Circles. Multi-coloured	5¼"l	1950s–60s
2226	Honey	Cactus Range. Also flowers on lid		1950s–60s
2227	Bulb Pot	Rope Range white matt with green	12"l	1950s–60s
2228/9	No information			
2230	Jardiniere	Round Pattern. White	3½"h	1950s
2231–3	Pots			1950s
2234–6	No information			
2237	Vase			1950s
2238	No information			
2239/40	Bowls			1950s
2241	No information			
2242	Bowl			1950s
2243	Pot			1950s
2244	Honey Pot	Lace Range. With lid		1950s
2245	Sweet Dish	Cactus Range. With Flower. Ass. Cols	5¼"l	1950s–60s
2246	Vase			1950s
2247	Wall Vase	Cactus Range. Green/Fawn Matt glaze		1950s–60s
2248	Flower Pot	Cactus Range. Green/Fawn Matt glaze		1950s–60s
2249	Bulb Bowl	Cactus Range. Green/Fawn Matt glaze		1950s–60s
2250	Pot			1950s
2251	Jardiniere	Cactus Range. Green/Fawn Matt glaze		1950s–60s
2252	Vase	Cactus Range. Green/Fawn Matt glaze		1950s–60s
2253	Pot			1950s
2254	Vase	Cactus Range. Green/Fawn Matt glaze		1950s–60s
2255	Vase	Lace Range		1950s
2256	Bowl			1950s
2257	No information			
2258	Vase			1950s
2259	Bowl	Shell Range	12"l	1950s–1970
2260	Vase	Floral Range Ass. Cols		1950s–60s
2261	Tray			1950s
2262	Wall Vase	Cactus Range Green/Fawn Matt glaze		1950s–60s
2263	No information			
2264	Jardiniere	Rope Range. White Matt with green	14"l	1950s–60s
2265	Vase	Rope Range. White Matt with green	5"h	1950s–60s

2266	Vase	Rope Range. White Matt with green	8"h	1950s–60s
2267	Vase	Floral Range. Ass. Cols		1950s–60s
2268	No information			
2269	Wall Pocket	Lace Range		1950s–60s
2270	Flower Pot	Lace Range	Small	1950s–60s
2271	Honey Pot	Lace Range		1950s–60s
2272	Vase			1950s
2273/4	No information			
2275	Posie	Log with Pixie or gnome. Matt/Shiny Glaze	5"l	1950s–1970s
2276	Posie	Basket with Pixie or gnome. Matt/Shiny Glaze	5"l	1950s–1970s
2277	Posie	Watering Can with Pixie or gnome. Matt/Shiny Glaze	3"h	1950s–1970s
2278	Posie	Flower Pot with Pixie or gnome. Matt/Shiny Glaze	3"h	1950s–60s
2279	Bowl			1950s
2280	Jardiniere	Rope Range	12"l	1950s–1970s
2281/2	Vases	Modern Slim design. Ass. Cols	7"h	1950s–60s
2283	No information			
2284	Posie	Trough. Lace Range		1950s–60s
2285	Tray			1950s
2286	No information			
2287	Vase			1950s
2288	Vase	Modern Style	7"h	1950s–60s
2289	Bulb Bowl	Square. With Pixie. Green/Fawn Matt	5½"l	1950s–60s
2290	No information			
2291	Pot			1950s
2292	No information			
2293	Wall Vase	Cactus Range. Green/Fawn Matt		1950s–60s
2294	No information			
2295	Bulb Bowl	Acorn. With Pixie. Green/Fawn Matt	7"dia	1950s–1982
2296	Jardiniere	Cactus Range Green/Fawn Matt		1950s–1960s
2297	Cheeseboard			1950s
2297	Posie	Lace Range. Round with flower holder		1950s–60s
2298	Cruet	Lace Range. Three pieces		1950s–60s
2299	Dish	Lace Range. Ass. Cols	Large	1950s–60s
2300	Jardiniere	Lace Range. Ass. Cols		1950s–60s
2301	Plant Pot	Lace Range. Ass. Cols		1950s–60s
2302–4	Vases			1950s
2305	Vase	Cactus Range. Green/Fawn Matt	Narrow	1950s–60s
2306	Wall Vase			1950s
2307	Bowl			1950s
2308	Bulb Bowl	Cactus Range. Green/Fawn Matt		1950s–60s
2309	Posie Holder	Brown & White		1950s
2310	Wall Vase			1950s
2311	Tray			1950s
2312	Vase	Floral Line. Ass. Pastel shades	Cone Shape	1950s–60s
2313	Holder			1950s
2314	Vase	In shape of tree	4¾"h	1950s
2315	Sweet dish	Floral line. Ass. Pastel shades	Small	1950s–60s
2316–8	Bowls	Floral line. Ass. Pastel shades		1950s–60s
2319	No information			
2320	Bulb Bowl	Rope Range. White Matt with green	7"dia	1950s–1970
2321	Vase	Hyacinth leaf Range. Grn,Fwn,Wht,Ylw	7"h	1950s–1982
2322	Wall Vase			1950s
2323	Candleholder	Lace Range. Ass. Cols.		1950s–60s
2324	No information			
2325	Sweet dish	Satin glaze	Small	1950s–60s
2326	Sweet dish	Satin glaze. As 2325 but larger		1950s–60s
2327	Cheese dish	Lace Range. Ass. Cols.		1950s–60s
2328	Vase			1950s
2329	Vase	Satin Glaze	5"h	1950s–1970
2330	Vase			1950s
2331	Dog	Sitting. Matt or Brundor (Shaded gloss)		1950s–60s
2332	Hose?	Perhaps mis-spelt Horse		
2333	Bowl	Nuleef Range. Matt colours		1950s–60s
2334	Vase	Nuleef Range. Matt colours	5½"h	1950s–60s
2335	Honey pot	Nuleef Range. Matt colours		1950s–60s
2336	Sweet dish	Nuleef Range. Matt colours	Small	1950s–60s

2337	Vase	Satin Glaze range		1950s–60s
2338	Vase			1950s
2339	Bulb Bowl	Round with Mushrooms, grass & pixie	9"dia	1950s–60s
2340	Jardiniere			1950s
2341	Jug	Nuleef Range. Matt cols	Large	1950s–60s
2342	Mug	Nuleef Range. Matt cols		1950s–60s
2343	Tankard	With Horses head. Dark brown glossy		1950s–1982
2344	Tankard			1950s
2345	No information			
2346	Bulb bowl	As 2339	7½"dia	1950s–60s
2347	No information			
2348	Toastrack	Nuleef Range. Matt colours		1950s–60s
2349	Cruet set on stand	Four pieces. Nuleef Range. Matt colours	9½"l 2¾"h	1950s–60s
2350	No information			
2351	Jugs	Nuleef Range. Matt colours. 3 sizes. Nos.1–3		1950s–60s
2352	Vase	Satin Glaze Range & Sablon Range	6"h	1950s–60s
2353	Lettuce dish	Two pieces. Nuleef Range. Matt cols		1950s–60s
2354	Twin Tray	With handle. Nuleef Range. Matt cols		1950s–60s
2355	Dish	Nuleef Range. Matt cols	8¼"l	1950s–60s
2356	Butter dish	Nuleef Range. Matt cols		1950s–60s
2357	Cheese dish	Nuleef Range. Matt cols		1950s–60s
2358	Triple tray	With handle Nuleef Range Matt cols		1950s–60s
2359	No information			
2360	Plant Pot	Nuleef Range. Matt colours		1950s60s
2361	Bulb Bowl	Nuleef Range. Matt colours		1950s–60s
2362	Sugar bowl	Nuleef Range. Matt colours		1950s–60s
2363	Cream Jug	Nuleef Range. Matt colours	Small	1950s–60s
2364	Posie trough	Nuleef Range. Matt colours		1950s–60s
2365	Bowl			1950s
2366	Wall Vase	Nuleef Range. Matt colours		1950s–60s
2367	Fruit Bowl	Nuleef Range. Matt colours		1950s–60s
2368	No information			
2369	Butter dish	Green		1950s
2370	Tray			1950s
2371	Bowl		Small	1950s
2372	No information			
2373	Vase			1950s
2374	No information			
2375	Tankard	With Hound. Dark Brown. Glossy	4½"h	1950s–1982
2376	Tankard	With Fox. Dark Brown. Glossy	4½"h	1950s–1982
2377	No information			
2378	Flower Pot	Sablon Range. White on black	4¾"h	1950s–60s
2379	Jardiniere	Sablon Range. White on black	8"l	1950s–60s
2380	Bowl			1950s
2381	Bowl	Fir Cone		1950s
2382	No information			
2383/4	Vases			1950s
2385	Posie Trough	Plume Range. Matt Pastel Cols		1950s–60s
2386	Wall Vase	Plume Range. Matt Pastel Cols		1950s–60s
2387	Bowl			1950s
2388	Flower Pot	Plume Range. Matt Pastel Cols		1950s–60s
2389	No information			
2390/1	Vases			1950s
2392	Pot			1950s
2393	Bowl			1950s
2394	Tankard	Plain		1950s
2395	Tankard			1950s
2396	Mother Duck	White with yellow hat and feet		1950s–60s
2397	Baby Duck	White with blue & white woolly hat		1950s–60s
2398	Baby Duck	White with wings out		1950s–60s
2399	Bowl			1950s
2400	Dish	Plume Range. Matt Pastel cols	Shallow	1950s–60s
2401	Bulb bowl	Plume Range. Matt Pastel cols		1950s–60s
2402	Plant Pot	Plume Range. Matt Pastel cols		1950s–60s
2403	Cheese Dish	Plume Range. Matt Pastel cols		1950s–60s
2404	Jardiniere			1950s
2405	Bowl			1950s
2406	Jardiniere	Plume Range. Matt Pastel cols. With handles		1950s–60s
2407	Jardiniere	Plume Range. Matt Pastel cols. With handles		1950s–60s

2408	Jardiniere	Plume Range. Matt Pastel cols. With handles		1950s–60s
2409	Cruet Set	Plume Range. Matt Pastel cols. Four pieces		1950s–60s
2410	Honey pot	Plume Range. Matt Pastel cols. With lid		1950s–60s
2411	Butter dish	Plume Range. Matt Pastel cols. With lid		1950s–60s
2412/3	No information			
2414–17	Bowls			1950s
2418	Vase			1950s
2419	Vase	Nuleef Range. Matt Ass. Cols	Cone shape	1950s–60s
2420	No information			
2421	Dog	Sitting. Barrel round neck. Matt & Gloss	4¾"h	1950s–1970
2422	Dog			1950s & 60s
2423	No information			
2424	Ashtray	Terriers head and tail. Matt cols.		1950s–60s
2425	Chimney	With cat, stork or owl. Matt cols	4"h	1950s–60s
2425	?Plaque	Dogs head		
2426	No information			
2427	Rabbit			1950s–60s
2428	Giraffe			1950s–60s
2429	Elephant			1950s–60s
2430	Vase	Palm tree with Hippo, Giraffe or elephant	4"h	1950s–60s
2431	Ashtray	Spaniels head & tail. Matt colours		1950s–60s
2432	Tankard	Horse		1950s–60s
2433/4	Tankards			1950s–60s
2435	Tankard Horse			1950s–60s
2436	Tankard			1950s–60s
2437	Tankard	Fox		1950s–60s
2438	Ashtray	Pekinese Head & tail. Matt colours	5¾"l	1950s–60s
2439	Vase	Nautilus Range. White matt with green	6"h	1950s–60s
2440	Jardiniere	Nautilus Range. White matt with green	6½"h	1950s–60s
2441	Vase	Nautilus Range. White matt with green	10"h	1950s–60s
2442	Vase			1950s–60s
2443	Owl	For chimney?		1950s–60s
2444	Stork	For chimney?		1950s–60s
2445	Vase			1950s–60s
2446/7	Vases	Satin glaze range	6"h	1950s–60s
2448	Vase			1950s–60s
2449	Vase	Nautilus Range. White matt with green	8¼"h	1950s–60s
2450	Pots			1950s–60s
2451	Dog	Sitting. With toothache. Fawn Matt	11"h	1950s–1970
2452	Vase	Hyacinth leaf Range. Ass. Cols & Glazes	9¼"h	1950s–1982
2453	Vase	Hyacinth lead Range. Ass. Cols & Glazes	11¼"h	1950s–1982
2454	Bowl			1950s
2455	Dog	Sitting. With toothache. Matt cols	8¼"h	1950s–1970
2456	Jardiniere	Hyacinth leaf Range. Ass.Cols & Glazes	10"h	1950s–1982
2457	Vase	Squirrel Range. Fawn & Grn with satin background	5¾"h	1950s–1960s
2458	Bowl			1950s
2459	Vase	Twin Squirrel Range. Fawn & Grn with satin background	5¾"h	1950s–1960s
2460	Vase			1950s
2461	Flower Pot	Assorted Matt Cols	4¾"h	1950s–1970
2462	No Information			
2463	Urn Vase	White matt with green	8¼"h	1950s–60s
2464	Vase			1950s
2465	Bowl	Moselle Range (with cupid) White Matt	9"h	1950s–1970
2466	Water Wheel			1950s
2467	Jardiniere	Various ranges. Curvy edge	7"l	1950s–60s
2468	Trough	Squirrel Range as 2457	5¾"l	1950s–60s
2469–71	No information			
2472	Vase			1950s
2473	Dog			1950s
2474	Bowl on stand	Moselle Range	10½"l	1950s–1970
2475	No information			
2476	Vase	With embossed lilac flowers	5"h	1950s
2477	Dog			1950s
2478	Trough	Hyacinth leaf Range. Ass. cols & Glazes	14¼"l	1950–1970
2479	No information			
2480	Wall Vase			1950s
2481	Bowl			1950s

2482	Bowl	Hyacinth leaf Range. Ass. cols & Glazes	6¾"l	1950s–1982
2483	Flower Pot	Hyacinth leaf Range. Ass. cols & Glazes	5"h	1950s–1982
2484	Jardiniere	Hyacinth leaf Range. Ass. cols & Glazes	13"l	1950s–1982
2485	Bowl	Hyacinth leaf Range. Ass. cols & Glazes	10½"l	1950s–1982
2486	Trough	Hyacinth leaf Range. Ass. cols & Glazes	8"l	1950s–1982
2487	Wall Vase	Hyacinth leaf Range. Ass. cols & Glazes	9"h	1950s–1982
2488	Jardiniere	Hyacinth leaf Range. Ass. cols & Glazes	8¼"l	1950s–1982
2489	Flower Pot	Hyacinth leaf Range. Ass. cols & Glazes	6"h	1950s–1982
2490	No information			
2491	Bowl			1950s
2492	No information			
2493	Dog	St. Bernard. Standing. Hand Painted	4½"h	1950s–1982
2494	Vase Urn	White with green	6¼"h	1950s–1960s
2495	Vase Urn	White with green	10¼"h	1950s–1960s
2496	No information			
2497	Dog	Springer Spaniel. Standing. Hand Painted	4¼"h	1950s–60s
2498–500	No information			
2501	Tray			1950s
2502	Dog	Collie. Standing. Hand painted	5½"h	1950s–1975
2503	Dog	Fox Terrier. Standing. Hand Painted	4"h	1950s–1970
2504	Dog	Boston Terrier. Standing. Hand Painted	4½"h	1950s–1970
2506	Vase			1950s
2507	Bowl	Squirrel Range. See 2459	5¾"l	1950s–60s
2508	No information			
2509	Bowl			1950s
2510	No information			
2511	Tray			1950s
2512	Bowl	Squirrel Range. See 2459	7½"dia	1950s–60s
2513	Bowl			1950s
2514	Vase Urn	White with green	7¼"h	1950s–1960s
2515	Vase			1950s
2516	Ashtray	Hound. Dark Brown. Glossy finish	6½"dia	1950s–1982
2517	Ashtray	Fox. Dark Brown. Glossy finish	6½"dia	1950s–1982
2518	Ashtray	Horse. Dark Brown. Glossy finish	6½"dia	1950s–1982
2519/20	Leaf	No information		1950s
2521	Bookends	Horse looking through stable door	4¼"h	1950s–1975
2522	Bookends	Wave with fish	3¾"h	1950s–60s
2523	Squirrel			1950s
2524	Dog	Bloodhound Sitting		1950s–60s
2527	Pot			1950s
2528	Dog	Setter. Standing. Hand Painted	4¾"h	1950s–1960s
2529	Squirrel			1950s
2530	No information			
2531	Trough			1950s
2532	No information			
2533	Ashtray	Round. Ass. colours		1950s–60s
2534/5	No information			
2536	Dog			1950s
2537	Dog	Greyhound. Sitting. Hand Painted	7½"l	1950s–S-I-P
2538	Dog	Airdale. Standing. Hand Painted	5"h	1950s–1975
2539	No information			
2540	Dog			1950s
2541/2	Bowl			1950s
2543/4	Vase			1950s
2544	Vase			1950s
2545	Dog	Smooth haired terrier. Standing. Hand Painted	4¼"h	1950s–1965
2546	Flower Pot	Laronde Range. Ass. Colours	5½"h	1950s–1960s
2547	No information			
2548	Vase	Cupid Plain 1950s		
2549	Cat	Sitting. Matt colours	5"h	1950–60s
2550	Pot			1950s
2551	Fern Pot	Matt colours	5½"h	1950s–1970
2552	Bookends			1950s
2553	Vase			1950s
2554	Jug			1950s
2555	Honey Pot			1950s
2556	Sugar Bowl			1950s
2557	Cream Jug			1950s

2558	Fern Pot			1950s
2559	Fern Pot	As number 2551	4″	1950–1970
2560	Shoe			1950s
2561	No information			
2562	Comport	Moselle Range. (With cupid) White Matt	7¾″h	1950s–1970
2563	Tray			1950s
2564	Vase	Moselle Range	8½″h	1950s–1970
2565	No information			
2566	Comport	Moselle Range	12″dia	1950s–1960s
2567	Flower Pot	Laronde Range. Ass. Cols	4¼″h	1950s–1960s
2568	Flower Pot	Laronde Range. Ass. Cols	4¾″h	1950s–1960s
2569	Bowl			1950s
2570	Beaker			1950s
2571	Teapot			1950s
2572	Seal			1950s
2573	Holder			1950s
2574	Bulldog			1950s
2575	Cheese dish			1950s
2576	No information			
2577	Jug	For Hot Water		1950s
2578	Bowl			1950s
2579	Cat			1950s
2580	Dog			1950s
2581–3	Jugs			1950s
2584	Dog	Sitting. Howling. Fawn Matt		1950s–60s
2585	Butter Dish	Plain		1960s
2586–88	Storage Jars			1960s
2589	Sugar Sifter			1960s
2590	Jug			1960s
2591	Cress Dish			1960s
2592	Mixing Bowl			1960s
2593	Wall Vase	Squirrel Range. As 2457	8″h	1960s
2594	No information			
2595	Dog	Dachshund. Caricature. Fawn		1960s
2596/7	No information			
2598	Bowl	Squirrel Range. As 2457	14″l	1960s
2599	Flower Holder			1960s
2600	Bowl	Squirrel Range. As 2457	19″dia	1960s
2601	Gondola Bowl			1960s
2602	No information			
2603	Tankard			1960s
2604/5	Teapots			1960s
2606	Bowl			1960s
2607	Wall Vase	Laronde Range. Ass. Cols	6½″h	1960s
2608	Trough	Laronde Range. Ass. Cols	7¾″l	1960s
2609	Vase	Laronde Range. Ass. Cols	7″h	1960s
2610	Bowl	Laronde Range. Ass. Cols	6½″l	1960s
2611	Basket	Laronde Range. Ass. Cols with handle	7¾″l	1960s
2612	Cruet	Laronde Range. Ass. Cols three pieces		1960s
2613	Bowl	Laronde Range. Ass Cols	14″l	1960s
2614	Jardiniere	Laronde Range. Ass. Cols	10½″l	1960s
2615	No information			
2616	Vase	Laronde Range. Ass. Cols	10″h	1960s
2617	Vase	Laronde Range. Ass. Cols	8″h	1960s
2618	Vase	Laronde Range. Ass. Cols	6″h	1960s
2619–21	No information			
2622	Mixing Bowl			1960s
2623	Dog	Spaniel		1960s
2624	No information			
2625	Bowl	Moselle Range. With Cupids	14″l	1960s
2626	Vase	Moselle Range. With Cupid	8¾″h	1960s–1982
2627	Holder			1960s
2628	No information			
2629/30	Bowls			1960s
2631	Jardiniere			1960s
2632	Vase			1960s
2633	Caster sugar shaker			1960s
2634/35	No information			

2636	Bowl	Laronde Range. Ass. Cols	11"dia	1960s
2637	No information			
2638	Bowl	Laronde Range. Ass. Cols	9¾"l	1960s
2639	Trough	Round. Brown & White		1960s
2640/1	No information			
2642	Tankard	Horse		1960s
2643	Jardiniere			1960s
2644	No information			
2645	Vase	Ivy Range. Deep Green	Large	1960s
2646	Vase	Ivy Range. Deep Green	Medium	1960s
2647	Trough	Ivy Range. Deep Green	Long	1960s
2648	Round Trough	Ivy Range. Deep Green	Small	1960s
2649	Jardiniere	Ivy Range. Deep Green	Medium	1960s
2650–54	No information			
2655	Vase	With lamb or other. Various cols	Appx 5"	1960s
2656	Vase	With lamb or other. Various cols	5"	1960s
2657	No information			
2658	Vase	With lamb or other. Various cols	Appx 5"	1960s
2659	Vase			1960s
2660	Vase	With dog or other. Various cols	Appx 5"	1960s
2661	Curved Trough	Ivy Range. Deep Green	Small	1960s
2662	No information			
2663	Plate			1960s
2664–6	No information			
2667	Bambi			1960s
2668	Lamb			1960s
2669–71	Novelty Dogs			1960s
2672	Dog			1960s
2673	Bowl			1960s
2674	No information			
2675	Dog	Old English Sheepdog. Standing. HP	5"h	1960s
2676	Vase			1960s
2677	No information			
2678	Jardiniere	On feet Curved edges. Blk/wht matt	10½"l	1960s
2679	Dog	Scottie. Standing. HP	3¾"l	1960s–1970
2680	Vase	Handle only		
2681	Anvil			1960s
2682	No information			
2683	Vase	Moselle range. With cupid	5½"l	1960s–1982
2684	Jardiniere/tray	On stand with handles. Shallow	7½"l	1960s
2685	Chest			1960s
2686	Ashtray			1960s
2687	Skis Rabbit			1960s
2688	Rabbit			1960s
2689	Skis Rabbit			1960s
2690/1	Bowls			1960s
2692	Vase			1960s
2693	Dog			1960s
2694	Vase Urn	White Matt or decorated	5"h	1960s–70s
2695	Vase Urn	White Matt or decorated	6"h	1960s
2696	Bowl	With stand and handles. White Matt or decorated	7½"l	1960s
2697/8	No information			
2699	Holder	Swan. Matt or glossy	7¼"l	1960s–1982
2700	No information			
2701	Bowl			1960s
2702	No information			
2703	Lemon Squeezer			1960s
2704	Fern Pot			1960s
2705	Jardiniere		5½"h	1960s
2706–8	No information			
2709	Vase			1960s
2710	Jardiniere	With two handles. Green	10"l	1960s
2711–13	No information			
2714	Fern Pot			1960
2715–19	No information			
2720	Wall Vase	Lantern. White	9¾"h	1960s
2721	Egg Separater			1960s
2722	Cat	Sitting. Brown & White as 2794 & 2795	Med	1960s

2723	Holder			1960s
2724	Vase			1960s
2725	Tray			1960s
2726	Cress dish and stand			1960s
2727	Holder	Swan. Matt or Glossy as 2699	9¼"l	1960s–1982
2728	No information			
2729	Bowl	Moselle Range. With Cupid	5½"l	1960s–1982
2730	Dog			1960s
2731	Dog			1960s
2732	No information			
2733	Veg			
2734	Dish			1960s
2735	Bowl			1960s
2736	Boy			1960s
2737	No information			
2738	Monkey Jug			1960s
2739	Jardiniere	With handles	20"l	1960s–1970
2740	Bowl	Bamboo Range		1960s
2741	Wall Vase	Bamboo Range		1960s
2742	Flower Pot	Bamboo Range		1960s
2743	Vase	Bamboo Range		1960s
2744	Planter			1960s
2745	Posy	Bamboo Range		1960s
2746	Jardiniere			1960s
2747	Flower Pot	Bamboo Range		1960s
2748	Twin Vase	Small		1960s
2749	Trough straight	Bamboo Range	6¼"l	1960s–70s
2750	Trough curved	Bamboo Range	8½"l	1960s–70s
2751	Vase		9¼"	1960s
2752	Vase	Bamboo Range	7½"	1960s
2753	Vase		10"	1960s
2754	Vase		6½"	1960s
2755	No information			
2756	Cat			1960s
2757	Seal			1960s
2758–62	Dogs			1960s
2763	Egg Cup			1960s
2764	Dog			1960s
2765	No information			
2766	Round trough	Bamboo Range	6¼"dia	1960s–70s
2767	'L'shape trough	Bamboo Range	6"l	1960s
2768	Bowl on pedestal	Corinthus Range	8"dia	1960s
2769	Pot			1960s
2770	Vase			1960s
2771	Wall Vase			1960s
2772	Vase			1960s
2773	No information			
2774	Jardiniere	Fan shape	10½"l	1960s
2775	Wall Vase			1960s
2776/7	Vases			1960s
2778	No information			
2779	Vase			1960s
2780	Jardiniere	Fan shape as 2774	7"l	1960s
2781	Vase			1960s
2782	Swan			1960s
2783	Bowl	Moselle Range. With cupid	5½"l	1960s–1982
2784	Bulb Bowl	Basket weave design	6"l	1960s–1970s
2785	Fern Pot	Various decorations	5½"h	1960s–S-i-P
2786	Vase			1960s
2787	Bowl			1960s
2788	Basket			1960s
2789	Crib			1960s
2790	Fern Pot	Various decorations	4¾"h	1960s–S-i-P
2791	Vase			1960s
2792	Jardiniere		Long	1960s
2793	Posy			1960s
2794	Cat	Brown & White sitting as No. 2722	Small	1960s
2795	Cat	Brown & White sitting as No. 2722	Large	1960s
2796	Fern Pot	Various decorations	4¼"h	1960s

2797	Dog			1960s
2798	Holder	Owl on treetrunk	about 2¾"h	1960s
2799	Holder	Gnome on piece of bamboo	about 3"h	1960s
2800	Holder	Fox on pine-cone	about 3"h	1960s
2801/2	No information			
2803	Vase			1960s
2804	Bowl	Various decorations	7½"h	1960s
2805	Bowl			1960s
2806	No information			
2807	Holder	Two monkeys with Coconut	about 3"h	1960s
2808	Pot			1960s
2809	Jug			1960s
2810	Bird stand			
2811	Jardiniere			1960s
2812	Bowl on pedestal	Corinthus Range	14½"l	1960s
2813	Monkey Jug			1960s
2814	Vase on pedestal	Corinthus Range	7"h	1960s
2815	Character Jug	Of Robert Burns		1960s
2815	Character Jug	Of William Shakespeare Re-numbered 4491 in 1969 and still in production.		
2816	Jardiniere			1960s
2817/8	No information			
2819	Vase on pedestal	Corinthus Range	10"h	1960s
2820	Vase			1960s
2821	No information			
2822	Figure			
2823	Bowl (Could have been figure previously)			1960s
2824	Figure			1960s
2825	Pot			1960s
2826	Bookend			1960s
2827	Vase on pedestal	Corinthus Range	8"h	1960s
2828	Bowl on pedestal	Corinthus Range	9¾"dia	1960s
2829	Holder	With girl, boy, other or nothing	about 5"h	1960s
2830	Flower Pot	Cone range		1960s
2831	Vase	Cone range		1960s
2832/3	Trough	Cone range		1960s
2834	Jardiniere	Cone range		1960s
2835	Bowl	Cone range		1960s
2836	Jardiniere	Cone range		1960s
2837	No information			
2838	Wall Vase			1960s
2839	No information			
2840	Vase			1960s
2841	Vase	Brown book with head of Shakespeare	about 6"h	1960s
2842	Figure			1960s
2843	No information			
2844	Vase			1960s
2845	Girl			1960s
2846	Vase	Lumpy design. Yellow	about 8"h	1960s
2847	Vase			1960s
2848	No information			
2849	Pot			1960s
2850/51	No information			
2852	Jardiniere			1960s
2853	No information			
2854	Bowl			1960s
2855–59	No information			
2860	Vase	Satin Glaze Range	8¼"h	1960s
2861	Vase			1960s
2862	Gondola Bowl			1960s
2863	Clog	Dutch decorations. Matt or gloss	4½"l	1960s
2864	Goblet Vase	Later used for Autumn Chinz	7"h	1960s–70s
2865	Goblet			1960s
2866	Bookend			1960s
2867–9	Shell			1960s
2870	Vase	Apple blossom Range Hand Painted on mottled background with satin finish	8¼"h	1960s–70s
2871	No information			
2872	Jardiniere	Apple Blossom Range see 2870	10½"l	1960s–70s

2873	Bowl			1960s
2874	Jardiniere	Apple Blossom Range see 2870	7"l	1960s–70s
2875	Trough	Apple Blossom Range see 2870	7¾"l	1960s–70s
2876	Vase	Apple Blossom Range see 2870	6¼"h	1960s–70s
2877	Flower Pot	Apple Blossom Range see 2870	5¾"h	1960s–70s
2878	Flower Pot	Apple Blossom Range see 2870	4¾"h	1960s–70s
2879	Pot			1960s
2880	Tray			1960s
2881	Goblet			1960s
2882	Bowl	Apple Blossom Range see 2870	7"l	1960s–70s
2883	Bowl	Apple Blossom Range see 2870	10¼"l	1960s–70s
2884	Bowl	Apple Blossom Range see 2870	14"l	1960s–70s
2885	Plate	Apple Blossom Range see 2870	9¼"dia	1960s
2886	Posy Bar			1960s
2887	Figure			1960s
2888	Character Jug	Of Uncle Sam Hand Painted		1960s
2889	Trough			1960s
2890	Bowl two handles			1960s
2891	Bowl plain			1960s
2892	Character Jug	Of Abraham Lincoln		1960s
2893	No information			
2894	Jardiniere			1960s
2895	Figure			1960s
2896	Vase	Satin Glaze Range	6"h	1960s–70s
2897	Stocking			1960s
2898	No information			
2899	Character Jug	Of John F. Kennedy		1960s
2900	Vase			1960s
2901	Chinese Vase			1960s
2902	Vase			1960s
2903	Figure			1960s
2904–9	No information			
2910	Pot			1960s
2911	No information			
2912	Giraffe	Sitting. Various Colours	5½"h	1960s
2913	Tray			1960s
2914/5	Vase			1960s
2916	Biscuit Jar			1960s
2917	Wall Vase			1960s
2918	No information			
2919	Bowl			1960s
2920	Vase			1960s
2921–29	No information			
2930	Colour code, denoting hand painted natural colours			
2931	Vase			1960s
2932	No information			
2933	Giraffe	Standing. Ass. Cols	6"h	1960s
2934–36	Vases			1960s
2937	Vase	Apple Blossom Range see No. 2870	10"h	1960s–1970s
2938	Dog	With long face. Various cols	4"h	1960s–1982
2939	Barrow			1960s
2940	Serviette Ring			1960s
2941	Jug two pint		6½"h	1960s
2942	Vase			1960s
2943	No information			
2944	Jug			1960s
2945	Beaker	Various decorations including Lime-grove	4¼"	1960s–1982
2946	Zebra			1960s
2947	Beaker			1960s
2948	Bowl			1960s
2949	Vase			1960s
2950	Dog	Long face, various colours	5¼"h	1960s–1982
2951	Dog	Long face, various colours	7¼"h	1960s–1982
2952	No information			
2953	Bowl			1960s
2954	Jardiniere	Magnolia Range. White Matt with Pink shading on Hand Painted base	9"l	1960s–1970
2955	Rabbit	Crouching with large eyes	Large	1960s
2956	Honey pot	Wyka Range. Various colours	4½"h	1960s

2957	Cheese dish			1960s
2958	Honey pot			1960s
2959	Butter dish			1960s
2960	Tray			1960s
2961	Salad Bowl			1960s
2962	Dog	Poodle. Sitting. White lustre	5¼"h	1960s–1982
2963/4	Shell			1960s
2965	Pot			1960s
2966/7	Teapot			1960s
2968	Sugar Bowl			1960s
2969	No information			
2970	Posy Bar			1960s
2971	Dog	Poodle. Playing. White lustre	6½"l	1960s–1970s
2972	Vase			1960s
2973	Dog	Dachshund. Curled up. Hand Painted	5"l	1960s
2974	Dog	Mongrel Puppy. Sitting. Hand Painted	5½"h	1960s–S-i-P
2975	Vase			1960s
2976	Teapot	Various Decorations including Lime-Grove	5¾"	1960s–1982
2977	Sugar Bowl	Various Decorations including Lime-Grove	3¼"h	1960s–1982
2978	Cream Jug	Various Decorations including Lime-Grove	3"h	1960s–1982
2979	No information			
2980	Rabbit	Standing. With bowtie. Various cols	6"h	1960s
2981	Vase	Magnolia Range. See No. 2954	9"h	1960s–1970s
2982	Teapot	Lime-grove Range	5"h	1960s–1975
2983	Vase	Plain	9"	1960s
2984	Basket			1960s
2985	Bowl			1960s
2986	Cress dish/Stand	Various decorations	9½"dia	1960s
2987	Basket			1960s
2988	Tray			1960s
2989	Bowl			1960s
2990	Cress dish/Stand			1960s
2991	No information			
2992	Vase	Magnolia Range. See No. 2954	6¼"h	1960s–1970s
2993	Jardiniere	Magnolia Range. See No. 2954	6¾"l	1960s–1970s
2994	No information			
2995	Flower Pot	Magnolia Range. See No. 2954	5"h	1960s–1970s
2996	Cream Jug	Wyka Range. Assorted Colours	2¾"h	1960s
2997	Vase	Wyka Range. Assorted Colours	10½"h	1960s
2998	Butter dish	Wyka Range. Assorted Colours	7"l	1960s
2999	Cheese dish			1960s
3000	Salad Bowl (Cress dish)	Wyka Range Ass. Cols	11"dia	1960s
3001	Cruet set	Wyka Range. Three pieces. Ass. Cols		1960s
3002	Sandwich Tray	Wyka Range. Assorted Colours	11½"l	1960s
3003	Twin Tray	Wyka Range. Assorted Colours	11½"l	1960s
3004	Triple Tray	Wyka Range. Assorted Colours	15"l	1960s
3005	Toast Rack	Wyka Range. Assorted Colours	9½"l	1960s
3006	Vase	Wyka Range. Assorted Colours	12½"h	1960s
3007	Cress dish/stand	Wyka Range. Assorted Colours	8¼"dia	1960s
3008	No information			
3009	Jug	Wyka Range. Assorted Colours	8"h	1960s
3010	Cheese dish	Wyka Range. Assorted Colours	7"l	1960s
3011	Vase	Wyka Range. Assorted Colours	8¼"h	1960s
3012	Beaker	Wyka Range. Assorted Colours	4½"h	1960s
3013	Sugar Bowl	Wyka Range. Assorted Colours	3¼"dia	1960s
3014–6	No information			
3017	Posy			1960s
3018	Trough	Fern decoration		1960s
3019	Pig	Money-box. Black Matt	4½"h	1960s–1982
3020	Pot			1960s
3021	No information			
3022	Flower Pot	Magnolia Range. See no. 2954	5¾"h	1960s–1970s
3023/4	No information			
3025	Vase	Slymcraft Range. Plain	6¼"h	1960s–1982
3026–28	Vases			1960s
3029	Vase	Slymcraft Range. Plain	11¾"h	1960s
3030	Vase	Slymcraft Range. Plain	7½"h	1960s–S-i-P
3031	Vase	Chesterfield Range. Ribbed	6"h	1960s

3032	Vase	Slymcraft Range. Plain	8¾"h	1960s
3033–35	Vases			1960s
3036	Vase	Slymcraft Range. Plain	7¾"h	1960s–1982
3037	Vase	Slymcraft Range. Plain	9¾"h	1960s–1982
3038	Vase	Slymcraft Range. Plain	9¾"h	1960s
3039	Vase	Slymcraft Range. Plain	9¾"h	1960s–S-i-P
3040	Vase	Slymcraft, and other decorations	3¼"h	1960s–1982
3041	Vase			1960s
3042	Vase	Slymcraft Range. Plain	7¾"h	1960s
3043	Vase	Slymcraft Range. Plain	5¾"h	1960s–S-i-P
3044	Vase	Slymcraft Range. Plain	7¾"h	1960s–1982
3045	Vase			1960s
3046	Vase	Slymcraft Range. Plain	7¾"h	1960s
3047	Vase	Slymcraft Range. Plain	9¾"h	1960s–1982
3048	Vase	Slymcraft Range. Plain	7¾"h	1960s–1982
3049	Vase	Slymcraft Range. Plain	12"	1960s
3050	Vase	Round Slymcraft Range. Plain	2¾"h	1960s
3051	Vase	Slymcraft Range. Plain	7½"h	1960s–1982
3052	Vase	Slymcraft Range. Plain	6½"h	1960s
3053	Vase	Chesterfield Range. Ribbed	10¼"h	1960s
3054	Vase	Chesterfield Range. Ribbed	8¼"h	1960s
3055	Vase	Slymcraft Range. Plain	9¾"h	1960s
3056	Vase	Slymcraft Range. Plain	9¾"h	1960s
3057	Flower Pot	Chesterfield Range. Ribbed	5"h	1960s
3058	Flower Pot	Chesterfield Range. Ribbed	6"h	1960s
3059	Vase	Slymcraft Range. Plain	7¾"h	1960s
3060	Vase			1960s
3061	Vase	Slymcraft Range. Plain	9¾"h	1960s
3062	Vase	Slymcraft Range. Plain	7½"h	1960s
3063	Vase	Slymcraft Range. Plain	5½"h	1960s–1982
3064	Vase	Slymcraft & other decorations	10"h	1960s–S-i-P
3065	Vase	Slymcraft Range. Plain	3½"h	1960s–1982
3066	Vase	Slymcraft Range. Plain	5¾"h	1960s–1982
3067	Vase	Slymcraft Range. Plain	10"h	1960s–1982
3068	Bowl	Slycraft Range. Plain	5½"dia	1960s
3069	Jardiniere	Chesterfield Range. Ribbed	9¼"l	1960s
3070	Vase			1960s
3071	Bowl	Slymcraft Range. Plain	7¾"a	1960s
3072	Jardiniere	Chesterfield Range. Ribbed	6¼"l	1960s
3073	Vase			1960s
3074	Dog			1960s
3075	Cat			1960s
3976	Flower Holder			1960s
3077	Dog	Dachshund. Sitting. Hand Painted	6½"h	1960s–1970s
3078	Dog	Dachshund. Sitting. Hand Painted	5"h	1960s–1970s
3079	No information			
3080	Basket			1960s
3081	Bowl			1960s
3082	Vase			1960s
3083	Bowl			1960s
3084	Trough			1960s
3085	Dish	Slymcraft Range. Plain	10¼"l	1960s
3086	Ashtray			1960s
3087	No information			
3088	Zebra			1960s
3089	Vase			1960s
3090/1	No information			
3092	Dog			1960s
3093	Dog	With toothache. Usually fawn	4"h	1960s
3094/5	No information			
3096	Dog	Terrier. Sitting	about 4½"h	1960s
3097	Rabbit or Chipmunk	Standing	about 5½"	1960s
3098	Vase	Lily Range. White flowers tinged with yellow on green leaves. Matt finish	6½"l	1960s
3099	Candle Holder			1960s
3100	Posy Trough	Chesterfield Range. Ribbed	7½"l	1960s
3101	Posy Holder	Lily Range. See No. 3098	10"l	1960s
3102	Cat			1960s

3103	No information			
3104	Vase			1960s
3105	Ashtray			1960s
3106	Toby Jug	No more information		1960s
3107	Vase			1960s
3108/9	No information			

THE FOLLOWING NUMBERS WERE ISSUED TO THE FALCON WARE FACTORY

3110	Dog	Poodle. Standing	4¾"h	1950s–1970s
3111	Wall Vase			1950s
3111	Girl figure	Pam. HP	3"h	1950s–60s
3112	Boy figure	Paul. HP	2¾"h	1950s–60s
3113	Boy figure	Pete HP	3¼"h	1950s–60s
3114	Dog	Mongrel Puppy, sitting. HP	3"h	1950s–60s
3115	Duck	With BIG feet Matt	1½"h	1950s–60s
3116	Dog	Mongrel Puppy, lying. HP	2¼"h	1950s–60s
3117	Duck	With BIG feet Matt	2"h	1950s–60s
3118	Dog	Mongrel Puppy, begging. HP	3½"	1950s–60s
3119	Foal	Running HP		1950s–60s
3120	Hare	Sitting up. Matt	4"h	1950s–60s
3121	Cat	With arched Back. Matt	2½"h	1950s–60s
3122	Ashtray	Round. With 3115		1950s–60s
3123	Dog	Mongrel. Sitting. Smiling HP	5¾"h	1950s
3124	Dog	Dachshund. Standing. HP	Long	1950s–1970s
3125	Dog			1950s
3126	Dog	Griffin. Lying. Matt	4"h	1950s
3127	Rabbit			1950s
3128	Dog	Corgi. Sitting. Matt & HP	4¼"h	1950s–S-i-P
3129	Horse	With saddle	5½"h	1950s
3130	Horse	Standing	5½"h	1950s
3131	Donkey			1950s
3132	Dog	With Panniers	2¼"h	1950s
3133	Dog	Corgi puppy sitting	2½"h	1950s–1975
3134	Dog	Corgi puppy on back	1½"h	1950s
3135	Dog	Corgi puppy playing	2"h	1950s
3136	Dog	Corgi standing	3¾"h	1950s–1970s
3137	Dog	Corgi puppy standing	2¾"h	1950s–1970s
3138	Donkey	With Baskets or Cart	3¾"h	1950s–1970s
3139	Donkey	Standing	4¼"h	1950s–1982
3140	Elelphant			1950s
3141	Monkey	Boxing	4¾"h	1950s
3142	Dog			1950s
3143	Dog			1950s
3144	Horse	Standing Grazing	5"h	1950s–1982
3145	Foal	Standing	4¼"h	1950s–1982
3146	Cockerel			1950s
3147	Laughing Donkey			1950s
3148	No information			
3149	Horse			1950s
3150	Foal	Standing	4"h	1950s–1982
3151	Cat	Sitting down Black/White		1950s–60s
3151	Vase			
3152	Horse or Zebra	Standing		1950s–60s
3153	Tigress	Sitting		1950s–60s
3154	Stag	Sitting		1950s–60s
3155	Horse	Standing	6½"h	1950s–1982
3156	Wall bird	Swallow Hand painted	Large 6"l	1950s–70s
3157	Wall bird	Swallow Hand painted	Medium 5"l	1950s–70s
3158	Wall bird	Swallow Hand painted	Small 5"l	1950s–70s
3159–61	No information			
3162	Grebe	To go with Bowl 702 HP	6"l	1950s–60s
3163	Cat			1950s
3164	Dog	Pekinese puppy sitting	2½"h	1950s–1975
3165	Dog	Pekinese standing	3"h	1950s–S-i-P
3166	Dog	Staffordshire Bull Terrier Standing	4½"h	1950s–S-i-P
3167	Cat	Sitting, with long neck	about 4"h	1950s–1960s
3168	Kitten in a ball of wool	Matt cols	about 3"h	1950s–60s
3169	Dog	Golden Retriever. Standing	5¼"h	1950s–S-i-P
3170	Dog	Alsation. Standing	5¾"h	1950s–1975

3171	Dog	Alsation. Standing	4"h	1950s–1960s
3172	Goat	Standing	5¼"h	1950s–1970s
3173	Dog	Chow. Standing	4¾"h	1950s–S-i-P
3174	Dog	Poodle Playing. White Lustre	5¾"h	1950s–60s
3175	Dog	Dachshund. On hind legs	5½"h	1950s–60s
3176	Horse	Standing	7¼"h	1950s–S-i-P
3177	Dog	Spaniel Puppy playing	about 5"h	1950s–60s
3178	Dog			1950s
3179	Dog	Sealyham? Puppy	about 4"h	1950s–60s
3180	Horse	Standing	9"h	1950s–1982
3181	No information			
3182	Dog	Goofy. Sitting with ears up	5¾"h	1950s–1970
3183	Dog	With toothache. Sitting	5¼"h	1950s–1970s
3184	No information			
3185	Bowl			1950s
3186	Tray			1950s

THE FOLLOWING ARE SYLVAC WARE FACTORY NUMBERS

3187	Cruet	Consisting of two longfaced dogs as pepper and salt. round bowl as mustard pot. All in a dogs basket. Four pieces		1960s
3188	Bowl	Chesterfield Range. Ribbed	7"l	1960s
3189	Posy trough	Slymcraft Range	14½"l	1960s–1982
3190	Bowl	Chesterfield Range. Ribbed	9¼"l	1960s
3191	Bowl			
3192	Vase			
3193	Bulb bowl	Oblong. Brick design	9"l	1960s–70s
3194	Bulb bowl	Oblong. Brick design	6¼"l	1960s–70s
3195	Bowl			
3196	Bowl	Magnolia Range. See No. 2954	8"dia	1960s–70s
3197	Basket			1960s
3198–02	No information			
3203	Jug	For hot water. 1¼"pint	5¾"h	1960s–70s
3204	Cream Jug	Various decorations	3¾"h	1960s–1982
3205	No information			
3206	Butter Dish	Lime-Grove Range and others	7"l	1960s–1982
3207	Cheese dish	Lime-Grove Range and others	8½"l	1960s–1982
3208	Sandwich Tray	Lime-Grove Range and others	12½"l	1960s–1982
3209	Honey pot	Lime-Grove Range and others	4"h	1960s–1982
3210	No information			
3211	Jardiniere			1960s
3212	Bowl			1960s
3213	Bowl	Magnolia Range. See No. 2954	13½"l	1960s–70s
3214	Bowl	Magnolia Range. See No. 2954	9¼"l	1960s–70s
3215	Flower Pot	Magnolia Range. See No. 2954	7½"l	1960s–70s
3216	Vase	Magnolia Range. See No. 2954	10"h	1960s–70s
3217	Vase	Magnolia Range. See No. 2954	8"h	1960s–70s
3218	Trough	Magnolia Range. See No. 2954	6½"l	1960s–70s
3219	Tankard	With horses Amber Glaze	5"h	1960s–70s
3220	Tankard	With fish Amber Glaze	5"h	1960s–70s
3221	Jardiniere	Magnolia Range. See No. 2954	12"l	1960s–1970s
3222	Bowl			1960s
3223	Log			1960s
3224	Bowl			1960s
3225	Jardiniere	Slymcraft Range	14"l	1960s–1982
3226	Tankard	With Ducks Amber Glaze	5"h	1960s–70s
3227	Bowl			1960s
3228	Vase			1960s
3229	No information			
3230	Vase		7"h	1960s
3231	Candle Holder			1960s
3232	Vase			1960s
3233	Bowl	As a log	8"l	1960s
3234	Bowl	As a log	4½"l	1960s
3235	Bowl	As a log	4¼"l	1960s
3236	Vase			1960s
3237	Tray			1960s
3238	Cup	Various decorations	3"h	1960s–1982
3238	Saucer	Various decorations	5½"dia	1960s–1982
3239	Elephant	Money Box		1960s

3240	Pig			1960s
3241	Dog			1960s
3242	No information			
3243	Bowl		8¾"l	1960s
3244	Bowl		6"l	1960s
3245	Pot			1960s
3246	Bowl			1960s
3247	Vase	Lily Range. See No. 3098	10"h	1960s
3248	No information			
3249	Bowl			1960s
3250	Vase			1960s
3251	Bowl			1960s
3252	Vase			1960s
3253	Cup			1960s
3254	Bowl			1960s
3255	Vase	Chesterfield Range. Ribbed	10"h	1960s
3256	Vase	Chesterfield Range. Ribbed	8"h	1960s
3257	Plate			1960s
3258	Cream Jug			1960s
3259/60	Bowl			1960s
3261	Plate	Misty Morn Range	10"dia	1960s–1982
3262	Plate	Teddy Nursery Range and Zooline Nursery Ware	8"dia	1960s–S-i-P
3263	Plate	Teddy Nursery Range and Zooline Nursery Ware and also other ranges	6½"dia	1960s–S-i-P
3264	Cereal Dish	Teddy Nursery Range and Zooline Nursery Ware and also other ranges	6¼"dia	1960s–S-i-P
3265	Fruit Dish			1960s
3266	Plate	Bread & Butter. Various ranges	11"dia	1960s–1982
3267	Cake Stand			1960s
3268	Cake Stand	Various decorations. Two tier	9½"dia	1960s–1982
3269	Fruit Bowl	Various decorations	8½"dia	1960s–1982
3270	Soup Bowl			1960s
3271/2	No information			
3273	Tankard	With fox	3¾"h	1960s–1982
3274	Tankard	With hound. Also Stoke City?	3¾"h	1960s–1982
3275/6	Dog			1960s
3277	Vase			1960s
3278	Tankard	With horse	3¾"h	1960s–1982
3279	Possibly G.B. Shaw Character Jug. Re-numbered 4492			1960s–70s
3280	Bowl	As log	6"l	1960s
3281	Cup			1960s
3282	No information			
3283	Vase	Lily Range. See No. 3098	8¼"h	1960s
3284	Vase			1960s
3285	Jardiniere	Lily Range. See No. 3098	10"l	1960s
3286	Vase	Lily Range. See No. 3098	12"h	1960s
3287	Bowl	Lily Range. See No. 3098	9¾"l	1960s
3288	Flower Pot	Lily Range. See No. 3098	8"dia	1960s
3289	Posy Trough	Lily Range. See No. 3098	7¼"l	1960s
3290	Jardiniere	Lily Range. See No. 3098	11¾"l	1960s
3291	Flower Pot	Lily Range. See No. 3098	7"dia	1960s
3292	Bowl	Lily Range. See No. 3098	6½"l	1960s
3293–5	No information			
3296	Cruet	Various ranges. Four pieces	3¾"h	1960s–1982
3297	Cheeseboard & knife	Various Ranges	9¾"l	1960s–70s
3298	Vase			1960s
3299	Toast Rack	Various Ranges	7½"l	1960s–1982
3300–02	No information			
3303	Vase			1960s
3304	Beaker			1960s
3305	Vase			1960s
3306	Tankard			1960s
3307	Cat			1960s
3308	Jardiniere			1960s
3309	Jardiniere	With handles	15½"l	1960s–70s
3310	Jardiniere	With handles	9"l	1960s–1982

3311 C	Bowl	With bird		1960s
3312 RT	Vase	Plain	7"c.h	1960s
3313 SC	Flower Holder	Oval with cupid	4¼"c.h	1960s
3314 SC	Dog	Smooth haired fox-terrier sitting		1960s
3315 JL	Coffee Pot	2¼"pint Various Ranges	9"h	1960s–1982
3316 RT	Vase	Shape as 3312 Large Size	9"c.h	1960s
3317 SC	Dog	Wire haired fox-terrier standing	6"c.h	1960s
3318 SC	Dog	Wire haired fox-terrier lying down curled up		1960s
3319 SC	Dog	Silly Pup sitting		1960s
3320 SC	Dog	Mongrel		1960s
3321 SC	Dog	Alsation. Sitting	6"h	1960s–1970s
3322 JL	Rabbit	Lop eared	Medium Size	1960s
3323 JL	Vase	Lager Shape Set of 3 with 3252	S/s 6¾"c.h	1960s
3324 JL	Vase	Lager Shape Set of 3 with 3252 Large Size	11"c.h	1960s
3325 SC	Flower Holder	Round with Cupid		1960s
3326 JL	Rabbit	Lop eared	Large Size	1960s
3327 JL	Rabbit	Ears erect		1960s
3328 JL	Rabbit	Ears erect	8"	1960s
3329 SC	Vase	Shell	7"	1960s
3330 JL	Vase		8"	1960s
3331 SC	Flower Pot	Round. Ribbed	c.h.1¾"	1960s
3332 SC	Flower Pot	Square. Ribbed	c.h.1¾"	1960s
3333 SC	Flower Holder	Cupid	c.h.5"	1960s
3334	Flower Holder	Sea Shell. Base of 3260	c.l.5½"	1960s
3335 SC	Dog	Spaniel Sitting		1960s
3336 SC	Flower Pot	Square. Ribbed	1¾"	1960s
3337 JL	Pig or Hippo		3½"l	1960s
3338 SC	Dog	West Highland. Sitting		1960s
3339 RT	Osprey	Prestige Pieces. HP	8½"h	1960s–1982
3340	Jardiniere or Ginger Jar	With cover	6"	1960s
3341 JL	Jardiniere	Opelle Range. Oval Fluted		1960s
3342 JL	Vase		7"	1960s
3343 JL	Vase		5½"	1960s
3344 JL	Vase		5"	1960s
3345 JL	Jardiniere		Small Size	1960s
3346 JL	Pig	Pigs head money-box		1960s
3347	Vase		8"	1960s
3348 JL	Jardiniere		10½"	1960s
3349 RT	Jardiniere	Pebble Range	9¾"l	1960s–70s
3350 JL	Vase	Pebble Range	6¾"h	1960s–70s
3351 JL	Planter			1960s
3352 RT	Ginger Jar	Embossed		1960s
3353 JL	Coffee Pot		Small Size	1960s
3354 RT	Jar	Plain with cover. Square		1960s
3355 JL	Bowl	Pebble Range	6¾"dia	1960s–70s
3356 RT	Bowl	Oblong		1960s
3357 RT	Vase or Jar	Blossom		1960s
3358 JL	Vase	Pebble Range	9"h	1960s–70s
3359 RT	Vase/Jar	Square. Engraved pattern		1960s
3360 RT	Flower Holder	Pebble Range	11½"l	1960s–70s
3361 RT	Fern Pot	Pebble Range	4½"h	1960s–70s
3362	Vase	Flat sides	c.h.5½"	1960s
3363 JL	Trough		8½"l	1960s
3364 RT	Vase	Plain	8"	1960s
3365 JL	Posy Bar		6½"	1960s
3366 JL	Posy Bar		4"	1960s
3367 RT	Vase/Jar	Square. Engraved Pattern		1960s
3368 JL	Vase	Pebble Range	11¼"h	1960s–70s
3369 RT	Vase	Rope handles. Shape 3364	8"	1960s
3370 SC	Bowl	Seahorse? on Stand	10"	1960s
3371 RT	Vase	Rope handles. Pattern 3369	11"	1960s
3372 RT	Tea Caddy	Elephant Head handle		1960s
3373 JL	Jardiniere	Pattern 3363	Small Size	1960s
3374 RT	Vase	As 3362. Engraved Pattern	5½"	1960s
3375 RT	Vase	3362 Shape. Embossed. Incised	5½"	1960s

3376 JL	Jardiniere	Pattern 3351		1960s
3377 C	Fern Pot		5"	1960s
3378 C	Tray	Feather Range. Blue/Pink/Green shading on matt background, with Lustre finish	7½"l	1960s–70s
3379 JL	Vase	Rope Handles. Alpine Pattern 3369	8"	1960s
3380 JL	Vase	Rope Handles. Alpine Patter 3369	8"	1960s
3381 JL	Jardiniere	Alpine Pattern	11"	1960s
3382 JL	Vase	Alpine Pattern	6"	1960s
3383 SC	Mule	Sitting		1960s
3384 SC	Mule	Standing	6½"h	1960s
3385 JL	Vase	Rope seams. Alpine Pattern	8"	1960s
3386 JL	Jardiniere	Rope seams. Alpine Pattern	Small size	1960s
3387 JL	Bowl	Oval Rope seams. Alpine Pattern	Small size	1960s
3388 JL	Bowl	Oval Rope seams. Alpine Pattern	Large size	1960s
3389 JL	Pot	Rope seams	Large size	1960s
3390 JL	Pot	Rope seams	Small size	1960s
3391 JL	Posy Bar	Rope seams	Small size	1960s
3392 SC	Cat	With long neck. Embossed with flowers	12¾"h	1960s–70s
3393 RT	Duck		4½"	1960s
3394 SC	Pipe Ashtray	Golden Brown with silver edge and woodgrain	4¾"l	1960s–70s
3395 J	Fern Pot	Pattern 3351	Small Size	1960s
3396 JL	Fern Pot	Pattern 3351	Large Size	1960s
3397 JL	Jug/Vase	Pattern 3351	10"	1960s
3398 JL	Vase	Pattern 3351	9"	1960s
3399 JL	Vase	Pattern 3351	8"	1960s
3400 JL	Vase	Pattern 3351 Alpine	6"	1960s
3401 JL	Bowl	Oval Pattern 3351	Large Size	1960s
3402 JL	Bowl Oval	Pattern 3351	Small size	1960s
3403 SC	Cat	Long neck	7"	1960s
3404 SC	Cat	Caricature. Long neck. Ass. Cols	6½"h	1960s–70s
3405 SC	Jar	Flower pattern	6"	1960s
3406 SC	Cat	Back paw to ear	4"	1960s
3407 SC	Cat	Back paw to ear	4"	1960s
3408 SC	Beaker	Plain		1960s
3409 SC	Pipe Ashtray	As 3394	4¾"l	1960s–70s
3410 SC	Box Ashtray			1960s
3411 JL	Mug			1960s
3412 JL	Vase			1960s
3413 SC	Beaker	Wheat pattern		1960s
3414 SC	Vase	Sea Horse	8"	1960s
3415 JL	Flower Pot	Pebble Range	6"h	1960s–70s
3416 JL	Vase			1960s
3417 SC	Jar with cover			1960s
3418 SC	Dog	Pup Shetland Collie		1960s
3419 JL	Jardiniere	Pebble Range	6½"l	1960s–70s
3420 JL	Posy Trough	Pebble Range	7¾"l	1960s–70s
3421 JL	Honey Pot	Plain		1960s
3422 SC	Dog	Spaniel 'Funnies' Large head small body	Approx 3"h	1960s
3423 SC	Dog	Sheepdog 'Funnies' Large head small body	Approx 3"h	1960s
3424 SC	Dog	Pekinese 'Funnies' Large head small body	Approx 3"h	1960s
3425 SC	Dog	Alsation 'Funnies' Large head small body	Approx 3"h	1960s
3426 SC	Dog	Dachshund 'Funnies' Large head small body	Approx 3"h	1960s
3427 SC	Dog	St. Bernard 'Funnies' Large head small body	Approx 3"h	1960s
3428 SC	Dog	Poodle 'Funnies' Large head small body	Approx 3"h	1960s
3429 SC	Dog	Bulldog 'Funnies' Large head small body	Approx 3"h	1960s
3430 SC	Dog	Shetland Collie 'Funnies' Large head small body	Approx 3"h	1960s
3431 SC	Dog	Scottie 'Funnies' Large head small body	Approx 3"h	1960s
3432 SC	Dog	Yorkshire Terrier 'Funnies' Large head small body	Approx 3"h	1960s
3433 SC	Dog	Yawning 'Funnies' Large head small body	Approx 3"h	1960s
3434 JL	Bowl	Pebble Range	13½"l	1960s–70s
3435 SC	Ash box	Horses		1960s
3436 SC	Ash box	Fish		1960s
3437 SC	Ash box	Duck		1960s
3438 RT	Plinthe Cyder AD			1960s
3439 JL	Bowl	Pebble Range	9¾"l	1960s
3440 JL	Bowl	Pebble Range	6½"l	1960s

3441 RT	Vase	Plain	6"	1960s
3442 SC	Jar			1960s
3443 SC	Vase	Oval Alternate plain squares	8"	1960s
3444 SC	Vase	Alternate plain squares		1960s
3445 SC	Seahorse stand			1960s
3446 SC	Basket			1960s
3447 RT	Dog	Cairn Terrier 'Wendy'	5"h	1960s
3448 SC	Vase or Decanter			1960s
3449 JL	Vase		6"	1960s
3450 JL	Vase		8"	1960s
3451 JL	Vase		10"	1960s
3452 RT	Cup	Tea embossed		1960s
3453 JL	Trough			1960s
3454	Tray	Round Two handles 6 dishes		1960s
3455 JL	Pot	Pattern 3450	Large size	1960s
3456 JL	Pot	Pattern 3450	Small size	1960s
3457 SC	Cat	Long Neck Plain. Ass. Cols	12"	1960s–70s
3458 JL	Jardiniere	Pattern 3450	Small size	1960s
3459 JL	Otter	With fish Prestige Pieces. HP	9½"l	1960s–82
3460 SC	Vase	Seahorse		1960s
3461 JL	Bowl	Oblong Pattern 3450	Large size	1960s
3462 JL	Bowl	Oblon Pattern 3450	Small size	1960s
3463 JL	Bulb Bowl	Square		1960s
3464 JL	Planter		15"	1960s
3465 JL	Bowl	Opelle Range		1960s
3466 JL	Wall Vase	Opelle Range		1960s
3467 RT	Ash tray	Peter Rumsey Abergavenny		1960s
3468 RT	Cup			1960s
3469	Boots Reserved			
3470 SC	Posy Bar	Seahorse	Small size	1960s
3471 SC	Posy Bar	Seahorse	Large size	1960s
3472 SC	Vase	Seahorse	6"	1960s
3473	Jardiniere	Seahorse	Small size	1960s
3474 SC	Bowl	Seahorse	Large size	1960s
3475 SC	Bowl	Seahorse	Small size	1960s
3476	Planter			1960s
3477 JL	Jardiniere	Plain	Small size	1960s
3478	Shaving Mug	Plain		1960s
3479 SC	Bowl			1960s
3480 JL	Fern Pot	Pebble Range	5¼"h	1960s–70s
3481 JL	Tray	Pebble Range	5¼"l	1960s–70s
3482 JL	Tray	Pebble Range	12¾"l	1960s–70s
3483 JL	Vase	Flat front	5"	1960s
3484 C	Tray	Feather Range See No. 3378	13¾"l	1960s–70s
3485 C	Bowl	Feather Range See NO. 3378	12"	1960s
3486 JL	Grapefruit or Sundae dish		3½"h	1960s
3487 JL	Vase	Panel on Front, Plain	10"	1960s
3488	Tankard	Plain ½ pint. Nottingham Forrest Football Club Centenary. 1865–1965	3¾"h	1960s
3489	Bowl	Ribbed with cover. Powder Bowl		1960s
3490 RT	Vase	Incised Tudor Blue on White	6"	1960s
3491 RT	Vase	Tudor Panel on front incised	8"	1960s
3492 RT	Vase	Tudor. Incised	10"	1960s
3493 RT	Jardiniere	Tudor. Incised	Large Size	1960s
3494 RT	Jardiniere	Tudor. Incised	Small Size	1960s
3495 RT	Bowl Low	Tudor. Incised		1960s
3496 RT	Pot	Tudor. Incised	Large Size	1960s
3497 RT	Pot	Tudor. Incised	Small Size	1960s
3498 RT	Posy Trough	Tudor. Incised	Large Size	1960s
3499 RT	Posy Trough	Tudor. Incised	Small Size	1960s
3500 RT	Dog	Labrador Standing	5"h	1960s–S-i-P
3501 SC	Vase			1960s
3502 W	Twin Tray	Feather Range See No. 3378		1960s
3503 W	Triple Tray	Feather Range See No. 3378	12"l	1960s–70s
3504 W	Tray	Feather Range See No. 3378	12¼"l	1960s–70s
3505 W	Cruet	Feather Range See No. 3378		1960s
3506 W	Twin Tray	Feather Range See No. 3378	11"l	1960s–70s
3507 W	Cress dish/stand	Feather Range See No. 3378	10"dia	1960s–70s

3508 W	Cheese dish	Feather Range See No. 3378		1960s
3509 W	Cooky Jar	Feather Range See No. 3378		1960s
3510 W	Tray 4 sections	Feather Range See No. 3378	14½"l	1960s–70s
3511 W	Butter dish Square	Feather Range See No. 3378		1960s
3512 W	Twin Preserve dish	Feather Range See No. 3378	11"l	1960s–70s
3513 W	Beaker	Feather Range See No. 3378		1960s
3514 W	Honey Pot	Feather Range See No. 3378		1960s
3515 W	Tray	Feather Range See No. 3378	5½"l	1960s
3516	Teacup			1960s
3517	Pot	Panel on front plain	Large Size	1960s
3518	Pot	Panel on front plain	Small Size	1960s
3519 JL	Cup			1960s
3520 JL	Butter Dish	Plain. Square		1960s
3521 JL	Posy Bar			1960s
3522 SC	Dog	Spaniel		1960s
3523 SC	Vase	New Shell Range	8"	1960s
3524 SC	Vase	New Shell Range	10"	1960s
3525 SC	Jardiniere	New Shell Range	Large Size	1960s
3526 SC	Jardiniere	New Shell Range	Small Size	1960s
3527 SC	Wall Vase	New Shell Range		1960s
3528 SC	Posy Trough	New Shell Range	11"	1960s
3529 SC	Flower Holder	New Shell Range		1960s
3530 SC	Bowl	New Shell Range	Small Size	1960s
3531 SC	Bowl	New Shell Range	Large Size	1960s
3532 SC	Posy Bar	New Shell Range		1960s
3533 SC	Bowl with foot	New Shell Range	6"	1960s
3534 SC	Bowl with foot	New Shell Range	9"	1960s
3535 JL	Jardiniere	Plain	Large Size	1960s
3536 JL	Posy Bar	Plain		1960s
3537 SC	Bowl			1960s
3538 JL	Vase	Plain	6"	1960s
3539 RT	Vase	Tudor incised	6"	1960s
3540 JL	Vase	Plain	8"	1960s
3541 RT	Vase	Tudor	8"	1960s
3542 RT	Ashtray with MR. SYLVAC and dog with toothache issued to retail outlets		about 10"h	1960s
3543 JL	Cup			1960s
3544 JL	Cup	Plain		1960s
3545 RT	Bowl			1960s
3546 RT	Tankard	½ Pint Jersey Channel Islands	3¾"h	1960s
3547 W	Cup and Saucer	Magnolia Range		1960s
3548/9 JL	Vases	Plain	8"	1960s
3550 RT	Vase/Lamp		15½"	1960s
3551 JL	Vase		8"	1960s
3552 RT	Dog	Pug. Standing	4½"h	1960s–S-i-P
3553 JL	Vase	Urn. Vintage Range	7"h	1960s–81
3554 RT	Butter dish	Butterfly handle		1960s
3555 JL	Bowl	Evening fantasy Range	3⅞"dia	1960s–70s
3556 RT	Log	Novelty with fawn Blue & White	Small Size	1960s
3557 RT	Vase	Lily Range	8"	1960s
3558 SC	Vase		13"	1960s
3559 JL	Vase	Urn Vintage Range	5"h	1960s
3560 RT	Dog	White, jumping over fawn wall, oblong	3¼"h	1960s
3561 SC	Dog	Bassett Hound. Sitting	5¾"l	1960s–S-i-P
3561	Cockerel			
3562 SC	Vase	New Shell range	12"	1960s
3562	Cockerel			
3563 SC	Dog	Bassett Hound. Sitting up	6¾"h	1960s–70s
3564 RT	Cup	Butterfly Handle		1960s
3565 SC	Dog	Scottie for novelties	2¾"	1960s
3566 RT	Barrel Ash Box			1960s
3567 SC	Dog	Spaniel to go with 1996 Basket	2½"	1960s
3568 SC	Giraffe		10"	1960s
3569 JL	Jug	One pint. Lime-grove Range	5½"h	1960s–82
3570 SC	Elephant	Sitting		1960s
3571 RT	Basket and kitten novelty			1960s
3572	Jardiniere	Plain		1960s

3573	Bowl	Grapefruit		1960s
3574 RT	Cricketers	Schweppes Ad		1960s
3575 SC	Hare	Shell Pattern		1960s
3576 RT	Honey Pot	Plain with Butterfly handle	4½"h	1960s
3577 SC	Jardiniere	Rose Pattern		1960s
3578 JL	Vase	Urn Vintage Range	9¼"	1960s–198
3579 JL	Vase	Urn Vintage Range	11¼"	1960s–198
3580 SC	Frog	Shell Pattern	4"	1960s
3581 JL	Vegetable Dish			1960s
3582 JL	Porridge or Soup dish			1960s
3583 SC	Penguin	Shell Pattern		1960s
3584 JL	Jug/Vase		11"	1960s
3585 SC	Toucan	Shell Pattern		1960s
3586 SC	Dog	Lying down Shell Pattern		1960s
3587 SC	Vase		8"	1960s
3588 RT	Bowl	Fluted	11"	1960s
3589 JL	Cheeseboard with container			1960s
3590 RT	Pot	Raffia	4"	1960s
3591 SC	Vase		6"	1960s
3592 JL	Bowl		11"	1960s
3593 RT	Vase or Bottle		6"	1960s
3594 JL	Meat Dish	Oval	15½"	1960s
3595 SC	Vase	Plain	8"	1960s
3596 JL	Jug	Feather Range See no 3378		1960s
3597 RT	Pot			1960s
3598 SC	Vase	Oval	8"	1960s
3599 JL	Sugar Bowl	Feather Range See No. 3378		1960s
3600 JL	Cream Jug	Feather Range See No. 3378		960s
3601 JL	Jug	Feather Range See No. 3378		1960s
3602 SC	Vase	Embossed		1960s
3603 SC	Vase			1960s
3604 JL	Jug	Butterfly Handle		1960s
3605 RT	Pot	Plain		1960s
3606 JL	Cream Jug	Butterfly Handle		1960s
3607 JL	Sugar Bowl	Butterfly Handle		1960s
3608 RT	Bowl	Fluted		1960s
3609 JL	Coffee Canister			1960s
3610 SC	Cat	Shell Pattern		1960s
3611 JL	Gravy Boat and Stand			1960s
3612 SC	Mouse	Shell Pattern	4"	1960s
3613 RT	Honey Pot	Hive	4½"	1960s
3614 SC	Dog	Sitting	5"	1960s
3615 SC	Dog	Sitting	5"	1960s
3616 RT	Pot	Embossed		1960s
3617 RT	Beaker with two handles. Teddy Nursery Range and Zooline Nursery Ware		3½"h	1960s–S-i-P
3618 SC	Jardiniere	(Glass)	11"	1960s
3619 JL	Cruet	Butterfly Handle		1960s
3620 JL	Teapot	Butterfly Handle		1960s
3621 RT	Ashtray	Oblong	6"	1960s
3622 SC	Vase/Jar	Triangle		1960s
3623 RT	Pot	Embossed		1960s
3624 RT	Bowl	Privet Range	7"l	1960s–81
3625 RT	Bowl	Stones		1960s
3626 RT	Top Hat		4"	1960s
3627 SC	Jar	Plain Round		1960s
3628 JL	Coffee Pot			1960s
3629 SC	Vase	Triangle. Embossed		1960s
3630 JL	Coffee Pot			1960s
3631 RT	Vase		8"	1960s
3632 RT	Tankard	½ pint Finished in leather	5"	1960s–1982
3633 JL	Meat Dish		12"	1960s
3634 JL	Beaker			1960s
3635 JL	Sugar Bowl			1960s
3636 RT	Cheese & Biscuit Tray		14½"dia	1960s–70s
3637 SC	Vase/Jar	Embossed	6"	1960s
3638 SC	Bowl	Stonewall Pattern	9½"	1960s
3639 RT	Jardiniere	With handles	13"w	1960s
3640 JL	Coffee Pot	Embossed		1960s

3641 RT	Ash tray			1960s
3642 SC	Dog	Bassett Hound. Sitting	5"l	1960s–82
3643 SC	Vase	Stonewall Pattern	9"	1960s
3644 RT	Mixing Bowl	Plain		1960s
3645 RT	Tray			1960s
3646 JL	Beaker	Embossed		1960s
3647 JL	Coffee Pot	Web Pattern		1960s
3648/9 JL	Sugar Bowls			1960s
3650 JL	Beaker	Web Pattern		1960s
3651 SC	Jardiniere	Teardrops. Two Handles	13"	1960s
3652 JL	Jardiniere	Plain	Small Size	1960s
3653 SC	Jardiniere	Stonewall Pattern		1960s
3654 JL	Jardiniere	Plain	11"	1960s
3655 JL	Vase	Plain	10"	1960s
3656 JL	Vase	Plain	8"	1960s
3657 JL	Vase	Plain	6"	1960s
3658 JL	Pot		Small Size	1960s
3659 JL	Pot		Large Size	1960s
3660 SC	Ashtray	Three feet	8"	1960s
3661 RT	Tankard	With leather finish 1 pint		1960s
3662 SC	Vase	Plain	6"	1960s
3663 JL	Bowl	Plain. Pedestal	Small Size	1960s
3664 JL	Beaker	Pedestal		1960s
3665 JL	Bowl		Medium Size	1960s
3666 JL	Bowl		Large Size	1960s
3667 JL	Sugar Bowl			1960s
3668 JL	Teapot			1960s
3669 JL	Cream Jug			1960s
3670 JL	Coffee Pot	Fluted		1960s
3671 JL	Cup	Plain Pedestal		1960s
3672 JL	Cup	Embossed Pedestal		1960s
3673 JL	Cheese dish	Round. Pedestal		1960s
3674 SC	Ashtray	Tyre		1960s
3675 JL	Grandfather Clock		2"	1960s
3675	Dog			
3676 RT	Vase/Jar			1960s
3677 JL	Cheese dish	Square. Pedestal with knob		1960s
3678 RT	Vase	Palm	8"	1960s
3679 JL	Cheese dish	Butterfly Handle. Oblong		1960s
3680 SC	Pot	New Shell Pattern		1960s
3681 RT	Bowl	Fluted	Medium Size	1960s
3682 RT	Ashtray		4"	1960s
3683 RT	Lamp	Pebble Design	12"	1960s
3684 SC	Jardiniere	New Shell Pattern	7"h	1960s
3685 JL	Honeypot	Plain		1960s
3686 JL	Butter dish	Oblong. Pedestal		1960s
3687 JL	Coffee pot	Pedestal	Large Size	1960s
3688 JL	Beaker			1960s
3689 SC	Jardiniere			1960s
3690 RT	Vase	Palm pattern	8"	1960s
3691 RT	Bowl	With Cover	4"	1960s
3692 SC	Jardiniere		Large Size	1960s
3693 SC	Vase	Chequers		1960s
3694 SC	Vase		8"	1960s
3695 SC	Jardiniere		Small Size	1960s
3696 SC	Bowl	On foot		1960s
3697 SC	Bowl	Oval	10"	1960s
3698 SC	Jardiniere		Small Size	1960s
3699 SC	Flower Pot		Large Size	1960s
3700 SC	Flower Pot		Medium Size	1960s
3701	Flower Pot	Chequers	Small Size	1960s
3702 SC	Posy Bar			1960s
3703	Posy Trough		Small Size	1960s
3704 SC	Planter or Trough			1960s
3705 SC	Vase		6"	1960s
3706 SC	Menu Card		6"	1960s
3707 SC	Posy	Pedestal		1960s
3708 JL	Cheese/Butter dish	Square knob changed to 3554 Butterfly		1960s

3709	Name Tabs/Place Cards		3″	1960s
3710 RT	Bowl	Palm	Small Size	1960s
3711 RT	Vase	Harp	5″	1960s
3712 JB	Ashtray	Square	2″h	1960s
3713 JL	Cruet	Pedestal		1960s
3714 RT	Jardiniere	Palm. Two Handles	Large Size	1960s
3715 RT	Flower Pot	Palm Pattern	6″h	1960s–70s
3716 RT	Bulb Bowl	Palm Pattern Oval	10¼″l	1960s–70s
3717 RT	Posy or Slipper	Palm Pattern		1960s
3718 RT	Flower Holder	Palm Pattern	Large Size	1960s
3719 RT	Posy Boat	Palm Pattern	Small Size	1960s
3720 RT	Posy Bar	Palm Pattern		1960s
3721 RT	Wall Vase	Palm Pattern		1960s
3722 RT	Flower Pot	Palm Pattern	4¾″h	1960s–70s
3723 RT	Jardiniere	Palm Pattern		1960s
3724 RT	Vase	Palm Pattern	10″	1960s
3725 RT	Vase	Palm Pattern	6″	1960s
3726 RT	Bowl	Palm Pattern Oval	6¾″	1960s–70s
3727 JL	Jug	Pedestal. One Pint		1960s
3728 JL	Cream Jug			1960s
3729 JL	Cream	Web Pattern		1960s
3730 JB	Ashtray	Square	3″h	1960s
3731 JL	Vase	Oslo Range Blue-Orange-White	9¾h	1960s–70s
3732 JL	Vase	Oslo Range Blue-Orange-White	8″h	1960s–70s
3733 JL	Vase	Oslo Range Blue-Orange-White	6″h	1960s–70s
3734 JL	Bowl	Oslo Range Blue-Orange-White	Large Size	1960s
3735 JL	Bowl	Oslo Range Blue-Orange-White	7¾″dia	1960s–70s
3736 JL	Bowl	Oslo Range Blue-Orange-White	5¾″dia	1960s–70s
3737 JL	Fern Pot	Oslo Range Blue-Orange-White	4¾″h	1960s–70s
3738 JL	Fern Pot	Oslo Range Blue-Orange-White	6¾″h	1960s–70s
3739 JL	Posy	Oslo Range Blue-Orange-White		1960s
3740 JL	Jardiniere	Oslo Range Blue-Orange-White	6¼″l	1960s–70s
3741 JL	Jardiniere	Oslo Range Blue-Orange-White	9¼″l	1960s–70s
3742 RT	Mug-One handle	Teddy Nursery Range and Zooline Nursery Ware	3¼″h	1960s–S-i-P
3743 JL	Bowl	Oslo Range See No. 3731	3¾″dia	1960s–70s
3744 RT	Bread & Butter Plate	Butterfly Range		1960s
3745	Sandwich Tray	Butterfly Range		1960s
3746 RT	Teapot	Butterfly Range		1960s
3747 RT	Mug	Half-Pint Tudor Range		1960s
3748 RT	Mug	Half-Pint		1960s
3749 RT	Mug	Half-Pint Embossed		1960s
3750 RT	Mug	Pineapple		1960s
3751 RT	Mug	Fluted		1960s
3752 JL	Vase		10″	1960s
3753 SC	Vase/Jar			1960s
3754 SC	Money-box	Cats Head		1960s
3755 RT	Bird		4″	1960s
3756 RT	Birds head	Pie Filler	2″	1960s
3757 JL	Cup	Pedestal		1960s
3758 SC	Jar	Flower Pattern		1960s
3759 RT	Plate	Fluted	10″	1960s
3760	Ashbowl		5½″	1960s
3761 JL	Tray	Oblong	15″	1960s
3762 RT	Horse			1960s
3763 SC	Money-box	Life-boat mans head		1960s
3764 JL	Jar	Square		1960s
3765 SC	Dog	Scottie. Sitting		1960s
3766 SC	Dog	Poodle. Sitting	6″	1960s
3767 SC	Dog	Corgi. Sitting	6″	1960s
3768 RT	Triple Tray			1960s
3769 JL	Jardiniere	Plain	10½″	1960s
3770 SC	Money-box	Cat's head		1960s
3771	Cheese dish	Oblong Wishing Well		1960s
3772	Honey-pot	Wishing Well		1960s
3773	Butter Dish	Square. Wishing Well		1960s
3774–3787	These numbers were left for further Wishing Well items, but were probably never used.			
3788	Egg Cup	Teddy Nursery Range & Zooline	3″dia	1960s–S-i-P

3789 JL	Stork			9″	1960s
3790 JL	Stork			6″	1960s
3791	Baby Plate	Teddy & Zooline Nursery Ranges		6″dia	1960s–S-i-P
3792 JL	Vase				1960s
3793	Vase/Jar	Square. Plain			1960s
3794 RT	Vase	Round			1960s
3795 SC	Vase	Round			1960s
3796 JL	Jardiniere				1960s
3797 SC	Vase/Jar				1960s
3798 SC	Dog	Spaniel. Sitting			1960s
3799 SC	Character Jug	Life-boat Man. Seaman Jones			1960s
3800 RT	Vase	Square			1960s
3801 SC	Vase/Jar	Round			1960s
3802 SC	Money-box	Seaman Jones		Small Size	1960s
3803 RT	Lamp	Tudor		10″	1960s
3804 RT	Lamp	1807 Vase Right way up		9¾″h	1960s
3805 RT	Lamp	1807 Vase Upside down		9¾″h	1960s
3806 RT	Bowl	Oblong		10½″l	1960s
3807 SC	Fern Pot	Wall Pattern		5½″h	1960s–70s
3808 SC	Fern Pot	Wall Pattern		4¾″h	1960s–70s
3809 SC	Fern Pot	Wall Pattern		4½″h	1960s–70s
3810 SC	Vase	Wall Pattern		10″	1960s
3811 SC	Vase	Wall Pattern		8″	1960s
3812 SC	Vase	Wall Pattern		6″	1960s
3813 SC	Bowl	Wall Pattern Oblong		Small Size	1960s
3814 SC	Twin Bowl	Wall Pattern		13″	1960s
3815 SC	Bowl	Wall Pattern Oblong		12″	1960s
3816 SC	Jardiniere	Wall Pattern		Small Size	1960s
3817 SC	Bowl	Wall Pattern Oblong		14″	1960s
3818 SC	Tray	Wall Pattern Oblong		7″	1960s
3819 SC	Posy Bar	Wall Pattern		14″	1960s
3820 SC	Posy Bar	Wall Pattern		Small Size	1960s
3821 RT	Bowl	Oblong		7½″l	1960s
3822 RT	Bowl	Oval		11″	1960s
3823 RT	Bowl	Oval		Large Size	1960s
3824 RT	Jardiniere	Privet Pattern			1960s
3825 RT	Vase	Privet Pattern		7″	1960s
3826 SC	Bowl	Wall Pattern Oblong		12″	1960s
3827 SC	Dog	Spaniel Sitting with slipper in mouth		5″h	1960s
3828 RT	Coffee Pot				1960s
3829 SC	Dog	Scottie			1960s
3830 SC	Posy or Slipper	Wall Pattern			1960s
3831 SC	Tray	Wall Pattern		13″	1960s
3832 RT	Jug	Plain			1960s
3833 RT	Jar	Plain			1960s
3834 RT	Jug	Embossed			1960s
3835 SC	Bowl	Oblong Plain			1960s
3836 RT	Coffee pot				1960s
3837 SC	Money box	Teddy Bear Police			1960s
3838 SC	Bowl	Manhattan Range Oblong		10¼″l	1960s–70s
3839 SC	Money box	Bunnies Bank			1960s
3840 SC	Money box	Cowboy			1960s
3841 SC	Money box	Indian			1960s
3842 RT	Vase	Privet Pattern		8½″h	1960s–1981
3843 JL	Bowl and Fish				1960s
3844 RT	Vase	Privet Pattern		10½″h	1960s–1981
3845 RT	Vase	Privet Pattern		6″	1960s
3846 RT	Bowl	Privet Pattern Oval		10″	1960s
3847 RT	Cat	Plain. Laughing. No fur		6″	1960s
3848 SC	Dog	Scottie		4″	1960s
3849 RT	Fish on Pedestal				1960s
3850 JL	Vase	Linton Range		4″	1960s
3851 JL	Vase	Linton Range		6″	1960s
3852 JL	Vase	Linton Range		8″	1960s
3853 JL	Vase	Linton Range		Large Size	1960s
3854 JL	Posy	Linton Range		Small Size	1960s
3855 JL	Planter	Linton Range		12″	1960s
3856 JL	Jardiniere	Linton Range		Small Size	1960s
3857 JL	Jardiniere	Linton Range		Large Size	1960s

3858 JL	Pot	Linton Range	Small Size	1960s
3859 JL	Pot	Linton Range	Large Size	1960s
3860 JL	Bowl	Linton Range	Small Size	1960s
3861 JL	Bowl	Linton Range	Large Size	1960s
3862 JL	Posy Slipper	Linton Range		1960s
3863 JL	Vase	Begonia Range	4″	1960s
3864 JL	Vase	Begonia Range	6″	1960s
3865 JL	Vase	Begonia Range	8″	1960s
3866 JL	Vase	Begonia Range	10″	1960s
3867 JL	Posy	Begonia Range	Small Size	1960s
3868 JL	Planter	Begonia Range		1960s
3869 JL	Jardiniere	Begonia Range	Small Size	1960s
3870 JL	Jardiniere	Begonia Range	Large Size	1960s
3871 JL	Pot	Begonia Range	Small Size	1960s
3872 JL	Pot	Begonia Range	Large Size	1960s
3873 JL	Bowl	Begonia Range	Small Size	1960s
3874 JL	Bowl	Begonia Range	Large Size	1960s
3875 JL	Slipper	Begonia Range		1960s
3876 JL	Tray	Begonia Range		1960s
3877 JL	Vase	Texture Range	4″	1960s
3878 JL	Vase	Texture Range	6″	1960s
3879 JL	Vase	Texture Range	8″	1960s
3880 JL	Vase	Texture Range	10″	1960s
3881 JL	Posy	Texture Range	Small Size	1960s
3882 JL	Planter	Texture Range		1960s
3883 JL	Jardiniere	Texture Range	Small Size	1960s
3884 JL	Jardiniere	Texture Range	Large Size	1960s
3885 JL	Pot	Texture Range	Small Size	1960s
3886 JL	Pot	Texture Range	Large Size	1960s
3887 JL	Bowl	Texture Range	Small Size	1960s
3888 JL	Bowl	Texture Range	Large Size	1960s
3889 JL	Slipper Posy	Texture Range		1960s
3890 JL	Tray	Texture Range		1960s
3891	Not used			
3892 RT	Cat	Laughing. With fur. As 3847		1960s
3893 JL	Tray	Coral		1960s
3894 RT	Bowl	Privet Range. Round		1960s
3895 RT	Fern Pot	Privet Range	4⅞″h	1960s–81
3896 RT	Fern Pot	Privet Range	5¾″h	1960s–81
3897 JL	Vase	Coral	6″	1960s
3898 JL	Jardiniere	Coral	Medium Size	1960s
3899 RT	Posy Ring	Privet Range	5½″dia	1960s
3900 RT	Posy Bar	Privet Range		1960s
3901 JL	Vase	Coral	8″	1960s
3902 JL	Posy Bar	Coral		1960s
3903 RT	Jardiniere	Privet Range	Large Size	1960s
3904 JL	Vase	Coral	10″	1960s
3905 JL	Jardiniere	Coral	Small Size	1960s
3906 JL	Pot	Coral		1960s
3907 JL	Jardiniere	Coral	Large Size	1960s
3908 RT	Sugar Bowl	To match coffee pot 3828		1960s
3909 RT	Cream Jug	To match coffee pot 3828		1960s
3910 JL	Pot	Coral	Large Size	1960s
3911 RT	Dish		7x4x1½″	1960s
3912	Squirrel	Sitting. No paws		1960s
3913 RT	Dog	Jack Russell. Standing	3½″h	1960s–S-i-P
3914 RT	Egg Cup	Avon Range	1½″h	1960s
3915 RT	Bread & Butter Plate	Square Lisbon		1960s
3916 GM	Vase		Medium Size	1960s
3917 GM	Vase		Small Size	1960s
3918 GM	Fox			1960s
3919/20 RT	Mugs	Plain. Half-Pint		1960s
3921 GM	Dog	Hunchback	7″	1960s
3922 RT	Mug	Half-pint		1960s
3923 GM	Dog	Spaniel Crouching	5″l	1960s
3924 GM	Vase	Plain	10″	1960s
3925 GM	Deer	Bambi		1960s
3926 RT	Mug			1960s

3927 GM	Fox			1960s
3928 RT	Lamp			1960s
3929 GM	Vase	Tree. Twin Rabbits	12″	1960s
3930 RT	Bull	Standing. Prestige Pieces	14½″l	1960s–82
3931 RT	Jar	Plain	6″	1960s
3932 GM	Vase		12″	1960s
3933 GM	Dog	Pomeranian		1960s
3934 GM	Pot	Cactus Range	3″	1960s
3935 GM	Money box	Squirrel Sitting. Re-numbered to 5105		1960s
3936 GM	Pot	Cactus Range	3″	1960s
3937 RT	Tankard	Wisdom & Providence	5″h	1960s
3938 GM	Vase	Manhatten Range	6¼″h	1960s–70s
3939 GM	Vase	Manhatten Range	8″h	1960s–70s
3940 GM	Bowl	Manhatten Range	6¼″l	1960s–70s
3941 GM	Fern Pot	Manhatten Range	6½″dia	1960s–70s
3942 GM	Fern Pot	Manhatten Range	5¾″dia	1960s–70s
3943 GM	Fern Pot	Manhatten Range	5″dia	1960s–70s
3944 GM	Jardiniere	Manhatten Range	7½″l	1960s–70s
3945 GM	Posy Trough	Manhatten Range	7½″l	1960s–70s
3946 GM	Vase	Manhatten Range	8″	1960s
3947 GM	Vase	Manhatten Range	10¼″h	1960s–70s
3948 GM	Tray	Manhatten Range	12¾″l	1960s–70s
3949 GM	Bowl	Manhatten Range	10″l	1960s–70s
3950 GM	Tray	Manhatten Range	6¼″l	1960s–70s
3951 GM	Posy trough	Manhatten Range	5″l	1960s–70s
3952 GM	Posy trough	Manhatten Range	10¼″l	1960s–70s
3953 RT	Ashtray	Shaped as Maple leaf. Montreal	5½″dia	1960s
3954 RT	Mug	Maple Pattern		1960s
3955 RT	Tray	Maple leaf		1960s
3956 GM	Jardiniere	Manhatten Range	11½″l	1960s–70s
3957 GM	Fox			1960s
3958	Lamp	Hyacinth Leaf Range		1960s
3959	Lamp	3880 Vase	10″	1960s
3960 RT	Cat	Prowling Manx	6″	1960s
3961	Lamp	Macklestone Pot	Small Size	1960s
3962	Lamp		12″	1960s
3963	Lamp Extension		8″	1960s
3964 GM	Jardiniere	Boar Fight	10″	1960s
3965 RT	Jardiniere	Embossed	Medium Size	1960s
3966 RT	Vase	Three feet	9″	1960s
3967 RT	Jardiniere			1960s
3968 GM	Dog	Dachshund		1960s
3969 RT	Vase			1960s
3970 RT	Vase	Embossed	10″	1960s
3971 GM	Wall Vase	Horse-shoe		1960s
3972 GM	Vase		4″	1960s
3973 RT	Mug	To coffee set		1960s
3974 RT	Vase		5″	1960s
3975 RT	Tankard	Wisdom & Providence	4¼″h	1960s–70s
3976	Lamp/Vase	Macklestone	10″	1960s
3977 RT	Cheese dish	Totem Range	7½″l	1960s–1970s
3978 RT	Tankard	Wisdom & Providence	5¾″h	1960s–70s
3979	Lamp/Vase	Macklestone		1960s
3980 RT	Vase	Plain		1960s
3981 RT	Beaker	Coffee		1960s
3982 GM	Honey pot	Totem Range	4¾″h	1960s–70s
3983 RT	Jardiniere		13½″	1960s
3984 GM	Cat			1960s
3985 RT	Coffee Perculator	Sono	Small Size	1960s
3986 GM	Butter Dish	Totem Range	6″l	1960s–70s
3987 GM	Posy Bar	Totem Range		1960s
3988 RT	Dog	Irish Terrier. Standing	5″h	1960s–70s
3989 RT	Bowl		Small Size	1960s
3990 GM	Pot		Large Size	1960s
3991 RT	Tray	Tulip		1960s
3992 GM	Jardiniere		Small Size	1960s
3993 RT	Vase		6″	1960s
3994 RT	Vase		3½″	1960s
3995 RT	Vase	Maple leaf Range	10¼″h	1960s–S-i-P

3996 RT	Ashtray	Round. Suede finish	5¼"dia	1960s–1982
3997 GM	Vase	Plain	8"	1960s
3998 RT	Vase	Urn. Olympus Range	4"h	1960s–70s
3999 RT	Vase	Embossed	10"	1960s
4000 GM	Vase	Plain	6"	1960s
4001 RT	Jardiniere	Maple Range	10¼"l	1960s–S-i-P
4002 RT	Fern Pot	Maple Range	5¼"dia	1960s–S-i-P
4003 RT	Pot	Fluted		1960s
4004 RT	Fern Pot	Maple Range	7"dia	1960s–S-i-P
4005 RT	Pot		3"	1960s
4006 RT	Fern Pot	Maple Range	5¼"dia	1960s–S-i-P
4007 GM	Bulb Bowl	Plain	Large Size	1960s
4008 RT	Jardiniere	Maple Range	7"l	1960s–S-i-P
4009 RT	Ashtray	Suede Finish	7⅝"dia	1960s–1982
4010 RT	Vase	Maple Range	6"h	1960s–S-i-P
4011 RT	Vase	Maple Range	8"h	1960s–S-i-P
4012 GM	Jardiniere	Manhattan Range	9"l	1960s–70s
4013 RT	Bowl	Maple Range	7½"dia	1960s–S-i-P
4014 GM	Cruet	Totem Range 4 piece	3½"h	1960s–70s
4015 GM	Bowl	Plain	Small Size	1960s
4016 GM	Posy Bar	Plain	9"	1960s
4017 GM	Bulb Bowl	Round Plain		1960s
4018 RT	Bowl	Maple Range	6¼"l	1960s–S-i-P
4019 RT	Bowl	Manhatten Range	3¾"dia	1960s–70s
4020	Fruit dish	Totem Range		1960s
4021 RT	Coffee Perculator	(Mono)		1960s
4022 GM	Two Oil/Vinegar Bottles	With stoppers on tray. Totem Range	7¾"l	1960s–70s
4023 RT	Posy Trough	Maple Range	8"l	1960s–S-i-P
4024 RT	Bowl	Manhatten Range	8½"dia	1960s–70s
4025	Coffee Perculator			1960s
4026 GM	Sugar Bowl			1960s
4027 RT	Ashtray	Round	6½"	1960s
4028 GM	Cream Jug	Coffee		1960s
4029 GM	Toast Rack	Totem Range	7¼"l	1960s–70s
4030 GM	Cheese Board and knife	Totem Range	9¾"l	1960s–70s
4031 GM	Four Egg cups & stand	Totem Range	6½"dia	1960s–70s
4032 RT/GM	Hors d'Oeuvre tray	3 sections. Totem	13¼"l	1960s–70s
4033 GM	Sugar Bowl	Totem Range	4"dia	1960s–70s
4034 GM	Beaker	Toronto Totem Range		1960s
4035 RT/GM	Hors d'Oeuvre tray	2 sections	10¼"l	1960s–70s
4036 GM	Sandwich Tray	Totem Range	13"l	1960s–70s
4037 GM	Coffee Pot	Totem Range	8¼"h	1960s–70s
4038 GM	Beaker	Totem Range	4"h	1960s–70s
4039 RT/GM	Cream Jug	Totem Range	4"h	1960s–70s
4040 RT/GM	Jug	Totem Range	5¼"h	1960s–70s
4041 RT	Storage Jar	New Kitchen Ware 2588	Large Size	1960s
4042 RT	Storage Jar	New Kitchen Ware 2511	Small Size	1960s
4043 RT	Jug	New Kitchen Ware 2582	Large Size	1960s
4044 RT	Jug	New Kitchen Ware 2544	Medium Size	1960s
4045 RT	Jug	New Kitchen Ware 2590	Small Size	1960s
4046 RT	Teapot	New Kitchen Ware 2571	Large Size	1960s
4047 RT	Teapot	New Kitchen Ware 2604	Small Size	1960s
4048 RT	Coffee Jug	New Kitchen Ware 2809		1960s
4049 RT	Cheese Dish	New Kitchen Ware		1960s
4045 RT	Butter Dish	New Kitchen Ware		1960s
4051 RT	Sugar Bowl	New Kitchen Ware		1960s
4052 RT	Beaker	New Kitchen Ware		1960s
4053 RT	Sugar Shaker	New Kitchen Ware		1960s
4054 RT	Honey Pot	New Kitchen Ware		1960s
4055	Mixing Bowl	New Kitchen Ware Plain	Large Size	1960s
4056	Mixing Bowl	New Kitchen Ware Plain	Small Size	1960s
4057	Egg Separator	New Kitchen Ware		1960s
4058	Lemon Squeezer	New Kitchen Ware		1960s
4059	Pepper & Salt	New Kitchen Ware		1960s

4060 GM	Vinegar Bottle	New Kitchen Ware		1960s
4061 RT	Spice Jar	New Kitchen Ware	3¼″	1960s
4062	Not used			
4063	Vase			1960s
4064	Vase			1960s
4065	Mug Tea Taster			1960s
4066 RT	Ashtray		Small Size	1960s
4067 RT	Coffee pot	Plain		1960s
4068	Vase	Acorn with squirrel handle, no snip Old Number 1959	8½″h	1960s–1982
4069	Vase	Stork handle Old Number 1960, no snip	10″h	1960s–1982
4070	Vase	Rabbit handle Old Number 1978 no snip	8½″	1960s–70s
4071 RT	Egg cup	Double	Small Size	1960s
4072 RT	Lemon Squeeze/coffee strainer			1960s
4073 GM	Beaker	Plain		1960s
4074 RT/GM	Preserve Jar	Plain		1960s
4075 RT/GM	Preserve Jar	Totem Range		1960s
4076 RT	Coffee Pot			1960s
4077	Manx Cat	Shrink 3960	Small Size	1960s
4078 GM	Pot	Square Foot	Second Size	1960s
4079 GM	Pot	Urn Plain	Third Size	1960s
4080 GM	Pot	Urn Olympus Range	6¼″h	1960s–70s
4081 GM	Pot	Urn Olympus Range	7″h	1960s–70s
4082 RT	Coffee Percolator	(Mono)	Small Size	1960s
4083 GM	Pot	Square Foot Plain	First Size	1960s
4084 GM	Pot	Urn Olympus Range	9½″h	1960s–70s
4085 GM	Bowl	Square Foot Plain		1960s
4086 GM	Bowl	Olympus Range	10¼″dia	1960s
4087 RT	Jug	(Mono) Coffee 4021		1960s
4088 RT	Sugar Bowl	(Mono) Coffee 4021		1960s
4089 RT	Cream	(Mono) Coffee without handle	3½″	1960s
4090 RD	Tankard	Fish		1960s
4091 GM	Vase	Plain	8″	1960s
4092 GM	Vase	Plain	10″	1960s
4093 GM	Vase	Olympus Range	8″h	1960s–70s
4094 RT	Lamp	Manhatten		1960s
4095	Cup and Saucer	Totem Range		1960s–70s
4096 GM	Vase	Plain	5″	1960s
4097 RT	Dog	King Charles Spaniel Sitting	4¾″h	1960s–S-i-P
4098 GM	Vase	Olympus Range	10″h	1960s–70s
4099 RT	Coffee Strainer	With handle		1960s
4100 GM	Vase	Plain	12″	1960s
4101 RT	Coffee Strainer	No handles		1960s
4102 RT	Coffee Strainer	Totem Range	5″dia	1960s–70s
4103 GM	Vase	Olympus Range	5″h	1960s–70s
4104 GM	Bowl on Stand	Plain Square Foot	7½″	1960s
4105 GM	Vase	Olympus Range	12″h	1960s–70s
4106 GM	Coffee Pot	Totem goes with 4102	6¼″h	1960s–70s
4107 GM	Bowl on Stand	Round Foot	7½″	1960s
4108 JR	Mug			1960s
4109 GM	Bowl on Round Stand	Embossed	7½″	1960s
4110 GM	Vase	Horseshoe	5″	1960s
4111 RT	Ashtray	Log		1960s
4112 GM	Lamp/Candlestick		8″	1960s
4113 GM	Dog	Great Dane	6″	1960s
4114 RT	Vase		8″	1960s
4115 GM	Bowl	Olympus Range	7″h	1960s–70s
4116 GM	Vase	Seaweed and Shells	8″	1960s
4117 RT	Vase	Floral Pattern	8″	1960s
4118 RT	Ashtray	Plain Square		1960s
4119 RT	Vase	Fruit Pattern	8″	1960s
4120 GM	Ashtray	Square	5½″	1960s
4121 RT	Vase	Cornflower	8″	1960s
4122 GM	Lamp/Bowl on Stand		Large Size	1960s
4123 GM	Bowl on Stand	Plain	Small Size	1960s
4124 GM	Jug	Plain, Square		1960s
4125 GM	Ashtray	With Golf Ball	5½″dia	1960s–1982

4126 RT	Vase	Embossed	8″	1960s
4127 GM	Vase	Sycamore Range	6″h	1960s–70s
4128 GM	Vase	Sycamore Range	6½″	1960s
4129 GM	Bowl	Sycamore Range	8½″dia	1960s–70s
4130 GM	Bowl	Olympus Range	4″h	1960s–70s
4131 GM	Bowl	Olympus Range	5″h	1960s–70s
4132 GM	Fern Pot	Hyacinth Range	7″dia	1960s–82
4133 GM	Storage Jar			1960s
4134 GM	Teapot	Plain for Totem		1960s
4135 GM	Teapot	Plain		1960s
4136 RT	Ashtray	Square. Briar		1960s
4137 GM	Cup/Mixing Bowl			1960s
4138 RT	Vase	Plain	6″	1960s
4139 GM	Spice Jar/Honey Pot			1960s
4140 GM	Teapot	Totem Range Two/three cup	5″h	1960s–70s
4141	Saucer	Totem Range to 4095 cup		1960s–70
4142 GM	Breakfast Cup			1960s–70s
4143 GM	Storage Jar	Totem Range	7″h	1960s–70s
4144 GM	Teapot	Totem Range 6/8 Cups	6½″	1960s–70s
4145 GM	Ashtray	Totem Range	4″	1960s
4146 GM	Mixing Bowl	Totem Range	8½″l	1960s–70s
4147 GM	Mixing Bowl	Totem Range	11½″l	1960s–70s
4148 GM	Spice Jar	Totem Range	3¾″h	1960s–70s
4149 GM	Cheese Dish	Totem Range	8¼″l	1960s–70s
4150 GM	Storage Jar	Totem Range	8″h	1960s–70s
4151 GM	Egg Separator	Totem Range	3½″h	1960s–70s
4152 RT	Vase	Marina Range (Shells)	8″h	1960s–70s
4153 RT	Fern Pot	Marina Range	7″dia	1960s–70s
4154 RT	Tray	Marina Range	6½″l	1960s–70s
4155 RT	Fern Pot	Marina Range	4½″h	1960s–70s
4156 RT	Fern Pot	Marina Range	5½″h	1960s–70s
4157 RT	Vase	Marina Range	6¼″h	1960s–70s
4158 RT	Posy	Marina Range	8″l	1960s–70s
4159 RT	Flower Holder	Marina Range	8½″dia	1960s–70s
4160 RT	Jardiniere	Marina Range	10½″l	1960s–70s
4161 RT	Bowl	Marina Range	6½″l	1960s–70s
4162 RT	Jardiniere	Marina Range	7″l	1960s–70s
4163 RT	Vase	Marina Range	5″h	1960s–70s
4164 RT	Vase	Flora Range	8″	1960s–70s
4165 RT	Vase	Flora Range	6″h	1960s–70s
4166 RT	Jardiniere	Flora Range	9¼″l	1960s–70s
4167 RT	Posy Ring	Flora Range	6″	1960s
4168 RT	Jardiniere	Flora Range	2½″l	1960s–70s
4169 RT	Fern Pot	Flora Range	5½″h	1960s–70s
4170 RT	Fern Pot	Flora Range	4¾″h	1960s–70s
4171 RT	Bowl	Flora Range	6½″l	1960s–70s
4172 RT	Posy	Flora Range	8″l	1960s–70s
4173 RT	Bowl	Flora Range	4½″dia	1960s–70s
4174 RT	Vase	Flora Range	10″h	1960s–70s
4175 RT	Bowl	Flora Range	9¼″dia	1960s–70s
4176 GM	Sugar Shaker	Totem Range	5½″h	1960s–70s
4177 GM	Sauce boat/stand	Totem Range	9″l	1960s–70s
4178 RT	Posy	Marina Range (Shells)	5¼″l	1960s–70s
4179 GM	Jug	Totem Range	6¼″h	1960s–70s
4180 RT	Coffee Perculator	Incised		1960s–70s
4181	Jardiniere			1960s
4182 GM	Four Egg Cups and stand	Lime-grove	6½″dia	1960s–1982
4183 RT	Tankard	Half-Pint Plain		1960s
4184 RT	Jar	Hound Head		1960s
4185 RT	Sugar Bowl	As 1140. Ireland	2½″h	1960s–70s
4186 RT	Cream	As 1134. Ireland	2½″h	1960s–70s
4187 RT	Sugar Bowl	As 1135. Ireland	Large Size	1960s–70s
4188 RT	Money box	Pig. As 1132 Ireland		1960s–70s
4189 RT	Beaker	Plain		1960s–70s
4190 RT	Coffee Perculator	Basket Pattern		1960s
4191 RT	Beaker	Country Scenes		1960s
4192 RT	Tankard	Leather		1960s
4193 GM	Sauce Boat/Stand	Totem Range	7¾″l	1960s–70s

4194 RT	Coffee Perculator	Basket Pattern	Large Size	1960s–70s
4195	Tray round	Aurora Range	6½"dia	1960s–70s
4196	Tray triangle	Aurora Range	6½"dia	1960s–70s
4197	Tray Square	Aurora Range	6½"dia	1960s–70s
4198	Tray Oblong	Aurora Range & Evening Fantasy	7"l	1960s–1982
4199 RT	Vase	223 Shape Crazy Paving	8½"	1960s
4200	Tankard	Pewter Plain		1960s
4201	Pot	Marina Range	4"	1960s–70s
4202 GM	Coffee Pot	Totem Range Straight Spout	10¾"h	1960s–70s
4203 RT	Vase	Plain		1960s
4204	Fern Pot	Marina Range	5"h	1960s–70s
4205 GM	Bowl	Sycamore Range	6½"l	1960s–70s
4206 GM	Vase	Sycamore Range	8"	1960s–70s
4207 GM	Jardiniere	Sycamore Range	7¼"l	1960s–70s
4208 GM	Vase	Sycamore Range	10"h	1960s–70s
4209 GM	Jardiniere	Sycamore Range	11"l	1960s–70s
4210 GM	Bowl	Sycamore Range	5"dia	1960s–70s
4211 GM	Fern Pot	Sycamore Range	5½"dia	1960s–70s
4212 GM	Fern Pot	Sycamore Range	6¼"dia	1960s–70s
4213 GM	Posy Trough	Sycamore Range	7¾"l	1960s–70s
4214 GM	Bowl	Sycamore Range	6"dia	1960s–70s
4215 RT	Vase	Sycamore Range	6"h	1960s–70s
4216	Sugar Bowl			1960s
4217	Pot stand	To 4265 Pot		1960s
4218 GM	Covered Bowl	Agincourt Range	4¼"h	1960s–1982
4219	Not used			
4220	Storage Jar	Totem Range	6½"h	1960s–70s
4221 RT/GM	Plate	Totem Range	10"	1960s–70s
4222 RT/GM	Plate	Totem Range	8"	1960s–70s
4223 RT/GM	Plate	Totem Range	5"	1960s–70s
4224	Tea Pot	Totem Range 4/5 Cup	5¾"h	1960s–70s
4225	Lemon Squeezer	Totem Range	5¾"dia	1960s–70s
4226	Flower Holder	Horseshoe Wales	5"h	1960s
4227	Flower holder	Horseshoe Scotland	5"h	1960s
4228	Flower holder	Horseshoe Devon	5"h	1960s
4229	Flower holder	Horseshoe Cornwall	5"h	1960s
4230	Flower holder	Horseshoe Somerset	5"h	1960s
4231 RT	Posy Trough	With deer. Woodland Range	4¼"l	1960s–82
4232 RT	Jardiniere	Embossed Whirl Pattern		1960s
4233 RT	Vase	With Squirrel. Woodland Range	4½"h	1960s–82
4234 RT	Rabbit			1960s
4235 RT	Coffee Pot.	Totem Range		1960s
4236 RT	Flower Holder	Horseshoe Cheddar	5"	1960s
4237 RT/GM	Coffee Perculator	Totem Range	8¾"h	1960s–70s
4238 RT	Coffee Perculator	Plain		1960s
4239 RT	Vase with deer.	Woodland Range.	2¼"h	1960s–70s
4240 RT	Basket with deer.	Woodland Range	5½"l	1960s–82
4241 GM	Vase with squirrel.	Woodland Range	6"h	1960s–82
4242 RT	Vase with rabbit	Woodland Range.	9¼"h	1960s–82
4243 GM	Twin Vase with rabbit.	Woodland Range.	7"h	1960s–82
4244 RT	Tray	Aurora Range	7"l	1960s–70s
4245	Tankards. Age of Chivalry. Ass. Designs.		4½"h	1960s–70s
4246 GM	Ash Tray Horseshoe Re-numbered 5382		6"l	1960s–70s
4247 RT	Vase/Lining		7"	1960s
4248 RT	Lining			1960s
4249 RT	Sweet Tray.	With animal		1960s
4250 RT	Squirrel			1960s
4251 RT	Dog	Corgi	3"	1960s
4252 RT	Dog	Spaniel	3"	1960s
4253 GM	Tankard	Pewter Coloured	3¾"h	1960s–70s
4254 GM	Tankard	Assorted decorations	4¾"h	1960s–82
4255 GM	Tankard	Pewter Col. Agincourt Range	5½"h	1968–82
4256 RT	Beaker			1960s
4257 RT	Beaker			1960s
4258 GM	Vase			1960s
4259 GM	Jug covered.	Pewter Col.Agincourt Range	10¼"h	1960s–82
4260	Mug Coffee.	Embossed		1960s
4261 RT	Lining		5"	1960s

4262 RT	Honey Pot	Pixie		1960s
4263 RT	Vase	Plain	8″	1960s
4264 RT	Vase	Autumn Chinz Range	6″h	1960s–70s
4265 RT	Fern Pot	Autumn Chinz Range	4¾″h	1960s–82
4266 RT	Vase	Oak Leaves	8″	1960s
4267 RT	Tankard	Pewter Coloured	6¼″h	1960s–70s
4268 RT	Tankard	Pewter Coloured	5″h	1960s–70s
4269 RT	Honey pot	Embossed		1960s
4270 RT	Tankard	Pewter Col. Agincourt Range	4⅜″h	1960s–82
4271 GM	Jug	Pewter Col. Agincourt Range	4¼″h	1960s–82
4272 RT	Jug	Pewter Col. Agincourt Range	6″h	1960s–70s
4273 GM	Tankard	Pewter Col. Agincourt Range	4¼″h	1960s–82
4274 GM	Tankard	Pewter Col. Agincourt Range	3½″h	1960s–70s
4275 GM	Tankard	Pewter Col. Agincourt Range	3″h	1960s–70s
4276 GM	Posy Bar			1960s
4277 GM	Jardiniere		11″	1960s
4278 GM	Bowl		Small Size	1960s
4279 GM	Pot		Large Size	1960s
4280 GM	Bowl		8″	1960s
4281 GM	Posy Bar		7″	1960s
4282 GM	Posy			1960s
4283	Mug	Plain		1960s
4284 GM	Vase Collon	No 1	Large Size	1960s
4285	Vase Collon	No 2	Small Size	1960s
4286	Vase York			1960s
4287	Fern Pot with deer	Woodland Range	4″h	1960s–82
4288 RT	Tray with deer	Woodland Range	6″l	1960s–70s
4289 RT	Bowl with squirrel	Woodland Range	7½″dia	1960s–82
4290	Twin Vase with deer	Woodland Range	3¼″h	1960s–82
4291	Fern Pot with squirrel	Woodland Range	5″h	1960s–70s
4292	Bowl with rabbit	Woodland Range	7½″l	1960s–82
4293	Ashtray with deer	Woodland Range	4¼″l	1960s–82
4294 GM	Bowl	Plain Oval	8″	1960s
4295 GM	Tankard	Pewter Col.	5″	1960s–70s
4296 GM	Tankard	Pewter Col	2½″h	1960s–70s
4297 RT	Flower Holder.	Horseshoe Ireland	5″h	1960s
4298	Pot		Small Size	1960s
4299	Vase	Harmony Range	8″h	1960s–70s
4300	Posy Trough	Harmony Range	7½″l	1960s–70s
4301	Vase	Harmony Range	10″h	1960s–70s
4302	Fern Pot	Harmony Range	7″dia	1960s–70s
4303	Fern Pot	Harmony Range	6¼″dia	1960s–70s
4304	Vase	Harmony Range	10¼″h	1960s–70s
4305	Jardiniere	Harmony Range	8½″l	1960s–70s
4306	Vase	Harmony Range	6″h	1960s–70s
4307	Jardiniere	Harmony Range	10¾″l	1960s–70s
4308	Bowl	Harmony Range	9½″l	1960s–70s
4309	Fern Pot	Harmony Range	7½″dia	1960s–70s
4310	Bowl	Harmony Range	6¼″l	1960s–70s
4311 GM	Tankard	Pewter Col. Agincourt Range	6″h	1960s–82
4312 RT	Honey Pot	Plain		1960s
4313	Mug	Plain Totem Shape		1960s
4314 RT	Honey Pot	Embossed		1960s
4315 GM	Pepper & Salt	Plain Pewter Col	5½″h	1960s–70s
4315 GM	Mustard Pot	Plain Pewter Col	2½″dia	1960s–70s
4316 RT	Ashtray	Horseshoe Ireland	6″l	1960s–82
4317 GM	Tankard	Pewter Cols. Agincourt Range	4¼″h	1960s–1982
4318 GM	Tankard	Agincourt Range	5⅛″h	1960s–1982
4319 RT	Vase	Aurora Range	8″h	1960s–70s
4320–2 RT	Vases		8″	1960s–70s
4323 GM	Fern Pot	Aurora Range	5″h	1960s–70s
4324 GM	Fern Pot	Aurora Range	5½″h	1960s–70s
4325 GM	Fern Pot	Aurora Range	6″h	1960s–70s
4326 GM	Fern Pot	Appolo Range	7½″h	1960s–70s
4327 GM	Vase	Aurora Range	6″h	1960s–70s
4328 GM	Vase	Aurora Range	10″h	1960s–70s
4329 GM	Vase	Aurora Range	4″h	1960s–70s

4330 GM	Jardiniere	Aurora Range	11″	1960s–70s
4331 GM	Jardiniere	Aurora Range	7½″l	1960s–70s
4332 GM	Bowl	Appolo Range	6½″l	1960s–70s
4333 RT	Coffee Perculator			1960s
4334 RT	Pot	Manhatten Shape		1960s
4335 RT	Tray Shell		6″	1960s
4336 GM	Bowl	Harmony Range	4¼″dia	1960s–70s
4337 GM	Tray	Oval		1960s–70s
4338 GM	Fern Pot	Harmony Range	5″dia	1960s–70s
4339 RT	Coffee Beaker	Embossed	3¾″h	1960s–82
4340	Vase	Harmony Range	8¼″h	1960s–70s
4341	Not used			
4342 RT	Coffee Beaker	Embossed	3¾″h	1960s–82
4343 RT	Coffee Beaker	Embossed	3½″h	1960s–82
4344 RT	Coffee Beaker	Plain		1960s–70s
4345 GM	Bowl	Appolo Range	9½″l	1960s–70s
4346 GM	Vase	Embossed Plain shape		1960s–70s
4347 GM	Jardiniere			1960s–70s
4348 RT	Coffee Beaker	Embossed	3¾″h	1960s–82
4349 GM	Pot	Olympus M/s 4081		1960s–70s
4350 GM	Pot	Olympus S/s 4081		1960s–70s
4351 GM	Pot	Olympus L/s 4081		1960s–70s
4352 GM	Tankard	Plain		1960s–70s
4353	Not used			
4354 RT	Tray Shell	Three feet	Small Size	1960s–70s
4355 RT	Ash tray Horseshoe. Horse head		6″l	1960s–70s
4356/7 GM	Plates Oval	Totem Range		1960s–70s
4358 RT	Honey pot.	Plain. No lid		1960s–70s
4359 RT	Tray	Plain Shell	6″	1960s–70s
4360 GM	Money box	Pig		1960s–70s
4361 GM	Re-numbered to 5106 (Owl Money Box)			
4362 GM	Tankard	Starway pattern	3¾″h	1960s–70s
4363 GM	Pot	Plain	Large Size	1960s–70s
4364–6 GM	Vases	Plain	6″	1969–70s
4367 GM	Vase		8″	1960s–70s
4368 GM	Jug	Pewter colour		1960s–70s
4369 RT	Lining ¼″pint			1960s–70s
4370 GM	Coffee Pot	Plain		1960s–70s
4371 GM	Jardiniere	Evening Fantasy Range	9½″l	1960s–70s
4372 GM	Cup	Changed to 4508		
4373 GM	Vase	Plain		1960s–70s
4374 RT	Vase	Embossed		1960s–70s
4375 GM	Vase	Riverside Range. With swan	8″H	1960s–82
4376 RT	Pot			1960s
4377 GM	Vase	Riverside Range. With swan	6″h	1960s–82
4378 GM	Coffee pot.	Starway pattern	10½″h	1960s–70s
4379 GM	Jardiniere	Evening Fantasy Range	9½″l	1960s–70s
4380 GM	Pot	Plain	Large Size	1960s–70s
4381 GM	Ash tray	Round	6″	1960s–70s
4382 GM	Sugar Bowl			1960s–70s
4383 RT	Cigarette Box		4½″x3″	1960s–70s
4384	Cream Jug	Starway Pattern	4″h	1960s–70s
4385 RT	Vase	Riverside Range. With swan	4″h	1960s–82
4386	Beaker.	Given new number 4508		
4387 RT	Novelty Tankard. Fish Head.		6″h	1960s–70s
4388	Ashtray. Square. Evening Fantasy Range		4¾″ dia	1960s–70s
4389 RT	Tobacco Jar			1960s–70s
4390 GM	Sugar Bowl	Starway Pattern	4″dia	1960s–70s
4391/2	Not used			
4393	Vase.	Riverside Range. With swan.	3⅜″h	1960s–82
4394 RT	Bowl.	Riverside Range. With swan.	7⅝″l	1960s–82
4395 RT	Candlestick	Riverside Range. With swan.	2¾″h	1960s–70s
4396	Candlestick	Hollyberry Range	4¼″dia	1960s–70s
4397 RT	Ashtray	Square	4″	1960s–70s
4398	Tray	Hollyberry Range	8″l	1960s–70s
4399	Tray	Hollyberry Range	6″l	1960s–70s
4400 OM	Toby Jug	Mine Host		1960s–70s
4401 OM	Toby Jug	New Toby	7¼″h	1960s-S-i-P
4402 OM	Toby Jug	New Toby	5¼″h	,,

4403 OM	Toby Jug	New Toby	3¾"h	1960s-S-I-P
4404 OM	Toby Jug	Old Toby	8"h	,,
4405 OM	Toby Jug	Old Toby	4"h	,,
4406 OM	Toby Jug	Old Toby	3"h	,,
4407 OM	Character Jug	Coachman	5½"h	,,
4408 OM	Character Jug	Coachman	4"h	1960s–1975
4409 OM	Character Jug	Auld Mac	4½"h	1960s-S-i-P
4410 OM	Character Jug	Auld Mac	2½"h	1960s–1975
4411 OM	Character Jug	Squire	4"h	1960s-S-i-P
4412 OM	Character Jug	Squire	2½"h	1960s–1975
4413 OM	Character Jug	Jolly Roger	Medium Size	1960s–70s
4414 OM	Character Jug	Jolly Roger	Small Size	1960s–70s
4415 OM	Character Jug	Gaffer	3¾"h	1960s-S-i-P
4416 OM	Character Jug	Gaffer	2½"h	,,
4417 OM	Character Jug	Fisherman.Not seen until the 1980 Catalogue	2¼"h	S-i-P
4418 OM	Character Jug	Nellie	Small Size	1960s
4419 OM	Character Jug	James	Small Size	1960s
4420 OM	Character Jug	Colonel	3¼"h	1960s-S-i-P
4421 OM	Character Jug	Silas Sly	3¼"h	1960s–1975
4422 OM	Character Jug	King Neptune	4¼"h	1960s–1975
4423 OM	Character Jug	King Neptune	3¼"h	1960s-S-i-P
4424 OM	Character Jug	King Neptune	2"h	1960s–1975
4425 OM	Character Jug	King Neptune	Extra Large Size	1960s
4426 OM	Character Jug	Santa Claus. Seen only in the Crown Winsor Catalogue Ex/L/s		S-i-P
4427 OM	Character Jug	Santa Claus Seen only in the Crown Winsor Catalogue Ex/L/s		S-i-P
4428 OM	Character Jug	Santa Claus Medium Size	3¼"h	1960s-S-i-P
4429 OM	Character Jug	Santa Claus	Small Size	1960s
4430 OM	Character Jug	Mr. Pickwick	Extra Large Size	1960s
4431 OM	Character Jug	Mr. Pickwick	4¼"h	1960s-S-i-P
4432 OM	Character Jug	Mr. Pickwick	3¼"h	,,
4433 OM	Character Jug	Mr. Pickwick	2"h	,,
4434 OM	Character Jug	Tony Weller	Extra Large Size	1960s
4435 OM	Character Jug	Tony Weller	4½"h	1960s–1975
4436 OM	Character Jug	Tony Weller	3¼"h	1960s-S-i-P
4437 OM	Character Jug	Tony Weller	2¼"h	1960s–1975
4438 OM	Character Jug	Sam Weller	Extra Large Size	1960s
4439 OM	Character Jug	Sam Weller	4¼"h	1960s–1975
4440 OM	Character Jug	Sam Weller	3¼"h	1960s-S-i-P
4441 OM	Character Jug	Sam Weller	2"h	1960s–1975
4442 OM	Character Jug	Mrs. Bardell	Extra Large Size	1960s
4443 OM	Character Jug	Mrs. Bardell	Large Size	1960s
4444 OM	Character Jug	Mrs. Bardell	Medium Size	1960s
4445 OM	Character Jug	Mrs. Bardell	Small Size	1960s
4446 OM	Character Jug	Mr. Winkle	Extra Large Size	1960s
4447 OM	Character Jug	Mr. Winkle	4½"h	1960s–1975
4448 OM	Character Jug	Mr. Winkle	3¼"h	1960s-S-i-P
4449 OM	Character Jug	Mr. Winkle	2¼"h	1960s–75
4450 OM	Character Jug	Watchman	4½"h	1960s–75
4451 OM	Character Jug	Watchman	3½"h	1960s–75
4452 OM	Character Jug	Watchman	2¼"h	1960s-S-i-P
4453 OM	Character Jug	Cavalier	Medium Size	1960s
4454 OM	Character Jug	Cavalier	Small Size	1960s
4455 OM	Character Jug	George	Medium Size	1960s
4456 OM	Character Jug	George	Small Size	1960s
4457 OM	Character Jug	Simon	3¾"h	1960s–75
4458 OM	Character Jug	Simon	2½"h	1960s–75
4459 OM	Character Jug	Mr. Wolfe	3½"h	1960s-S-i-P
4460 OM	Character Jug	Mr. Wolfe	2¼"h	1960s-S-i-P
4461 OM	Character Jug	Mandolin Player	Large Size	1960s
4462 OM	Character Jug	Mandolin Player	8"h	1960s-S-i-P
4463 OM	Character Jug	Mandolin Player	Small Size	1960s
4464 OM	Character Jug	Louis	Small Size	1960s
4465 OM	Character Jug	Madam Marie Pompador		1960s
4466 OM	Character Jug	Charles	2¾"h	1960s-S-i-P
4467 OM	Character Jug	Cabby	2¾"h	1960s-S-i-P
4468 OM	Character Jug	Milady	Medium Size	1960s

4469 OM	Character Jug	Muskateer	5⅞"h	1980s-S-i-P
4470 OM	Character Jug	Ann Hathaway	5¼"h	1960s–75
4471 OM	Character Jug	Ann Hathaway	3¼"h	1960s-S-i-P
4472 OM	Character Jug	Ann Hathaway	Small Size	1960s
4473 OM	Character Jug	William Shakespeare	4¾"h	1960s–75
4474 OM	Character Jug	William Shakespeare	3"h	1960s-S-i-P
4475 OM	Character Jug	William Shakespeare	S/s	1960s
4476 GM	Character Jug	Churchill-Re-modelled	4¼"h	1980s-S-i-P
4477 OM	Character Jug	Welsh Lady	3"h	1960s-S-i-P
4478 OM	Character Jug	Shylock	6½"h	1960s-S-i-P
4479 OM	Character Jug	Falstaff	6¼"h	1960s-S-i-P
4480 OM	Character Jug	Touchstone	Large Size	1960s
4481 OM	Character Jug	Romeo	Large Size	1960s
4482 OM	Character Jug	Juliet	Large Size	1960s
4483 OM	Character Jug	Irish Leprachaun	Medium Size	1960s
4484 OM	Character Jug	Duffy the Pixie	Medium Size	1960s
4485 OM	Character Jug	Hamlet		1960s
4486 RT	Character Jug	Dick Turpin	4¾"h	1960s–75
		Also seen in 1950s Catalogue un-numbered		
4487 RT	Character Jug	Cavalier	4¾"h	1960s-S-i-P
		Old number 306 (1950s)		
4488 RT	Character Jug	Henry VIII	4"h	1960s-S-i-P
		Also seen in 1950s Catalogue un-numbered		
4489 RT	Character Jug	Yeoman of the Guard	4¼"h	1960s-S-i-P
		Also seen in 1950s Catalogue No. 312		
4490 RT	Character Jug	Life-Guard	5"h	1978-S-i-P
4491 RT	Character Jug	William Shakespeare	5"h	1960s-S-i-P
		Old Number 2815		
4492 RT	Character Jug	George Bernard Shaw	5½"h	1960s–75
		Old Number 3279		
4493 GM	Character Jug	Chelsea Pensioner	4¼"h	1978-S-i-P
4494 GM	Character Jug	Grenadier Guardsman	5"h	1978-S-i-P
4495 GM	Character Jug	Leprechaun	4½"h	1980-S-i-P
4496 GM	Character Jug	Fisherman	5"h	1980-S-i-P
4497 GM	Character Jug	Harrods Doorman (For Harrods only)		1981
4498/9	Not used			
4500 GM	Teapot			1969–70s
4501 GM	Beaker.Concorde	New number for 4386		1969–70s
4502 GM	Cruet			1969–70s
4503 GM	Sugar Bowl			1969–70s
4504 GM	Cream Jug			1969–70s
4505 GM	Butter Oblong			1969–70s
4506 GM	Cheese Dish			1969–70s
4507	Sandwich Tray			1969–70s
4508	Cup			1969–70s
4509 GM	Sandwich Tray	Oval	9"	1969–70s
4510 GM	Coffee Pot	1½ pints		1969–70s
4511	Plate	Oval		1969–70s
4512	Coffee Pot	2½ pint	Large Size	1969–70s
4513	Honey Pot			1969–70s
4514	Plate		8"	1969–70s
4515–20	Not used			
4521 RT	Pot Plain		Large Size	1969–70s
4522 RT	Teapot			1969–70s
4523	Vase	Rose Pattern	6"	1969–70s
4524 RT	Ashtray	Riverside Range. With swan	4½"dia	1969–1982
4525 GM	Cheese dish	With Cat and Mouse	6½"l	1969–1982
4526 RT	Fern Pot	Rhapsody Range	6½"dia	1969–1982
4527 RT	Ash tray		9¼"	1969–70s
4528 RT	Vase & stand to accommodate dog on front		8¾"h	1969–70s
4529 RT	Vase	Gossamer Range	7"h	1969–70s
4530	Honey pot	Hollyberry Range	4"h	1969–70s
4531 RT	Dolphin		8"	1969–70s
4532 RT	Vase			1969–70s
4533	Not used			
4534	Vase		10"	1969–70s
4535 RT	Vase	Privet Range	5"h	1969–1981
4536 RT	Fern Pot	Privet Range	4"h	1969–1981
4537 RT	Vase	Privet Range	4"h	1969–1981

4538 RT	Posy Bar	Privet Range	4″	1969–70s
4539 RT	Fern Pot	Privet Range	3¼″h	1969–1981
4540 RT	Vase	Privet Range	7⅛″h	1969–1981
4541 GM	Cow Cream Jug			1969–70s
4542 RT	Posy Vase		10″	1969–70s
4543 GM	Cow Butter Dish		8″	1969–70s
4544 RT	Bowl Triangle	Privet Range		1969–70s
4545	Vase	Spectrum Range	7¾″h	1969–70s
4546	Egg Cup Stand	Fox		1969–70s
4547 RT	Floating Bowl	Riverside Range with swan	10¼″dia	1969–70s
4548 RT	Vase	Plain	8″	1969–70s
4549 GM	Apple Sauce Bowl	With face	4¾″h	1969–1982
4550 RT	Vase	Plain Tristan	6″	1969–70s
4551 GM	Vase	Chintz Range	Medium Size	1969–70s
4551 GM	Bread Sauce Bowl	with face Number changed to 4557		
4552	Vase	Same as 4548	8″	1969–70s
4553 GM	Beetroot Bowl	With face	4¼″h	1969–1982
4554	Vase	Rhapsody Range	8¼″h	1969–1982
4555 RT	Jardiniere	Autumn Chintz	7″l	1969–1970s
4556	Vase	Autumn Chintz	10″h	1969–70s
4557	Bread Sauce Bowl	with face (Previously 4551)	4″h	1969–1982
4558	Vase	Autumn Chintz	6″h	1969–70s
4559	Jardiniere	Autumn Chintz	10⅛″l	1969–70s
4560	Posy Bar	Autumn Chintz	7⅝″l	1969–70s
4561 GM	Fern Pot	Gossamer Range	5½″dia	1969–70s
4562	Pot	Tristan		1969–70s
4563	Vase	Tristan	8″	1969–70s
4564	Vase	Tristan		1969–70s
4565 GM	Cucumber Bowl	With face	6″h	1969–1982
4566 RT	Novelty Tankard	Fish head as 4387	5⅛″h	1969–70s
4567 RT	Novelty Tankard	Fish head as 4387	4⅜″h	1969–70s
4568	Vase	Evening Fantasy	8″h	1969–70s
4569	Urn	Evening Fantasy	6¼″h	1969–70s
4570 GM	Novelty Tankard	Skull	4″h	1969–1982
4571 RW	Perculator			1969–70s
4572 GM	Sauce Boat/Stand	Pisces Range	7¾″l	1969–1982
4573 TR	Vase	Assyria Range	8″h	1969–70s
4574 GM	Novelty Tankard	Drinking Horn	5⅝″h	1969–1982
4575	Bowl	Autumn Chintz	4¾″h	1969–70s
4576	Cheese dish	Hollyberry Range	7¼″l	1969–70s
4577	Cruet-Four Pieces	Hollyberry Range	6¾″l	1969–70s
4578	Not used			
4579	Posy	Hollyberry Range	6¾″l	1969–70s
4580	Posy (Ring)	Hollyberry Range	7″dia	1969–70s
4581 RT	Vase	Tristan	10″	1969–70s
4582	Candlestick-to fit	4580-Hollyberry Range	3″dia	1969–70s
4583 GM	Bowl	Tristan		1969–70s
4584 GM	Novelty Tankard	Riding Boot	5¾″h	1969–70s
4585 GM	Cruet Duck			1969–70s
4586 RT	Vase	Tristan		1969–70s
4587 GM	Hot Milk Jug	Starway Range	5¾″h	1969–70s
4588 RT	Vase	Tristan	6″	1969–70s
4589	Cheese Dish	Cow		1969–70s
4590	Bowl	Tristan	5″dia	196970s
4591	Bowl	Tristan Oval	6″	1969–70s
4592	Vase		6″	1969–70s
4593 GM	Jardiniere	Tristan	Large Size	1969–70s
4594	Vase	Gossamer Range	9″h	1969–70s
4595	Jardiniere	Tristan	Small Size	1969–70s
4596	Fern Pot	Gossamer Range	6¼″dia	1969–70s
4597 GM	Jardiniere	Tristan	Large Size	1969–70s
4598 GM	Posy Bar	Tristan		1969–70s
4599	Vase	Gossamer Range	5″h	1969–70s
4600 GM	Butter Dish	Round Barrel (cow?)		1970s
4601	Pot	Hoop.2 Handles.6 Feet.		1970s
4602 RT	Vase			1970s
4603 RT	Jardiniere	Gossamer Range	9½″l	1970s
4604 RT	Bowl	Gossamer Range	4″dia	1970s
4605 RT	Posy Trough	Gossamer Range	7″l	1970s

4606 RT	Jardiniere	Gossamer Range	6"l	1970s
4607 GM	Jardiniere	Plain	10"	1970s
4608	Vase	Rhapsody Range	6"h	1970s
4609 GM	Jardiniere		Small Size	1970s
4610 GM	Vase	Plain	10"	1970s
4611 GM	Bowl	Plain	9"	1970s
4612 GM	Fern Pot	Rhapsody Range	5¾"dia	1970–1982
4613 RT	Fern Pot	Rhapsody Range	8¾"dia	1970–1982
4614 RT	Jardiniere	Rhapsody Range	10¾"l	1970–1982
4615 RT	Jardiniere	Rhapsody Range	7"l	1970–1982
4616 RT	Bowl/cover	Fish		1970s
4617 GM	Vase	Plain	10"	1970s
4618 GM	Vase		6"	1970s
4619 GM	Vase	Plain	8"	1970s
4620 RT	Bowl	Rhapsody Range	9"dia	1970–1982
4621	Tankard	Plain 4342 Shape		1970s
4622	Tankard	Hound Head		1970s
4623	Tankard	Fox Head		1970s
4624	Tankard	Horse Head		1970s
4625	Vase	Plain	6"	1970s
4626 GM	Vase		8"	1970s
4627 GM	Lochness Monster	Souvenir of Scotland		1970s
4628 GM	Drinking Horn		8"	1970s
4629	Vase	Hollyberry Range	6"h	1970s
4630 GM	Vase	Plain	6"	1970s
4631 GM	Vase	Spectrum Range	6"h	1970s
4632 GM	Boot	Riding Boot one pint size		1970s
4633	Beaker	Hollyberry Range	3½"h	1970s
4634	Tray	Hollyberry Range	9½"l	1970s
4635 GM	Bowl (Low Foot)	Spectrum Range		1970s
4636 GM	Vase	Spectrum Range	10"	1970s
4637 GM	Fern Pot	Spectrum Range	6"dia	1970s
4638 RT	Vase	Rhapsody Range	10"h	1970–1982
4639 RT	Bowl	Rhapsody Range	9"dia	1970s
4640 GM	Pot	Spectrum Range	Medium Size	1970s
4641 RT	Bowl	Rhapsody Range	5¼"dia	1970–1982
4642 GM	Posy Bar	Spectrum Range	7¾"l	1970s
4643 GM	Jardiniere	Spectrum Range	6½"l	1970s
4644 GM	Fern Pot	Spectrum Range	3½"dia	1970s
4645 RT	Bowl	Rhapsody Range	9½"l	1970–1982
4646	Jardiniere	Hollyberry Range	7½"l	1970s
4647 GM	Bowl	Spectrum Range	5½"dia	1970s
4648 GM	Jardiniere	Hollyberry Range	10"l	1970s
4649 GM	Comport	Spectrum Range	8¾"dia	1970s
4650 RT	Badger		4"	1970s
4651 GM	Vase	Spectrum Range	4¾"h	1970s
4652 GM	Bowl	Spectrum Range	7¼"dia	1970s
4653 GM	Bowl	Spectrum Range		1970s
4654–9 GM	Vases	Plain	6"	1970s
4660 GM	Jardiniere		Small Size	1970s
4661 GM	Vase		8"	1970s
4662 GM	Vase		10"	1970s
4663 GM	Vase		8"	1970s
4664	Vase	Hoop.2 Handles.6 Feet		1970s
4665 RT	Bowl	Rhapsody Range	4½"dia	1970–1982
4666 RT	Bowl 2 Handles	Rhapsody Range	5"h	1970–1982
4667 RT	Flower Holder		6"	1970s
4668 GM	Cup	Starway Range	3"h	1970s
4669 GM	Cruet (Two piece)	Pisces Range	3½"h	1970s–1982
4670	Bowl	Round. Plain. With foot	3¼"	1970s
4671 RT	Posy Ring		6½"dia	1970s
4672 RT	Horseshoe Posy		6½"dia	1970s
4673 RT	Posy Bar		4½"	1970s
4674	Posy Bar		6¾"l	1970s
4675 RT	Posy Bar		8¾"l	1970s
4676 RT	Posy Bar		13¼"l	1970s
4677 RT	Posy tray		7¾"l	1970s
4678	Fern Pot	Assyria Range	7"dia	1970s
4679–81	Not used			

150

4682 RD	Mug	Owl Embossed		1970s
4683 GM	Sauce boat & Stand. Mint		5½"l	1970–1982
4684 GM	Fish Plate Round	Pisces Range	9½"dia	1970–1982
4685 GM	Fish Plate Oval	Pisces Range	12½"l	1970–1882
4686 GM	Saucer	Starway Range	5½"dia	1970s
4687/8	Not used			
4689 GM	Vase		8"	1970s
4690 GM	Plate	Assyria Range	12¼"dia	1970s
4691 GM	Bowl-Oval-Barrel	Two handles		1970s
4692 GM	Vase		6½"	1970s
4693 GM	Vase	Assyria Range	6¼"h	1970s
4694/5 GM	Vases	Plain	6½"	1970s
4696 GM	Pot	Plain-Three feet		1970s
4697 GM	Pot	Stag Fighters. Three feet.		1970s
4698 GM	Bowl	On Foot		1970s
4699 GM	Bowl Two Handles	Assyria Range	5½"dia	1970s
4700 GM	Honey Pot	Plain		1970s
4701 GM	Vase		7"	1970s
4702 GM	Vase	Etruscan Range. Three feet.	8"h	1970s-S-i-P
4703 GM	Tray/Saucer	Leaf		1970s
4704 GM	Vase	Plain		1970s
4705	Fish Plate	Pisces Range	5"dia	1970s–1982
4706 GM	Fish Plate	Pisces Range	6¾"dia	1970s–1982
4707 RT	Horse & Rider	Previously Falcon Ware No 21.	9"l	1970s
4708 RT	Pony & Rider	Re-numbered from Falcon Ware.	5¾"l	1970s
4709 RT	Hound lying down.	Goes with 4707	4"l	1970s
4710 RT	Hound on scent.	Goes with 4707	3½"l	1970s
4711 RT	Hound standing.	Goes with 4707	4"l	1970s
4712 GM	Honey Pot	Golf Ball	3½"a	1970s
4713 GM	Honey Pot	Football	3½"a	1970s
4714 GM	Honey Pot	Cricket Ball	3½"a	1970s
4715 GM	Honey Pot	Rugby Ball	4¾"h	1970s
4716 GM	Honey Pot	Tennis Ball		1970s
4717	Hockey			1970s
4718	Honey Pot	Bowls		1970s
4719 GM	Tankard	Golf Ball	3¾"h	1970–1982
4720 GM	Tankard	Cricket Ball	3¾"h	1970s
4721 GM	Tankard	Football	3¾"h	1970s
4722 GM	Tankard	Rugby Ball	4½"h	1970s
4723 GM	Tankard	Tennis Ball	3¾"h	1970s
4724 GM	Tankard	Hockey Ball	3¾"h	1970s
4725 GM	Tankard	Bowls	3¾"h	1970s
4726 RT	Tankard	Sailing	4"h	1970s
4727 GM	Tankard	Fishing	3¾"h	1970s
4728 GM	Tankard	Football	3¾"h	1970s
4729/30	Not used			
4731	Bowl On Foot			1970s
4732	Bison Standing		8"l	1970s
4733	Buffalo Standing		9½"l	1970s
4734	Honey Pot	Barrel-Six Feet		1970s
4735	Tankard			1970s
4736	Tankard	Scottish (Thistle)		1970s
4737–43	Not used			
4744 RT	Jug	Ash Leaf	4"h	1970s
4745 RT	Jug	Horsechestnut leaf	4"h	1970s
4746 RT	Jug	Leaf	4"h	1970s
4747 RT	Jug	Acorn leaf	4"h	1970s
4748/9	Not used			
4750 GM	Coleslaw bowl	With face	4¾"h	1970–1982
4751 GM	Tomato Sauce bowl.	With face	4¾"h	1970s
4752 GM	Piccalilli Sauce bowl.	With face	5"h	1970–1982
4753 GM	Chutney bowl	With face	5"h	1970–1982
4754 GM	Parsley Sauce bowl	With face	4¾"h	1970–1982
4755 GM	Pickled Cabbage bowl.	With face	5¼"h	1970–1982
4756	Onion Bowl	With face L/s 516	4¾"h	1970–1982

4757	Pot	Hoop. Six feet. 2nd Size		1970s
4758 GM	Bottle 10″			1970s
4759	Mint Sauce Jug			1970s
4760 GM	Egg Separater	Humpty Dumpty	4½″h	1970s
4761	Bowl Hoop		5″dia	1970s
4762	Bowl Hoop Oval		7″l	1970s
4763/4	Pots	Hoop-2 handles-six feet		1970s
4765 GM	Stand		3¾″dia	1970s
4766 RT	Gnome		Large Size	1970s
4767 GM	Spirit Measure/Whisky Tot for leather range			1970s
4768 GM	Sweet tray	Scottish		1970s
4769 RT	Gnome	(New for 707)	Small Size	1970s
4770 GM	Candlestick	Chrys		1970s
4771 GM	Ice Jug	Without handle		1970s
4772 GM	Vase	Etruscan Range	6″h	1971-S-i-P
4773 GM	Vase	Etruscan Range	5″h	1971-S-i-P
4774 GM	Bowl	Etruscan Range	4″h	1971-S-i-P
4775	Vase		4″	1970s
4776 GM	Fern Pot	Etruscan Range	5½″dia	1971-S-i-P
4777 GM	Fern Pot	Etruscan Range	4½″dia	1971-S-i-P
4778	Fern Pot	Etruscan Range	6½″dia	1971-S-i-P
4779 GM	Bowl	Low	10″	1970s
4780	Bowl	Etruscan Range	6″	1971-S-i-P
4781	Bowl	Etruscan Range	7½″dia	1970s
4782	Bowl	On stand	Small Size	1970s
4783 GM	Miniature bowl on stand		2½″h	1971–1982
4784 GM	Miniature Vase	Rhapsody Range	2¾″h	1971–1982
4785 GM	Miniature Jug/vase		3″h	1971–1982
4786 GM	Miniature Vase		3″h	1971–1982
4787 GM	Miniature Vase		3″h	1971–1982
4788 GM	Miniature Jug.	Small size 3834	3″h	1970s
4789 GM	Vase	House in the Glen Range with Pixie or Rabbit	8″h	1970s
4790 GM	Twin Vase	House in the Glen Range with Pixie or Rabbit	7″h	1970s
4791 GM	Vase	House in the Glen Range with Pixie or Rabbit	6″h	1970s
4792	Moustache cup, with handle			1970s
4793	Coffee Pot	Starway Range		1970s
4794	Moustache cup, no handle			1970s
4795	Ice Jug with handle			1970s
4796	Vase		10″	1970s
4797 GM	Coffee Pot	Medway Range	8½″h	1970s
4798 RT	Bird			1970s
4799	Vase			1970s
4800 GM	Vase	Bamboo	8″	1970s
4801 GM	Beaker	Medway Range	3¾″h	1970s
4802 GM	Sugar Bowl	Medway Range	3½″h	1970s
4803	Vase	Medway Range	6″	1970s
4804 RT	Vase	Altered and re-numbered to 5186	8″	1970s
4806 GM	Cream Jug	Medway Range		1970s
4807 RT	Coffee Pot	Brazil Range(Coffee bean)	8¾″h	1970s
4808 GM	Jardiniere	Bamboo Oblong	7″	1970s
4809 RT	Teapot	Croft Range	5¾″h	1971-S-i-P
4810 RT	Miniature Tankard		3″h	1971–1982
4811 GM	Breakfast/Salad Plate	Croft Range	8″dia	1971-S-i-P
4812 RT	Honey Pot	Croft Range	4½″h	1971-S-i-P
4813 RT	Cream Jug	Croft Range	3¼″h	1971-S-i-P
4814 RT	Sugar Bowl	Croft Range	3½″dia	1971-S-i-P
4815 GM	Cheese dish	Croft Range	7″l	1971-S-i-P
4816 GM	Butter dish	Croft Range	5″dia	1971-S-i-P
4817 RT	Beaker	Croft Range	4½″h	1971-S-i-P
4818 RT	Cup	Croft Range	3″h	1971-S-i-P
4819 RT	Saucer	Croft Range	5½″dia	1971-S-i-P
4820 RT	Tea plate	Croft Range	6½″dia	1971-S-i-P
4821 RT	Breakfast/Salad Plate	Croft Range	8″dia	1971-S-i-P

4822 GM	Tea plate	Croft Range	6¾"dia	1971-S-i-P
4823 GM	Fern Pot	Fleur Range	4¾"h	1970s
4824 GM	Jardiniere	Fleur Range	6¾"l	1970s
4825 GM	Fern Pot	Fleur Range	4"h	1970s
4826 GM	Jardiniere	Fleur Range	9¼"l	1970s
4827 GM	Vase	Fleur Range	7"h	1970s
4828 GM	Vase	Fleur Range	5"h	1970s
4829 GM	Vase	Fleur Range	9"h	1970s
4830 GM	Bowl	Fleur Range	5"h	1970s
4831 RT	Novelty Thimble	Cottage	1¾"h	1971–1982
		Cottage Box for above thimble	2½"l	
4832 GM		Cruet/Stand (Four Pieces) Croft Range	9"l	1971-S-i-P
4832 GM	Cruet Salt/Pepper	Croft Range	3½"h	1971-S-i-P
4833 GM	Storage/Biscuit Jar	Croft Range	7½"h	1971-S-i-P
4834 GM	Tea pot 2/3 Cup	Croft Range	4¾"h	1971-S-i-P
4835 TH		Flower Holder (Leaf) Novelty attached	4"	1970s
4836 TH		Stand for novelties and Whisky Tot 4767		
		Plain round	4¼"	1970s
4837	Dog	Spaniel-Shrink from 115		1970s
4838	Twin Rabbit	Shrink from 1590		1970s
4839 RT	Bull Galloway		Small Size	1970s
4840 TH	Flower holder	Privet Range. Novelties		
		attached-twin rabbit, dog etc	4¾"	1970s
4841 RT	Top Hat	Cat and Dog		1970s
4842 GM	Jardiniere	Plain	Large Size	1970s
4843 GM	Cup	Medway Range	3"h	1970s
4844 GM	Saucer	Medway Range	6¼"dia	1970s
4845 RT	Vase	Dots and Lumps	6"	1970s
4846 RT	Dog St.Bernard			1970s
4847	Gnome			1970s
4848	Jardiniere	Bamboo Range		1970s
4849 RT	Flower Holder	Picture		1970s
4850 RT	Saucer	Brazil Range	5½"dia	1970s
4851 RT	Cup	Brazil Range	2¾"h	1970s
4852 RT	Sugar Bowl	Brazil Range	3½"a	1970s
4853 RT	Cream Jug	Brazil Range	4¼"h	1970s
4854 GM	Vase	Rock		1970s
4855–7 GM	Vases	Medway Range	5"h	1970s
4858/9 GM	Vase	Medway Range	7"h	1970s
4860	Vase	Medway Range	9"h	1970s
4861	Vase	Medway Range	6"h	1970s
4862	Vase	Medway Range	10"h	1970s
4863	Vase	Medway Range	7"h	1970s
4864	Not used			
4865 RT	Honey Pot	Basket Base only about	3"h	1970s
4866 RT	Strawberry	Lid for 4865 and 4871		1970s
4867 RT	Raspberry/			
	Bramble	Lid for 4865 and 4871		1970s
4868 RT	Plum	Lid for 4865 and 4871		1970s
4869 RT	Orange	Lid for 4865 and 4871 (not used)		
4870 RT	Lemon	Lid for 4865 and 4871 (not used)		
4871 RT	Honey Pot	Leaf design (lids as above)about	3"h	1970s
4872 RT	Shire Horse	With/without harness	13"l, 9¾"h	1971–1982
4873 RT	Tankard	Boot		1970s
4874 RT	Salt & Pepper	Medway Range	4¼"h	1970s
4875 RT	Tea Plate	Medway Range	6¾"a	1970s
4876 RT	Honey Pot	Medway Range	4½"h	1970s
4877 RT	Cheese dish	Medway Range	7½"l	1970s
4878 RT	Oval Steak Plate	Medway Range	10"	1970s
4879 RT	Soup Bowl	Medway Range	5½"a	1970s
4880 RT	Tea Pot 4/5 Cups	Medway Range	5½"h	1970s
4881 RT	Sandwich Tray	Medway Range	12¼"l	1970s
4882 RT	Butter Dish	Medway Range	5a	1970s
4883	Not used			
4884	Vase	previous number 4811	7"	1970s
4885	Log–Two Blue tits	Previous number 4822		1970s
4886 GM	Bowl	House in the Glen Range with gnome		
		or rabbit	8"l	1970s

4887 GM	Basket	House in the Glen Range with gome or rabbit	5½"l	1970s
4888 GM	Tray	House in the Glen Range with gome or rabbit	4½"a	1970s
4889 GM	Posy Round	House in the Glen Range with gome or rabbit	8¾"a	1970s
4890 GM	Posy	House in the Glen Range with gnome or rabbit	4¾"l	1970s
4891–4	Not used			
4895 GM	Honey Pot	with Lemon face		1970s
4896 GM	Honey Pot	with Orange face		1970s
4897 GM	Honey Pot	with Plum face	1970s	
4898 GM	Honey Pot	with Raspberry/Bramble		1970s
4899 GM	Honey Pot	with Strawberry face	4"h	1970s
4900	Not used			
4901 GM	Cereal Dish			1970s
4902 GM		Beef dripping holder with lid	3¾"h	1971–1982
4903 GM		Pork Dripping holder with lid	3¾"h	1971–1982
4904 GM		Lard Holder with lid	3¾"h	1971–1982
4905 GM	Soup Bowl			1970s
4906 GM		Holder for Pan scourer, Beef stock or chicken stock	3¼"h	1971–1982
4907	Sink Tidy Bowl			1970s
4908 RT	Soup Bowl.	Shrink from 4905. New handle S/s		1970s
4909–12	Not used			
4913 GM	Bath Salts container			1970s
4914 GM	Beaker Fish			1970s
4915 GM		Tartare Sauce bowl, as fish	3¾"h	1971–1982
		(False Teeth Holder, deleted)		
4916 GM	Soap Tray Fish			1970s
4917 GM	Spare Toilet roll holder			1970s
4918	Talcum Powder Shaker			1970s
4919 GM	Toothbrush Holder Fish			1970s
4920	Not used			
4921 RT	Hexagon Pot		Large Size	1970s
4922 RT	Hexagon Pot		Medium Size	1970s
4923 RT	Hexagon Pot		Small Size	1970s
4924 RT	Moustache Tankard	Plain/Shaving Mug		1970s
4925–7 RT	Moustache Cups			1970s
4928 GM		Rabbit for House in the Glen		1970s
4929 GM		Gnome for House in the Glen		1970s
4930	Swan Pomade			1970s
4931 GM		Tea strainer tea pot (Re-modelled smaller)	3½"h	1971–1982
4932 RT	Vase	Plain		1970s
4933 RT	Vase	Mushroom Shape	Large Size	1970s
4934 GM	Vase	Mushroom Shape Small Size	5"	1970s
4935 GM	Vase	Mushroom Shape Medium Size	6½"	1970s
4936	Vase			1970s
4937–44	Not used			
4945 GM	Ashtray Coffin			1970s
4946 RT	Vase	Incised	5"	1970s
4947 RT	Vase	Incised		1970s
4948 RT	Vase	Incised	10"	1970s
4949 GM	Bowl	Footed Incised		1970s
4950 GM	Vase	Square Foot	7"	1970s
4951 GM	Basket	Incised Floral		1970s
4952 RT	Vase	Incised	8"	1970s
4953–58	Not used			
4959 RT	Tankard	as 4924		1970s
4960–62 RT	Moustache Cups	as 4925–7		1970s
4963 RT	Shire Horse also as pair with 4978 and plough With harness		10¾"l	1972–1982
4964		Shaving Mug Shape as 3478 reduced ½"		1970s
4965 GM		False teeth holder Mosaic (covered)		1970s
4966 GM	Bath Salts	(covered)		1970s
4967 GM	Beaker			1970s
4968	Soap Tray			1970s

4969 GM	Toilet Roll Holder			1970s
4970 GM	Toothbrush Holder			1970s
4971 GM	Shaving Mug			1970s
4972 RT	Tray (For Galloway Bull) As 4288			1970s
4973 GM	Boy and dog			1970s
4974 GM	Chicken Pomander			1970s
4975 GM	Floral Ball	Pomander		1970s
4976 GM	Lantern Book end			1970s
4977 GM	Kittens in Boot		4¾"h	1972–1982
4978 RT	Shire Horse (see 4963)		10¼"l	1972–1982
4979 GM	Basket Vase.	Flower Embossed		1970s
4980–85	Not used			
4986 RT	Dog	Dachshund Standing	7¾"l	1972–1982
4987 RT	Basket	(Whicker base)	4"	1970s
4988 RT	Dog	West Highland Terrier. Standing	6¼"l	1972–1982
4989	Frog	Pomander (As 1399)	2½"h	1970s
4990	Mouse	Pomander (As 105)		1970s
4991	Squirrel	Pomander (Woodland)		1970s
4992 RT	Dog	Boxer	c.s.5¾"	1970s
4993 GM	Vase	Florence	c.s.5½"	1970s
4994 GM	Vase		c.s.5½"	1970s
4995 GM	Vase	Grapevine	c.s.5½"	1970s
4996 GM	Vase	Two handles	c.s.5½"	1970s
4997 GM	Vase		c.s.5½"	1970s
4998 GM	Vase	Cottage	c.s.5½"	1970s
4999 RT	Dog	Spaniel. Standing	9"l	1972–1982
5000 RT	Dog	Collie. Standing	9"l	1972–1982
5001 GM	Saucer	Fabric with Rose		1970s
5002 GM	Cup	Fabric with Rose		1970s
5003/4 GM	Vases	Banana Leaf		1974
5005 GM	Bowl	Banana Leaf	5½"h.c.s.	1974
5006 GM	Pot	Banana Leaf	7¼"a.6"h.c.s.	1974
5007 GM	Vase	Banana Leaf	11"h.c.s.	1974
5008 GM	Pot	Banana Leaf	5¾"h.c.s.	1974
5009 GM	Bowl	Banana Leaf	9"w.5½"h.c.s.	1974
5010 GM	Pot	Banana Leaf	10". 8"h.c.s.	1974
5011 GM	Plinth for 5010 Pot			1974
5012–4	Not used			
5015 GM	Vase	Faint Rib	8"c.s.	1972
5016–8	Not used			
5019 GM	Pot		6"h.7"a	1972
5020 GM	Bowl			1972
5021 GM	Bowl		5"c.s.	1972
5022 GM	Rose Bowl and cover			1972
5023 RT	Dog	Shetland Sheepdog. Sitting	6¼"h	1974-S-i-P
5024 RT	Dog	Shetland Sheepdog. Sitting	Large Size	1974
5025 RT	Dog	Poodle	12¼"h.c.s.	1974
5026 GM	Vase	Irregular shape	6¾"c.s.	1972
5027 RT	Dog	Yorkshire Terrier. Sitting	5½"h	1972-S-i-P
5028 GM	Log Flower Holder and kingfisher			1972
5029 GM	Pebble Flower Holder			1972
5030 RT	Tankard Half-Pint. Coco de mer			1972
5031 RT	Dog	Poodle	9"c.s.	1972
5032 RT	Dog	Boxer. Standing	7¾"l	1972–1982
5033 GM	Celery Holder		7½"l	1972–1982
5034 RT	Dog	Dalmation. Standing	9"l	1972-S-i-P
5035 RT	Horse	Hunter. Standing	11½"h	1972–1982
5036 GM	Money box	Dog		1972
5037 GM	Money box	Frog		1972
5038 GM	Tea bag holder		6"l	1972–1982
5039 RT	Money Box	Owl	9"c.s.	1972
5040 RT	Eagle	American		1972
5041 GM	Coffee bag holder		6"l	1972–1982
5042 GM	Spring Onion Holder		4½"h	1972–1982
5043 GM	Corn on the Cob dish		9"l	1972–1982
5044 OM	Resin Container	Triangle		1972
5045 OM	Resin Container	Fluted Cone		1972
5046 OM	Resin Container	Cone Plain		1972
5047 GM	Tea Bag Dispenser			1972

5048 GM	Horse Radish Bowl. With face		4¼"h	1972–1982
5049 RT	Dog	Beagle. Standing.	8½"l	1972-S-i-P
5050 RT	Pie Funnel.	Swans Head		1972
5051 GM	Vase		6½"c.s.	1972
5052 GM	Thimble	Pigs Head		1980
5053 RT	Thimble	Boxed Castle.	Thimble	1¼"h.Box 2⅝"h	1980–1982
5054 GM	Thimble	Rose		1980
5055 GM	Thimble	Daffodil		1980
5056 GM	Thimble	Heart		1980
5057 GM	Thimble	Boxed Leaning Tower of Pisa	Thimble	1⅜"h.Box 3¼"h	1980–1982
5058 GM	Thimble	Boxed Windmill.	Thimble	1¼"h.Box 4"h	1980–1982
5059 GM	Thimble	Boxed Circus Clown.	Thimble	1¼"h.Box 3½"h	1980–1982
5060 GM	Thimble	Boxed Wishing Well.	Thimble	1¼"h.Box 2¼"l	1980–1982
5061 GM	Thimble	Unicorn		1979
5062 GM	Thimble	Lion		1979
5063 GM	Cigarette Box	Treasure Chest		1972
5064 OM	Ashtray	Resin Container		1972
5065 GM	Ashtray	Ships Wheel		1972
5066 GM	Vase	Leaf Pattern	6"c.s.	1972
5067 GM	Vase	Leaf Pattern	9"c.s.	1972
5068 GM	Vase	Leaf Pattern	6¼"c.s.	1972
5069 GM	Pot	Leaf Pattern	6"h.7¼"w.c.s.	1972
5070 GM	Pot	Leaf Pattern	7"h.6"w.c.s.	1972
5071 GM	Vase	Leaf Pattern	8¾"h.c.s.	1972
5072 GM	Bowl	Leaf Pattern	7"h.c.s.	1972
5073 GM	Bowl	Low Leaf Pattern	3⅛"h.7½"w.c.s.	1972
5074 GM	Bowl	Oval Leaf Pattern	7½a.2"h.c.s.	1972
5075 GM	Vase		5¼"c.s.	1972
5076 RT	Dog	Spaniel. Standing	7¾"l	1972-S-i-P
5077 GM	Coffee Bag Dispenser			1972
5078 GM	Cup	Hammered Pattern		1972
5079 GM	Saucer	Hammered Pattern		1972
5080 GM	Plate	Hammered Pattern	7"c.s.	1972
5081 GM	Sugar Bowl	Hammered Pattern		1972
5082 GM	Cream Jug	Hammered Pattern		1972
5083 GM	Coffee Pot	Hammered Pattern		1972
5084 GM	B & B Plate	Hammered Pattern		1973
5085 GM	Sandwich Tray	Hammered Pattern		1973
5086 GM	Cruet	Salt & Pepper. Hammered Pattern		1973
5087 GM	Teapot	Hammered Pattern	Small Size	1973
5088 GM	Teapot	Hammered Pattern	Large Size	1973
5089 GM	Cream jug	Hammered Pattern	Small Size	1973
5090 GM	Beaker	Hammered Pattern		1973
5091 GM	Money Box	Tortoise		1978
5092 GM	Money Box	Owl		1978
5093 GM	Money Box	Squirrel		1978
5094/5	Not used			
5096 GM	Money Box	Bulldog	5¾"h	1978-S-i-P
5097 GM	Money Box	Frog	5¼"h	1978–1982
5098	Tankard	Half-Pint. Plain. Old Number 3278	3¾"h	1973
5099 GM	Moustache Tankard.	Old Number 3278	3¾"h	1973
5100 GM	Pen tray	Motivil		1973
5101 GM	Money Box	Tortoise	5¾"l	1973-S-i-P
5102 GM	Money Box	Elephant	5"l	1973–1982
5103 GM	Money Box	Bloodhound	5¼"h	1973–1982
5104 GM	Money Box	Teddy Bear	5¼"h	1973–1982
5105 GM	Money Box	Chipmunk. Old Number 3935	5¾"h	1973-S-i-P
5106 GM	Money Box	Owl Old Number 4361	4¾"h	1973–1982
5107 RT	Cat	Siamese. Sitting.	8½"l	1973-S-i-P
5108 RT	Dog	Afghan Hound. Standing	8¾"l	1973-S-i-P
5109 GM	Cucumber Bowl			1973
5110 GM	Grapefruit Bowl on stand			1973
5111 RT	Cat	Siamese. Sitting	8¾"h	1973-S-i-P
5112 RT	Dog	Alsation. Standing	9¾"l	1973-S-i-P
5113 GM	Character Jug	Friar Tuck	6¾"h	1973–1981
5114 GM	Character Jug	Robin Hood	6"h	1973–1981
5115 GM	Character Jug	Sheriff of Nottingham	6"h	1973–1981
5116 GM	Character Jug	Little John	6¾"h	1973–1981
5117 GM	Character Jug	Maid Marion	6¼"h	1973–1981

156

5118 GM	Character Jug	Allan A Dale	6¼"h	1973–1981
5119 OM	Duck	Mallard	6½"l	1973
5120 OM	Duck	Golden Eye	6"l	1973
5121 OM	Gosling			1973
5122 OM	Duck	Shoveller	6½"l	1973
5123 OM	Duck	Tufted		1973
5124 GM	Beaker			1973
5125 RT	Horse	Shire. Shrink from 4963	8¾"l	1973–1982
5126	Onion Bowl	With Face	4"h	1973–1982
5127	Beetroot Bowl	With face	4¼"h	1973–1982
5128 GM	Strawberry Bowl			1973
5129 GM	Raspberry Bowl			1973
5130 GM	Ash Bowl and cover			1973
5131 RT	Donkey	With saddle or panniers	10½"l	1973–1982
5132 GM	Vase	Candlegrease Range. Florence	8½"c.s.	1973
5133 GM	Vase	Candlegrease Range. Florence	3½"c.s.	1973
5134 GM	Vase	Candlegrease Range. Florence	10"c.s.	1973
5135 GM	Pot	Candlegrease Range. Florence	6½"c.s.	1973
5136 GM	Candlestick	Candlegrease Range. Florence		1973
5137 GM	Pot	Candlegrease Range. Florence	5½"c.s.	1973
5138 GM	Candlestick	Bowl (Two candles)	3½"h.7¼"w.c.s.	1973
5139 GM	Candlestick Jug		4⅛"h.c.s.	1973
5140 GM	Bowl	Footed	Small Size	1973
5141	Not used			
5142 GM	Jardiniere		Large Size	1973
5143 OM	Ham Stand	Rodek		1973
5144 OM	Ashtray	Rodek		1973
5145 GM	Ashtray	(Cane) Car attached		1973
5146 GM	Ashtray	(Charcoal grey) Aeroplane attached		1973
5147 GM	Muffin Dish	Stand & Cover		1973
5148 GM	Mayonnaise Jug/Stand		6½"l	1973–1982
5149	Pomander	Pickwick Taken from 4433	S/s	1973
5150 RT	Dog	Dobermann Pinscher Standing	8½"l	1973-S-i-P
5151 GM	Banana Split	(open tray)		1973
5152 GM	Elephant	Taken from 5102 money box		1973
5153–5 GM	Beakers Plain			1973
5156 GM	Beaker	Leaves & Berries		1973
5157 GM	Beaker	Diamond		1974
5158 GM	Beaker	Flowers		1974
5159 GM	Beaker	Sticks		1974
5160 GM	Beaker	Flowers		1974
5161 GM	Beaker	Leaves		1974
5162 GM	Beaker	Circles		1974
5163 GM	Beaker	Elongated triangles		1974
5164	Not used			
5165 GM	Bust of Sir Winston Churchill		9"c.s.	1974
5166 GM	Rhinoceros	Standing	10½"l	1974–1982
5167 RT	Dog	Labrador. Standing	9½"l	1974-S-i-P
5168 GM	Butter dish	Round Basket Base Sunflower lid.		1974
5169 GM	Butter dish	Oblong Basket Base Sunflower lid.		1974
5170 RT	Dog	Irish (red) Setter Standing	9¼"l	1974
5171 GM	Coffee Pot	Embossed Fluted		1974
5172 GM	Cream Jug	Embossed Fluted		1974
5173 GM	Cup	Embossed Fluted		1974
5174 GM	Salt & Pepper	Embossed Fluted		1974
5175 GM	Sugar Bowl	Embossed Fluted		1974
5176 RT	Saucer	Embossed Fluted		1974
5177 RT	Tea plate	Embossed Fluted	7"a	1974
5178 GM	Tea Pot	Embossed Fluted		1974
5179 RT	B & B Plate	Embossed Fluted		1974
5180 GM	Butter dish	Embossed Fluted		1974
5181 GM	Cheese dish	Embossed Fluted		1974
5182 GM	Honey Pot	Embossed Fluted	5"h	1974
5183 GM	Fruit Dish	Embossed Fluted		1974
5184	Not used			
5185 RT	Bowl	Dolphin Range	8½"l.3¾"h	1974
5186 RT	Vase	Dolphin Range	4½"h.c.s.	1974
5187 RT	Tray	Dolphin Range		1974
5188 RT	Vase	Dolphin Range	6½"h.c.s.	1974

5189 RT	Pot	Dolphin Range	4¾"h.c.s.	1974
5190 RT	Posy Bar	Dolphin Range	2"h.c.s.	1974
5191 RT	Basket	Dolphin Range	5"h.c.s.	1974
5192 RT	Twin Vase	Dolphin Range	3½"h.c.s.	1974
5193 GM	Bowl Plain		3½"h.c.s.	1974
5194 GM	Dog Bowl	Embossed	3"h.c.s.	1975
5195 GM	Cat Bowl	Embossed	3"h.c.s.	1975
5196 RT	Vase	Chestnut		1974
5197 RT	Galloway Bull		6"h.c.s.	1974
5198 GM	Character Jug	Fisherman	6"h.c.s.	1974
5199 GM	Character Jug	Clerk	6"h.c.s.	1974
5200 GM	Character Jug	Horse Dealer	6"h.c.s.	1974
5201 GM	Character Jug	Miner	6"h.c.s.	1974
5202 GM	Character Jug	Bricklayer	6"h.c.s.	1974
5203 GM	Character Jug	Cook	6"h.c.s.	1974
5204 GM	Beaker	Plain		1974
5205 RT	Dog	Welsh Sheepdog. Crouching	9¾"l	1974-S-i-P
5206 RT	Character Jug	John Kennedy		1974
5207 RT	Galloway Bull	Shrink from 5197	5½"h.c.s.	1974
5208 GM	Beaker	Orange Face		1974
5209 RT	Fox	Prestige Animals	10½"l	1974–1982
5210 GM	Gazelle	Modus 80 Antique gold or pewter coloured glaze	9½"l	1974–1982
5211 GM	Squirrel	Prestige Animals	7"h	1974–1982
5212 GM	Cheetah	As 5210	10"l	1974–1982
5213 GM	Horse	As 5210	8½"h	1974–1982
5214 RT	Loving Cup	Three handles American Scenes		1974
5215 RT	Tankard	George Washington Embossed		1974
5216 OM	Badger		11"l.5½"h.c.s.	1974
5217–19 GM	Tankards	¾-pint	4¾"h.c.s.	1974
5220	Not used			
5221 GM	Volvo Tankard			1981
5222 OM	Tankard	Indian Head		1981
5223–5 RT	Vases		9"h.c.s.	1974
5226 RT	Vase	Ribbed	11½"h.c.s.	1974
5227 RT	Vase	Plain	8"h.c.s.	1974
5228 RT	Vase		7"h.c.s.	1975
5229 GM	Hippopotamus	Standing	6"l	1975–1982
5230 GM	Camel	Sitting	5¼"l	1975–1982
5231 GM	Bear		6½"l.3½"h.c.s.	1975
5232 GM	Two Monkeys	Sitting Cuddling	4⅛"h	1975–1982
5233 GM	Lion Sitting		6¼"l	1975–1982
5234 GM	Giraffe	Sitting	5"h	1975–1982
5235 RT	Cushion	(For cat 5236)	10"x7"c.s.	1975-S-i-P
5236 RT	Cat	Tabby or White Also with 5235	8"l	1975-S-i-P
5237 RT	Cat	Standing Tabby or black	11½"l	1975-S-i-P
5238 GM	Bear	As 5210	7"h	1975–1982
5239 GM	Badger		12"l.c.s.6¼"h.	1975
5240 RT	Pot	Plain		1975
5241 RT	Cup			1975
5242 GM	Brush & Mop Holder		6⅛"h	1975–1982
5243 GM	Vase	Harvest Time Range. Hand Decorated Mouse on matt background	7¾"h	1977–1982
5244 GM	Basket	Harvest Time Range Ditto	6"l	1977–1982
5245 GM	Fern Pot	Harvest Time Range Ditto	5"h	1977–1982
5246 GM	Vase	Harvest Time Range Ditto	4½"h	1977–1982
5247 GM	Vase	Harvest Time Range Ditto	6"h	1977–1982
5248 GM	Posy Bowl	Harvest Time Range Ditto	5"l	1977–1982
5249 GM	Bowl	Harvest Time Range Ditto	6"a	1977–1982
5250 GM	Jardiniere	Harvest Time Range Ditto	6¾"l	1977–1982
5251 GM	Mouse		2½"h.c.s.	1977
5252 GM	Mouse		1½"h.c.s.	1977
5253	Not used			
5254 GM	Mouse			1980
5255 GM	Fox			1975
5256 GM	Vase		6¾"h.c.s.	1975
5257 GM	Rabbit			1975
5258	Dog	Great Dane. Standing	8⅞"l	1979-S-i-P
5259 OM	Dog	Schnauzer. Standing	7"l	1979-S-i-P

5260 GM	Dog	Whippet Standing	6"l	1979-S-i-P
5261 OM	Cat	Crouching	10½"l	1979-S-i-P
5262 GM	Cat	Sitting	7⅛"l	1979-S-i-P
5263 GM	Dog	Poodle. Standing.		1981-S-i-P
5264–66	Not used			
5267 GM	Vase	Squares and Circles	6½"h.c.s.	1975
5268 RT	Vase	Incised	8"h.c.s.	1975
5269 RT	Vase	Incised	7"h.c.s.	1975
5270 RT	Tankard	Leather Covered	4¼"h	1977–1982
5271 RT	Tankard	Leather Covered	3¼"h	1977–1982
5272 GM	Bowl	with lid -Odds and Ends, and Heather and Thistle Range	4¼"a	1975–1982
5273	Bowl	Embossed. Shrink from 4641	3½"h.c.s.	1975
5274 GM	Bowl	Vintage Range	7¾"a	1975–1981
5275 GM	Vase	Vintage Range	9"h	1975–1982
5276 GM	Fern Pot	Vintage Range	6⅞"h	1975–1982
5277 GM	Bowl	Vintage Range	10½"a	1975–1982
5278 GM	Vase	Vintage Range	6⅞"h	1975–1982
5279 GM	Vase	Bamboo. Single stem		1975
5280 GM	Vase	Vintage Range	10"h.c.s.	1975
5281 RT	Tankard	King Arthur & Knights of the round table	5¾"h	1975–1982
5282 RT	Tankard	Brass Rubbings, also 'Last piece made in Bottle oven 1978'	8¼"h	1975–1982
5283 RT	Tankard	Lining for leather holder	Gill size	1975
5284 RT	Tankard	Caernarvon, Edinburgh or Windsor Castles	5¾"h	1975–1982
5285 GM	Leaf	For ashtrays		1975
5286 GM	Dish	Cloth Holder With face	3¾"h	1975–1982
5287 GM	Eagle		9"h.c.s.	1975
5288 RT	Ashtray	(Geest) With centre piece		1976
5289 GM	Rabbit	Caricature Lop Ear	7"h	1975–1982
5290 GM	Rabbit	Caricature Lop Ear	5¼"h	1975–1982
5291 GM	Rabbit	Caricature Lop Ear Ditto	3⅞"h	1975–1982
5292 GM	Dog	Caricature with long neck	7⅛"h	1975–1982
5293 GM	Dog	Caricature with long neck	5½"h	1975–1982
5294 GM	Dog	Caricature with long neck	3⅞"h	1975–1982
5295 GM	Dog	Caricature, one ear up.	7"h	1975–1982
5296 GM	Dog	Caricature, one ear up.	5¼"h	1975–1982
5297 GM	Dog	Caricature, one ear up.	3¾"h	1975–1982
5298 GM	Cat	Caricature. Long neck	7⅛"h	1975–1982
5299 GM	Cat	Caricature. Long neck	5¼"h	1975–1982
5300 GM	Cat	Caricature. Long neck	3⅞"h	1975–1982
5301 GM	Dog	Sheep Dog. Very Ugly	9⅜"h.c.s.	1976
5302 GM	Dog	Sheep Dog. Very Ugly	5⅞"h.c.s.	1976
5303 GM	Dog	Sheep Dog. Very Ugly	4⅛"h.c.s.	1976
5304 RT	Dog	Corgi	8⅛"h.c.s.	1976
5305 GM	Rabbit	Straight Ears	Large Size	1976
5306 GM	Rabbit	Straight Ears	Medium Size	1976
5307 GM	Rabbit	Straight Ears	Small Size	1976
5308 GM	Tea bag pot		4½"h	1976–1982
5309 RT	Ashtray	Square. King Arthur & Queen	5¾" across	1976
5310 RT	Ashtray	Plain Oblong		1976
5311 RT	Ashtray	Plain Oval		1976
5312 RT	Dog	Corgi	7½"h.c.s.	1976
5313 GM	Girl & Dog	Country Craft Range	11"h.c.s.	1976
5314 GM	Girl & Goat	Country Craft Range	11¾"h.c.s.	1976
5315 GM	Gamekeeper	Country Craft Range	11⅜"h.c.s.	1976
5316 GM	Goose Girl	Country Craft Range	11⅛"h.c.s.	1976
5317 RT	Candlestick	Plain	7"h.c.s.	1976
5318 RT	Candlestick	Embossed	7"h.c.s.	1976
5319 RT	Dog	Chihuahua. Standing	5¾"h	1976-S-i-P
5320 RT	Dog	St. Bernard. Standing	9½"l	1976-S-i-P
5321 RT	Dog	Corgi. Standing	6¾"l	1976-S-i-P
5322 RT	Dog	Old English Sheepdog	7"l	1978-S-i-P
5323 GM	Dog	Sealyham. Standing	7½"l	1978-S-i-P
5324 RT	Dog	Pyrennean Mountain	10"l	1978-S-i-P
5325 GM	Jug	New Cavalier Range	8"h	1976–1982
5326 GM	Punch Bowl	New Cavalier Range	10½"a	1976–1982
5327 RT	Plaque/Plate	New Cavalier Range	10"a	1976–1982
5328 GM	Tankard	New Cavalier Range	5¾"h	1976–1982

5329 GM	Jug	New Cavalier Range	5⅞"h	1976–1982
5330 GM	Goblet	New Cavalier Range	5"h	1976–1982
5331 RT	Ashtray	New Cavalier Range	5⅞"a	1976–1982
5332 GM	Loving Cup	New Cavalier Range	5¼"h	1976–1982
5333 GM	Tankard	New Cavalier Range	4⅛"h	1976–1982
5334 GM	Decanter	New Cavalier Range	9¾"h	1976–1982
5335 GM	Hanging Bowl	Right Herbert	Small Size	1976–1982
5336 RT	Hanging Bowl	Right Herbert		1976–1982
5337 GM	Jug	Cordon Brun Kitchen Ware, Cream and Brown, decorated with kitchen utensils	6¼"	1976–1982

Some of this range is also called Winsor Kitchenware,
White with a Red, Grey or Black Band
and is still in production

5338 GM	Jug	Cordon Brun Kitchen Ware	5½"h	1976–1982
5339 GM	Jug	Cordon Brun Kitchen Ware	4¾"h	1976–1982
5340 GM	Jug	Cordon Brun Kitchen Ware	3¾"h	1976–1982
5341 GM	Storage Jar	Cordon Brun Kitchen Ware	6¾"h	1976–1982
5342 GM	Storage Jar	Cordon Brun Kitchen Ware	5"h	1976–1982
5343 GM	Salt & Pepper	Cordon Brun Kitchen Ware	4½"h	1976–1982
5344 GM	Salt Jar	Cordon Brun Kitchen Ware	7½"h	1976–1982
5345 GM	Covered Sugar/Honey	Cordon Brun Kitchen Ware	4"h	1976–1982
5346 GM	Coffee Pot	Cordon Brun Kitchen Ware	8¼"h	1976–1982
5347 GM	Tea Pot	Cordon Brun Kitchen Ware	5¾"h	1976–1982
5348 GM	Beaker	Cordon Brun Kitchen Ware	4¼"h	1976–1982
5349 GM	Covered Butter dish	Cordon Brun Kitchen Ware	5¼"l	1977–1982
5350 GM	Covered Cheese dish	Cordon Brun Kitchen Ware	7¼"l	1977–1982
5351 GM	Jam Pot holder	Cordon Brun Kitchen Ware	4½"h.c.s.	1977–1982
5352 RT	Cup	Cordon Brun Kitchen Ware	3½"h	1977–1982
5353 RT	Saucer	Cordon Brun Kitchen Ware	5½"a	1977–1982
5354 RT	Plate	Cordon Brun Kitchen Ware	6½"a	1977–1982
5355 RT	Plate	Cordon Brun Kitchen Ware	8"a	1977–1982
5356 RT	Egg Cup with Saucer	Cordon Brun Kitchen Ware	5"a	1977–1982
5357 RT	Sugar Sifter	Cordon Brun Kitchen Ware	5¼"h	1977–1982
5358 GM	Spoon Rest	Cordon Brun Kitchen Ware	8"l	1977–1982
5359 RT	Egg Separator	Cordon Brun Kitchen Ware	3¼"h	1977–1982
5360 RT	Lemon Squeezer	Cordon Brun Kitchen Ware	4½"h	1977–1982
5361 GM	Herb/Spice Jars	Cordon Brun Kitchen Ware	3¾"h	1977–1982
5362 GM	Mixing Bowl	Cordon Brun Kitchen Ware	6½"a	1977–1982
5363 GM	Fruit & Stand	Cordon Brun Kitchen Ware	4⅞"x2½"c.s.	1977
5364 RT	Double Egg Cup	Cordon Brun Kitchen Ware	4¼"l	1977–1982
5365 RT	Tea pot stand	Cordon Brun Kitchen Ware	6¼"a	1977–1982
5366 GM	Toast Rack	Cordon Brun Kitchen Ware	7½"l	1977–1982
5367 OM	Ashtray	Large Size		1977
5368 GM	Ashtray	Small Size		1977
5369 GM	Fern Pot	Bamboo Range	5¼"h	1977–1982
5370 GM	Vase	Bamboo Range	7¾"h	1977–1982
5371 GM	Fern Pot	Bamboo Range	6½"a	1977–1982
5372 GM	Vase	Bamboo Range	10"h	1977–1982
5373 GM	Vase	Bamboo Range	12"h	1977–1982
5374 GM	Vase	Bamboo Range	6"h	1977–1982
5375 GM	Bowl	Bamboo Range	8"h	1977–1982
5376 GM	Bowl	Bamboo Range	11¾"	1977–1982
5377 GM	Bowl	Bamboo Range	5¾"l	1977–1982
5378 GM	Fern Pot	Bamboo Range	7½"a	1977–1982
5379 GM	Fern Pot	Bamboo Range	8¾"a	1977–1982
5380 GM	Dog	English Sheepdog		1977
5381 GM	Dog	Skye Terrier	4½"h.c.s.	1977
5382 RT	Ashtray	Horseshoe	6"l	1977–1982
5383 GM	Honey Pot	Bee	4⅞"h	1977-S-i-P
5384 GM	Ashtray		8"x2"c.s.	1977
5385 GM	Pomander			1977
5386 GM	Tray	Lincoln Pattern		1977
5387 GM	Vase	Two Handles	8¾"h.c.s.	1977
5388 GM	Vase	One Handle		1977
5389 GM	Pot		6¼"h.c.s.	1977

5390 GM	Tray		13½"l.c.s.	1977
5391 GM	Vase		11"h.c.s.	1977
5392 RT	Vase	Plain	9"h.c.s.	1977
5393 RT	Ginger Jar	Canton Range With Lid	11½"h	1977–1982
5394 RT	Ginger Jar	Canton Range With Lid	9½"h	1977–1982
5395 RT	Ginger Jar	Canton Range With Lid	7"h	1977–1982
5396 RT	Vase	Canton Range With Lid	13"h	1977–1982
5397 RT	Vase	Canton Range With Lid	9¼"h	1977–1982
5398 RT	Fern Pot	Canton Range With Lid	9"h	1977–1982
5399 RT	Bowl	Canton Range With Lid	9½"a	1977–1982
5400 GM	Pepper & Salt	Severn Range(4 different decorations)	3½"h	1977–1982
5401 OM	Bathroom Jar	"Boots"		1977
5402 GM	Cheese Dish	Severn Range.See 5400.	8¾"l	1980–1982
5403 GM	Ashtray			1977
5404 RT	Ashtray	Leyland Lorry,for British Leyland		1977
5405 GM	Ashtray		3¾"x5¼"c.s.	1977
5406 RT	Bowl	Ribbed		1977
5407 RT	Ashtray		2½"h×3¼"w	1977
5408 RT	Tray		5½"c.s.	1977
5409 RT	Teapot	English Rose Range	5"h	1977–1982
5410 RT	Sugar Bowl	English Rose Range	4"a	1977–1982
5411 RT	Cream Jug	English Rose Range	3"h	1977–1982
5412 GM	Saucer	English Rose Range	5½"a	1977–1982
5413 GM	Tea plate	English Rose Range	6¾"a	1977–1982
5414 GM	Cup	English Rose Range	3"h	1977–1982
5415 GM	Salt & Pepper	English Rose Range	3⅜"h	1977–1981
5416 GM	Honey Pot	English Rose Range	4⅛"h	1977–1981
5417 GM	Cheese dish	English Rose Range	7⅝"h	1977–1981
5418 GM	Butter dish	English Rose Range	5¾"l	1977–1981
5419 GM	Tea Pot	Severn Range. See 5400	5½"h	1980–1982
5420 GM	Jug	Severn Range. See 5400	4"h	1980–1982
5421 GM	Beaker	Severn Range. See 5400	4"h	1980–1982
5422 GM	Honey Pot	Severn Range. See 5400	5"h	1980–1982
5423 GM	Teatime Set	Beaker 3"h Teapot	4½"h	1977–1981
5424 GM	Butter Dish	Severn Range. See 5400	5¾"l	1980–1982
5425 GM	Three			
	Tea Bag Pot		5½"h	1977-S-i-P
5426 GM	Two			
	Tea Bag Pot		4¾"h	1977-S-i-P
5427 GM	One			
	Tea Bag Pot		4"h	1977-S-i-P
5428 GM	Tea Pot Stand		6"a	1977-S-i-P
5429 GM	Jug	Severn Range. See 5400	4½"h	1980–1982
5430 GM	Jug	Severn Range. See 5400	4¾"h	1980–1982
5431 GM	Owl	Lamp Base	5¼"h.c.s.	1978
5432 GM	Tortoise	Lamp Base	4½"h.c.s.	1978
5433 GM	Hound	Lamp Base	6"h.c.s.	1978
5434 RT	Dog	Springer Spaniel Standing	8"l	1978–1982
5435 OM	Jug	Pipers Whisky		1978
5436 OM	Ashtray	Pipers Whisky		1978
5437 OM	Ashtray	Guinness		1978
5438 OM	Bell & Dove			1978
5439 GM	Soap Dish			1978
5440 OM	Tyre Ash Tray			1978
5441–6 GM	Miniature Vases		3½"h.c.s.	1978
5447 GM	Honey Pot	Anniversary Range	5"h	1978–1981
5448 GM	Goblet	Anniversary Range	5"h	1978–1981
5449 GM	Tea Pot	Anniversary Range	6¾"h	1978–1981
5450 GM	Plate	Anniversary Range	10"a	1978–1981
5451 GM	Powder Bowl	Anniversary Range	4½"l	1978–1981
5452 GM	Cream Jug	Anniversary Range	3¾"h	1978–1981
5453 GM	Cup	Anniversary Range		1978
5454 GM	Saucer	Anniversary Range		1978
5455 GM	Tea Plate	Anniversary Range		1978
5456 GM	Loving Cup	Anniversary Range	7½"a	1978–1981
5457	Bowl	Anniversary Range		1978
5458 GM	Heart shaped tray	Anniversary Range	5½"l	1978–1981
5459 GM	Candlestick	Anniversary Range	6¾"l	1978–1981
5460 GM	Bell	Anniversary Range	5¼"h	1978–1981

5461/2	Not used			
5463/4 GM	Egg cups	(not used)		
5465 GM	Egg Cup	Chicken	4"l	1978–1982
5466 GM	Four Egg Cups/			
	Stand Chickens		8"a	1978–1982
5467 OM	Yorkshire Hod			1978
5468 OM	Sea Monster			
	Cruet.	Four pieces.S.P.V.M.	13"l	1978–1982
5469–72 GM	Jug Vases	Hollington Range	9"h	1978–1981
5473–76 GM	Jug Vases	Hollington Range	6½"h	1978–1981
5477	Not used			
5478 GM	Egg Cup	Truck. Zooline Nursery Ware	2⅜"l	1981–1982
5479 GM	Salt	Engine. Zooline Nursery Ware	4"l	1981–1982
5480 GM	Honey Pot	Teddy Bear	1981	
5481 GM	Vase	High Tide Medium Size	8¼"h.c.s.	1979
5482 GM	Bowl	High Tide Large Size		1979
5483 GM	Pot	High Tide	Small Size	1979
5484 GM	Pot	High Tide	Large Size	1979
5485 GM	Vase	High Tide	Large Size	1979
5486 GM	Vase	High Tide	Small Size	1979
5487 GM	Basket	High Tide		1979
5488 GM	Flower Holder	High Tide		1979
5489 GM	Bowl	High Tide	Small Size	1979
5490 GM	Vase Acorn			1979
5491–4 GM	Vases			1982
5495–98	Not used			
5499 GM	Vase	Autumn Range		1979
5500 GM	Pot	Autumn Range	Medium size	1979
5501 GM	Vase	Autumn Range	9"h.c.s.	1979
5502 GM	Vase	Autumn Range	11"h.c.s.	1979
5503 GM	Covered Bowl	Autumn Range		1979
5504 GM	Posy Bowl	Autumn Range		1979
5505 GM	Pot	Autumn Range	Small Size	1979
5506 GM	Pot	Autumn Range	Large Size	1979
5507 GM	Covered			
	Trinket Box.	Autumn Range		1979
5508 GM	Candlestick	Autumn Range		1979
5509 GM	Vase	Autumn Range		1979
5510 OM	Vase/			
	Single Flower.			1979
5511 OM	Vase/			
	Single Flower.			1979
5512 GM	Vase/			
	Single Flower.	Solo Range	4¼"h	1979–1981
5513 OM	Vase/			
	Single Flower.	Solo Range	6¼"h	1979–1981
5514 OM	Vase/			
	Single Flower.	Solo Range	4"h	1979–1981
5515 OM	Vase/			
	Single Flower.	Solo Range	6⅛"h	1979–1981
5516 GM	Vase/			
	Single Flower.	Solo Range	6⅛"h	1979–1981
5517 GM	Brooch/Pendant.	Retriever, head only		1979–1982
5518 GM	Brooch/Pendant.	Cairn, head only		1979–1982
5519 GM	Brooch/Pendant.	Poodle, head only		1979–1982
5520 GM	Brooch/Pendant.	Bulldog, head only		1979–1982
5521 GM	Brooch/Pendant.	Spaniel, head only		1979–1982
5522 GM	Brooch/Pendant.	Collie, head only		1979–1982
5523–25 GM	Brooches/Pendants.	Horse, heads only		1979–1982
5526–28	Not used			
5529 OM	Salt/Pepper.	Half-Pint Beer Mug.		1979
5530 OM	Money Box	Half-Pint Beer Mug		1979
5531 GM	Salt	Half-Pint Beer Mug Froth		1979
5532 GM	Money Box	Half-Pint Beer Mug Froth		1979
5533	Pot	Plain		1979
5534	Not used			
5535 GM	Bell	Croft Range	4¾"h	1979–1982
5536 GM	Jug	Croft Range	7"h	1979-S-i-P
5537 GM	Coffee Pot	Croft Range	9"h	1979-S-i-P

5538 GM	Clock	Croft Range	8"a	1979–1981
5539–46	Not used			
5547 OM	Honey Pot	Clown		1979
5548 HH	Vinegar Bottle	Nosey Parker	5¾"h	1980
5549 HH	Pepper	Nosey Parker	5"h	1980
5550 HH	Salt	Nosey Parker	4¾"h	1980
5551 GM	Tray	To go with 2790 & 2785 Pot	Large/Med S.	1980
5552 GM	Tray	To go with 2996 S/s Pot	Small Size	1980
5553 GM	Cradle			1981
5554 GM	Bootees			1981
5555 GM	Stork			1981
5556–8	Not used			
5559 EB	Plaque	(As Disc)	Large Size	1981
5560 EB	Plaque	(As Disc)	Small Size	1981
5561/2	Not used			
5563 HH	Tray			1980
5564 HH	Toilet Roll Holder			1980
5565 HH	Bath Salt Jar & Cover			1980
5566 HH	Toothbrush Holder			1980
5567 HH	Bowl – Dentures			1980
5568–70	Not used			
5571 GM	Plant Pot	Giant Panda Range	4½"h	1981–1982
5572 GM	Twin Vase	Giant Panda Range	6¼"h	1981–1982
5573 GM	Vase	Giant Panda Range	9"h	1981–1982
5574 GM	Vase	Giant Panda Range	7½"h	1981–1982
5575 GM	Bowl	Giant Panda Range	8½"l	1981–1982
5576 GM	Money Box	Giant Panda Range	4¼"h	1981–1982
5577	Not used			
5578 GM	Panda	Sitting		1981
5579 GM	Panda	Standing		1981
5580 RT	Disc	Number altered 1977	Small Size	
5581 RT	Disc	Number altered 1977	Large Size	
5582 RT	Disc	Set of three wall plaques. Martingales, decorated with: Cries of London, French Paintings, Horses heads, Horse & Foal, Hunting Scenes, Sailing Ships. S/s incorporating high quality leather	16"l	1977–1982
5583 RT	Disc.	Set of three wall plaques. Martingales, decorated with: French Paintings, Horse & Foal, Gun Dogs, incorporating high quality leather.	L/s.25½"l	1977–1982
5584 GM	Trinket Box	Milady Range	5¼"l	1980–1982
5585 GM	Ring Stand	Milady Range	4½"a	1980–1982
5586 GM	Plant Pot	Milady Range	6¾"a	1980–1982
5587 GM	Oval Tray	Milady Range	10"l	1980–1982
5588 GM	Powder Bowl	Milady Range	4½"a	1980–1982
5589 GM	Candle Holder	Milady Range	5¼"a	1980–1982
5590 GM	Plant Pot	Milady Range	5½"a	1980–1982
5591 GM	Plant Pot	Milady Range	4¾"a	1980–1982
5592 GM	Vase	Milady Range	8"h	1980–1982
5593 GM	Vase	Milady Range	6"h	1980–1982
5594 GM	Mirror	Milady Range	8¾"l	1980–1982
5595 GM	Vase	Milady Range	6¾"h	1980–1982
5596 GM	Vase	1904 Range	8⅝"h	1981-S-i-P
5597 GM	Jug Vase	1904 Range	9"h	1981-S-i-P
5598 GM	Vase	1904 Range	9⅝"h	1981-S-i-P
5599 GM	Vase	1904 Range	9¼"h	1981-S-i-P
5600 GM	Vase	1904 Range	9⅛"h	1981-S-i-P
5601–5	Not used			
5606 GM	Vase	Belgravia Range	8¼"h	1981-S-i-P
5607 GM	Vase	Belgravia Range	6¾"h	1981-S-i-P
5608 GM	Vase	Belgravia Range	6"h	1981–1982
5609 GM	Jardiniere	Belgravia Range	6¼"h	1981-S-i-P
5610 GM	Bowl	Belgravia Range	7¾"h	1981-S-i-P
5611 GM	Flower Pot	Belgravia Range	4⅝"h	1981-S-i-P
5612 GM	Flower Pot	Belgravia Range	5"h	1981–1982

5613 GM	Flower Pot	Belgravia Range	5½″h	1981-S-i-P
5614 GM	Flower Pot	Belgravia Range	6½″h	1981-S-i-P
5615 GM	Flower Pot	Belgravia Range	7½″h	1981-S-i-P
5616–19	Not used			
5620 GM	Cup	Tapestry Range	3⅛″h	1980–1982
5621 GM	Saucer	Tapestry Range	5¾″a	1980–1982
5622 GM	Tea plate	Tapestry Range	6¾″a	1980–1982
5623 GM	Beaker	Tapestry Range	4½″h	1980–1982
5624 GM	Sugar Bowl	Tapestry Range	3¼″a	1980–1982
5625 GM	Cream Jug	Tapestry Range	3½″h	1980–1982
5626 GM	Teapot	Tapestry Range	5″h	1980–1982
5627 GM	Sandwich Tray	Tapestry Range	11¾″l	1980–1982
5628 GM	Cruet Two piece	Tapestry Range	3½″h	1980–1982
5629 GM	Butter Dish	Tapestry Range	5¼″l	1980–1982
5630 GM	Cheese Dish	Tapestry Range	7½″l	1980–1982
5631 GM	Honey Jar	Tapestry Range	3½″h	1980–1982
5632/3	Not used			
5634–7 GM	Tea pots	Two Large Size, Two small size		1982
5638–43	Not used			
5644 GM	Wedding Cake	Thimble		1981
5645–54	Not used			
5655 GM	Beaker	Pig		1981
5656 GM	Money Box	Teddy Bear/Panda	5¼″h	1981-S-i-P
5657 GM	Money Box	Pig	5¼″h	1981-S-i-P
5658 GM	Money Box	Rabbit	5¼″h	1981–1982
5659 GM	Money Box	Elephant	5¼″h	1981–1982
5660 GM	Money Box	Cat	5¼″h	1981–1982
5661 GM	Money Box	Bassett Hound	5¼″h	1981–1982
5662 GM	Money Box	Fish	5¼″h	1981–1982
5663–69	Not used			
5670 GM	Tea Pot	Tudor Cottage Ware	5½″h	1981-S-i-P
5671 GM	Sugar Bowl	Tudor Cottage Ware	3″a	1981-S-i-P
5672 GM	Cream Jug	Tudor Cottage Ware	3¼″h	1981-S-i-P
5673 GM	Butter Dish	Tudor Cottage Ware	5¾″l	1981-S-i-P
5674 GM	Cheese Dish	Tudor Cottage Ware	7″l	1981-S-i-P
5675 GM	Honey Jar	Tudor Cottage Ware	4½″h	1981-S-i-P
5676 GM	Cruet Two Piece	Tudor Cottage Ware	3¼″a	1981-S-i-P
5677–5995	Not used			
5996 GM	Holder-Newspaper-	Desk Top Range	4⅝″h	1978–1981
5997 GM	Tray – Matchbox	Desk Top Range	5⅜″h	1978–1981
5998 GM	Pen Holder-Matchbox	Desk Top Range	4⅛″h	1978–1981
5999 GM	Pen Holder-Sack	Desk Top Range	4¼″h	1978–1981
6000 OM	Tray-Scrap Paper	Desk Top Range	5¼″l	1978–1982
6001 OM	Box-Gift Parcel	Desk Top Range	4½″l	1978–1982
6002 OM	Pen Holder-Carrier Bag	Desk Top Range	4″h	1978–1982
6003 OM	Money Box-Parcel	Desk Top Range	4″l	1978–1982
6004 OM	Paper Weight-Letter	Desk Top Range	5¼″l	1978–1982
6005 OM	String Dispenser	Desk Top Range	3⅝″h	1978–1982
6006 OM	Beer Can	Desk Top Range		1978
6007–6127	Not used			
6128 GM	Money Box	Alphabet 'P'		No date

Final Number.

LINES WITHOUT NUMBERS, MOSTLY MADE IN THE FALCON POTTERY

Girl with flowers and hat.
Jeanette
Fox S/S
Girl Sitting
Girl Figure Water Carrier
Mine Host with Barrel and
Jugs
The wishing well range
The Springtime Range
Hat wall Vase
Some Dovecote Range
Hudson Tray
Cavalier Musical Jug
John Bull Character Jug

Punch Character Jug
Burleigh Range
Scottie Dog
Hereford Cider Mug
Five Cats
Two Pigs S/s and L/s
Another little drink Mug
Baby Playtime Range
Tavern in the Town Mug
Dogs head jug
Tulip Dish
Brooches and earrings
Polar Bears
Garden Seat

Crinoline Lady
The Breton Girl
Duck Family
Primula Posy Ring
Twist Candle stick
Toucan L/s and S/s
Bull & Bush Jug
Roma Basket
Empress Pot
Ashtray S/s
Cigarette Box
Crescent Basket
Ginger Jar & Cover 14″h
Crescent Boat

York Vase
Queen Vase
Collon Vase
Chang Vase No 1 & 2
Alex No 1 & 2 vase
Priscilla
Carthorse (Front leg up)
Princess Vase
Seville Vase
Ascot Vase
Metro Vase
Riga, Tyne, Whitley Vases
Straw Hat Wall Vase

WHERE TO BUY SYLVAC

**THE FOLLOWING ANTIQUE DEALERS SPECIALISE
IN SYLVAC WARE:**
OLIVE M. CAPLE   Telephone 01–644–4896
Attends Antique Fairs in the South East.

GOING FOR A SONG   **TELEPHONE 0538 382976**
2 Brook Street,   **Now at Anvil Antiques**
Leek,   **Cross Street**
Staffs.   **Leek, Staffs.**

COTTAGE CURIOS   Telephone 0843 602806
39 High Street,
St. Peters,
Broadstairs,
Kent.

CASTLE ANTIQUES   Telephone 0926 498068
1, Mill Street,
Warwick,
Warwickshire.

Please telephone for opening times or nearest venue.

INDEX